WHO DO YOU SAY?

Claus Bussmann

WHO DO YOU SAY?

JESUS CHRIST IN LATIN AMERICAN THEOLOGY

Translated from the German by Robert R. Barr

ORBIS BOOKS

Maryknoll, New York 10545

The Catholic Foreign Mission Society of America (Maryknoll) recruits and trains people for overseas missionary service. Through Orbis Books Maryknoll aims to foster the international dialogue that is essential to mission. The books published, however, reflect the opinions of their authors and are not meant to represent the official position of the society.

First published as *Befreiung durch Jesus? Die Christologie der lateinamerikanischen Befreiungstheologie,* copyright © 1980 by Kösel-Verlag GmbH & Co., Munich

English translation copyright © 1985 by Orbis Books, Maryknoll, NY 10545

Library of Congress Cataloging in Publication Data

Bussman, Claus.
  Who do you say?

  Translation of: Befreiung durch Jesus?
  Bibliography: p.
  Includes index.
  1. Jesus Christ—History of doctrines—20th century.
2. Liberation theology.   3. Theology, Doctrinal—Latin
American—History—20th century.   I. Title.
BT198.B8713   1984   232′.098   84-16476
ISBN 0-88344-711-8 (pbk.)

Contents

Introduction

What would possess a German theologian and biblical scholar to take up the study of the Latin American theology of liberation?[1]

Personal associations, surely—experiences in the course of journeys the length and breadth of Central and South America.

But there was another reason. Curiosity. And this was the main reason. Certain Latin American theologians had been heard to say they had found a "new way of doing theology,"[2] and our German theologian wanted to see whether it was so, and if so, how—since if it were so, then it might well point to a "new way of doing" biblical studies, too, as a tool of theology. Indeed, biblical scholars had already asked this question.[3] What was going on in Latin America could have important repercussions on First World theology itself.

Our plan had never been to try to carry out a comprehensive investigation of liberation theology's approach to matters biblical, not even when we first conceived it. We would examine one question only: how the theology of liberation handles its reference to Jesus Christ.

We had two most compelling reasons for making this option. First, Christology is recognized as a central theme in theology today. (And so, by the way, it is a theme in which the biblical scholar will be particularly interested.) Second, Christology has been the subject of a great many European and North American books, articles, and monographs in recent years: hence a comparison between Northern and Latin American theology seemed particularly feasible in this area.

And so to the task. But before long, our German theologian began to realize that he had posited his question itself quite from the standpoint of German biblical studies and Christology, and this was going to cause problems. In the first place, he began to see, liberation theologians have precious little interest in a historical search for Jesus of Nazareth. Frankly, they attribute scant importance to German or other First World work in this area.[4] As for a nice, clear distinction between the "historical Jesus" and the "kerygmatic Christ"—coin of the realm in German theology—one rarely even meets up with it in the theology of liberation. But by and large, liberation theologians like "Christology" much better than "Jesuology"—and so our researcher reorganized his questions to aim more carefully at "Christology" in this more restricted sense. Now his investigation acquired a more overtly systematic emphasis—an emphasis altogether in keeping with the

1

spirit of liberation theology, which, by the way, prizes the unity of theology very highly.

The question which finally lay before our theologian, then, was the one posed by Bishop Samuel Ruiz of San Cristóbal de las Casas (Chiapas, Mexico), to a congress of liberation theologians in Bogotá, in 1974: "How does the theology of liberation make a Christological use of Sacred Scripture?"[5]

In the pages which follow, we shall attempt to answer this question mainly by calling the Latin American authors themselves to the stand. The overwhelming bulk of their Christological thinking is still unknown in northern climes, and we have endeavored to supply a great deal of actual documentation. Our own commentary will be as sparing as possible.

Our chapters and subdivisions will be systematic, but loosely so: we have been careful not to force the arguments and interpretations, often so different one from another, into a tight schema. Our main intent has simply been to set forth the Christological argumentation of liberation theology in broad outline. We do at times broach critical questions, but these stay in the background.

The reader will notice that, along with our primary purpose—to present a survey of liberation Christology—we have a second purpose as well: to reconsider the question of theology's role in society. The Latin American theologians who have developed the theology of liberation are all in agreement that no theology has any business being "socially naive"—oblivious of the social situation in which it is working. Johannes B. Metz says we have to pay attention to whether a given theology was worked out before Auschwitz or after. Similarly—and even more so—theology must take account of the fact that today's world only *seems* to be one world. In reality, it is divided into rich nations and poor ones, and populated by free human beings and repressed ones. Whenever this rift is not grist for the theological mill, theology itself will be estranged from reality and hence irrelevant. Theologians will perhaps even be content with two theologies, one for the rich countries and one for the poor ones. Then theology itself will have become a mirror of the socio-political split in the world today.

This is where the theology of liberation steps forward and asks northern theology questions the latter dare not turn away from if it means to keep its credibility. If this book—intended for theologians and anyone else interested in theology—succeeds in making its readers aware of these questions, then our second purpose will have been attained. No one need become an enthusiastic disciple of the theology of liberation.

For our own part, our personal interest in this "new way of doing theology" would be described as a critical sympathy at best. But it is not a matter of whether one be friend or enemy of this new theology. It is a matter of whether, as theologian or Christian, one poses the problem that the theology of liberation has injected into theological discussion. This will also be the proper measure of all the critical questions readers will ask themselves in the course of reading this book, whether these questions be concerned with the historical details in the life of Jesus, or with liberation Christology itself.

But if anyone claims to conceive an aversion for the whole of liberation theology or Christology on grounds of erroneous details in one or another particular argumentation—Jesus' attitude toward the Zealots, for example—then he or she ought to wonder whether this is not pure rationalizing: a nice way out of having to ask the bothersome question of theology's role in the wealthy nations.

For the question will still be there, whether we like it or not. And the people who are asking it are committed Christians. Unless we want a divided Christology ("Has Christ been parceled out?"—1 Cor. 1:12), First World theology will have to begin to busy itself about a divided world, and about Christology in a divided world.

PART 1

THE THEOLOGY OF LIBERATION: A "NEW WAY OF DOING THEOLOGY"

Our heading employs a formula of Gustavo Gutiérrez, in which that theologian seeks to sum up what is new in the theology of liberation.[1] There is abundant material in English, some of it for theologians, some of it for a broader audience, by way of introduction to this new theology that has sprung up in Latin America.[2] In part 1, then, we shall offer only (1) a survey of the background and main features of liberation theology, (2) a series of critical questions directed toward it by various authors, and (3) a brief look at its most recent development.

Chapter 1

Antecedents

In the Beginning, a Memory[1]

Open Veins of Latin America is the provoking title of a book by Uruguayan journalist Eduardo Galeano[2] on the nearly five hundred years of outrageous injustices perpetrated in Latin America by, first, Europe (Spain and Portugal especially, then later England) and now the United States.

We find a testimonial to the early history of this exploitation in the letter written by Bartolomé de las Casas to Spanish King Charles I (as Charles V of the Holy Roman Empire) in 1542, ten years after the conquest of Peru by Francisco Pizarro and his company. It will be a good place for us to begin.

Daily in the land of New Castile, atrocities are committed at which Christian humanity shudders to look upon. Heaven's vengeance will fall upon those who bear the guilt. Our Lord Jesus Christ is hourly crucified in New Castile.

Drunk with power, and utterly devoid of any sense of responsibility, the new lords of this plantation state only indulge their unbridled caprices. I have heard that the Spaniards set bloodhounds at the Indians, both for entertainment, and to accustom the hounds to this manner of the hunt.

Young Indian women are torn from their poor families and forced to serve the Spaniards' lusts. Many a Spaniard keeps a harem. I must say, this would become the Crescent far better than the spotless Cross.

The Indians are debased by the Spaniards to the status of slaves. Thousands die in the metal mines. Their bodies are thrown in shallow graves, and no one looks after their families. It has been long indeed since anyone has bothered about bringing the Indians Christianity's salvation.

The granaries are emptied. The herds of Indian camels have been wiped out. Thousands of these camels were slaughtered to satisfy the cloyed appetites of our gourmets. Many Spaniards eat only the brains of this beast, which they extol as the finest delicacy. One might expect that they would leave the flesh to the Indians. But they throw it to the dogs. More Indian camels have been slaughtered in the last four years than in the previous four hundred. Now that the camels have learned that the Spaniards are their enemies, most have fled to the mountains for refuge.

Now the Indians go about without victuals, without the warm fleece that used to provide them protection against the cold, driven up onto the high plateau. There, equality reigns: even those who fought on the side of Castile suffer these deprivations. Thus, many an Inca nobleman now trudges as a beggar through the land of his erstwhile dominion. And if hunger drives him to steal something from the superfluities of the Conquistadors, and he is caught at it, the price he pays is death under the lash.

Many men, like the Missionaries to the Pagans, do good to the Indians. Many would even sacrifice themselves in the defense of the enslaved people. But they have no power to do so. All power is in the hands of those whose only concern is for their own advantage.

The Holy Father has bestowed the right of conquest on the Spaniards under the express condition that they convert the pagans. This condition is not being complied with. The Almighty will call to account those who bear this awful responsibility. For the fact is that this sacred task is being trampled under foot and set at naught.[3]

This primitive testimonial cites two factors in particular that have continued to poison intercontinental relationships from Bartolomé's days down to our own; (1) the inseparability of missionary activity from the Conquista;[4] (2) the Europeans' feeling of superiority (today, that of the Creoles and Mestizos of European extraction) toward the Indians.[5]

As we see in Las Casas, there was Christian opposition to the "superiority complex" of the conquistadors and colonials from the very beginning.[6] But the opposition was very often without result. The Spanish (or Portuguese) crown, under whose aegis the missionary enterprise proceeded, generally resolved conflicts of interest between evangelization and economic exploitation in favor of the latter.[7] The renowned Nuevas Leyes de Indias of 1542, the New Laws for the Indies, changed nothing here. Their prohibition of Indian slavery, for example, remained a dead letter in practice. Indeed, even official church people were often involved in the inhumane treatment meted out to the Indian population.[8] No wonder, then, that the Christian faith was so often hateful to the Indian aborigines, or that their opposition to the Europeans was directed not only against the soldiery, but against the missionaries as well.

Eloquent testimony to this effect is to be found in the illustrated chronicle of the Inca convert to Christianity, Guamán Poma de Ayela, which appeared in 1614.[9] There, for example, we see an Indian on his knees, surrounded by ravening wolves. The Indian is identified as a symbol of the suffering Christ. The wolves are the Spanish overlords and the missionary fathers. In another illustration, a Spanish landowner is boasting to a missionary priest of the hanging of an Indian chieftan—the latter, once more, representing Jesus hanging on the cross.

But without a doubt, the most revealing example of the European sense of superiority in matters ecclesial is the fact that for a long time no efforts whatever were made to form a native Latin American clergy (except in Mexico, where the project fell through).[10]

Throughout the entire first one hundred years following the Conquista, nothing changed in this respect. The first Secretary of the Sacred Congregation for the Propagation of the Faith, F. Ingoli (1622–1649), arrived at the following very negative judgment:

1. "The Spaniards are unwilling to have the truth about America become known in Europe. Hence the Indians are forbidden to visit Europe under severe penalty.

2. "The Spaniards are unwilling to ordain Indians to the priesthood or to permit them to pursue higher studies. They prefer to keep them in their uncivilized state, the more easily to make use of them. In all of this, their pretext is that they are inept by nature, and inclined to alcoholism."

Of course it was the Europeans who first made alcoholics of the Indians, forcing them to trade in alcohol, which was perfectly legal.

Now Ingoli scores colonial paternalism and exploitation:

3. "Indeed even the Spaniards actually born in the West Indies—called 'Creoles'—are, in the eyes of the European Spaniard, simply inept.

4. "The Indians are actually capable of receiving priestly orders. They are intelligent, they learn easily, they love discipline, they shun adultery, theft, disloyalty, and lying, they pay their debts, and they surpass the Europeans in piety."

5. Here Ingoli goes on to remark that the enslavement of the Indians—the conditioning of their evangelization on the rape of their liberty—together with their exclusion from the clerical state, are the reasons for the failure of the American mission to make any progress in the seventeenth century. It was not ever thus, avers the Secretary. And the Indians' relapse into paganism is more likely to result from their constant dependency and repression than it is from admittance to spiritual responsiblity. Says Ingoli:

"The means of salvation that would be constituted by the admittance of the Indians to Holy Orders would obviate the first difficulty [that of the ineptitude of the foreign bishops and missionaries with the native languages] automatically. Further, native priests would look after the spiritual well-being of their fellow Indians with more love than the missionaries and with less self-seeking than now plagues the missionary endeavor. It would no longer be necessary to dispatch Europeans to . . .

the West Indies to lord it over the natives there so as to enrich themselves on the pretext of the spiritual emolument of the Indians.''[11]

Much has changed since the independence movements of the early nineteenth century. But, according to Latin American liberation theologian Gustavo Gutiérrez, the situation today is no less abominable than it was in the beginning.

The Church in Latin America was born alienated. It has not, from the start and despite some valiant efforts to the contrary, been the master of its own destiny. Decisions were taken outside the subcontinent. After the wars of independence of the last century, a sort of ecclesiastical "colonial treaty" was established. Latin America was to supply "the raw materials": the faithful, the Marian cult, and popular devotions; Rome and the Churches of the Northern hemisphere were to supply the "manufactured goods": studies of Latin-American affairs, pastoral directives, clerical education, the right to name bishops—and even supply them— money for works and missions. In other words, the general dependent situation of Latin America is just as real in Church affairs.[12]

In a brief treatment of the historical relationship of Latin America to Europe such as we are here presenting, we can only offer highlights. For the economic side of the subject we refer the reader to the book by Galeano cited above. But one thing is certain. The story of the Latin American Indian from 1492 to the present is mostly one of suffering. The Indians have been economically exploited, culturally destroyed and Europeanized, and raped in matters of religion.[13] It is true that political power has been in the hands of Creoles and Mestizos since the early nineteenth century. But the lot of the full-blood Indian has not changed a whit since the Conquista, except perhaps for the worse.[14]

This history of pain and suffering, to which we have here made but the most summary allusion, is vivid and painful in the memory of a great many Latin Americans of our own day. This is precisely where, it seems to us, the first beginnings of the theology of liberation in Latin America must therefore be located.

Pablo Richard agrees:

The theology of liberation simply cannot be understood apart from its historical context. . . . The debate on the theology of liberation begins to be a fruitful one when it broadens into a debate on the history of Latin America, which is also part of the history of the church and its theology. We must give an account of our theology of liberation, not by attempting to answer abstract questions, but by transforming the process in which we live into a process within our whole Latin American history, at least from the time of Christopher Columbus until today.[15]

An Insight: Dependence and the Theory of Dependency

How does it happen that the countries of Latin America, even when they are very rich in good soil, natural resources, and raw materials, belong, by world standards, to the poor, or so-called "underdeveloped," countries— those whose gross national product, both total and per capita, are below the world average?

Various answers have been given to this question—generally not all at the same time, but, by and large, in succession, replacing one another as theories evolve and change. Here we shall give only the two most recent attempts at an answer, and only in brief outline.[16]

Up until the middle sixties of our own century, the prevailing theory with which social scientists attempted to answer the above question was the theory of "development." It was asserted that the countries of Latin America are presently passing through a stage of development which to-day's developed countries—the industrialized nations—had to pass through themselves long ago. Accordingly, it was posited that the Latin American countries will eventually become "developed" countries too, just as the United States, for example, or the nations of Western Europe have. And so a kind of strategy of "catch-up" (or, as we say, "aid to underdeveloped countries") was developed and implemented, consisting in the dispatch of experts and capital from the more developed countries to the underdeveloped ones, to assist the latter to develop.

But as it became evident that the gap between the developed and the underdeveloped countries was widening instead of growing smaller, this theory fell into disrepute. It began to be referred to, pejoratively, as "developmentalism," and is now no longer employed by Latin American economists and sociologists. In its place, the "theory of dependency" has arisen, according to which the underdeveloped condition of the nations of Latin America, far from being a stepping-stone to development, is precisely the result of the development of the developed countries of the world—the other side of the coin, so to speak, of the wealth of the United States and Western Europe.[17] The Latin American states, then, are "dependent"— they consitute a "periphery" of which the wealthy countries are the "centers."[18]

Here, the goal of the Latin American peoples is seen as "liberation." As long as the nature of the untoward Latin American situation was conceived in terms of underdevelopment, "development" was the watchword; but once that situation began to be seen as a state of dependency, "liberation" became the order of the day. *The theology of liberation takes its name from an economic and sociological analysis of the Latin American context.*[19]

It is true that there were efforts in the direction of a special theology for a context of dependency from the first appearance of the theory of dependency.[20] But no theological breakthrough occurred until people in Latin

America actually became aware of their factual dependency and the need they had to be liberated from it. Gustavo Gutiérrez characterizes the transition thus:

> When we characterize the Latin American situation as one of dependence and unfair domination, we are naturally led to talk about liberation, and to participate in the process that will lead to it. We are in fact dealing with a term that expresses the new stance adopted by Latin Americans, a stance that is gradually taking concrete shape in official documents. It is recapitulated forcefully in the Medellín conference and in the Thirty-Sixth Episcopal Assembly of Peru. Expressions such as "development" and "integration," with their attendant retinue of international alliances, agencies, and experts, are relegated to the shadows; for they involve a different vision of the Latin American situation.[21]

And this brings us to Medellín.

Reaction of the Church: Plenary Meeting of the Latin American Bishops' Conference in Medellín, Colombia, in 1968[22]

"Liberation is one of the Medellín documents' key concepts," writes Argentinian bishop Eduardo Pironio.[23] And indeed there is no escaping the fact that the theory of dependency as an explanation of the Latin American situation did exert its influence on the episcopal documents at Medellín. True, the bishops were not directly concerned with the theory of dependency there, any more than they were with explaining the Latin American situation with a theory of their own. They were attempting to reorientate their pastoral theory and practice along the lines of Vatican II.[24] But of course in order to do this they could not afford to take their eyes off the factual situation in Latin America even for a moment, and their formulations contain elements of the development theory as well as that of dependency. For example:

> Let us recall that the present historical moment our people are living is characterized in the social order and from an objective point of view by conditions of underdevelopment dramatized by the imposing phenomena of marginality, alienation, and poverty, and largely influenced, in the last analysis, by economic, political, and cultural structures dependent upon the industrialized metropolises which monopolize technology and science (Neo-Colonialism). From the subjective point of view it is characterized by the personal awareness of this situation that awakens among large sectors of Latin Americans attitudes of protest and the desire for liberation, development, and social justice.[25]

The bishops spoke boldly in their description and evaluation of the Latin American situation. They did not hesitate to use expressions like "institutionalized violence"[26] and "unjust structures,"[27] nor to come right out and say that an "erroneous conception concerning the right of ownership of the means of production prevails in Latin American economics today,"[28] that "Latin America will undertake its liberation at the cost of whatever sacrifice,"[29] and that "all liberation is an anticipation of the complete redemption of Christ."[30]

Here the seeds are sown for later theologies of liberation, of whatever stamp. These expressions will become their hallmark. Unlike the teachings of Vatican II, the Medellín conclusions are topical. They make no claim to validity outside Latin America. True, we do find a perspective that somehow includes other peoples "who find themselves in a similar situation to ours,"[31] but the direct, conscious appeal of these bishops is one of Latin Americans to Latin Americans. With all Latin Americans, they feel this moment in history to be a moment of breach, of rupture, and they embark on a search for new paths to follow, one of the goals of which is to "permeate all the process of change with the values of the Gospel."[32]

Were we to wish to extract the salient features of the Medellín documents, we might summarize them briefly as follows:

1. Their point of departure is an analysis of the social-political-economic analysis of the situation in Latin America.

2. In this analysis, the church comes to an awareness of the monstrously evil situation of broad sectors of the population, as well as of its own special responsibility for these marginalized human beings.

3. Hence the need for a reorientation of church practice in the spirit of the gospel: a turn toward the poor, a rediscovery of the prophetical task of the church, and the coresponsibility of all Christians for the upbuilding of a just, "liberated" society worthy of human beings.[33]

Chapter 2

The Theology of Liberation:
Blueprint and Basics[1]

In view of all the various assertions and positions of the authors cited in note 2 of part 1, we shall here pursue two goals: (1) we shall yield the floor to as many Latin American theologians as possible, so that they may favor us with their own estimates and evaluations; and (2) we shall attempt to discern, amid all the divergencies in detail, the common elements in obtaining the theses of the theology of liberation.[2]

A Point of Departure in the Analysis
of the Latin American Situation

The theology of liberation takes up a thesis propounded in Medellín[3] and carries it further: For a great many liberation theologians, what is original in the theology of liberation consists partly in a refusal to ignore the context of oppression and the dimension of praxis.[4] Thus the social sciences become necessary tools of the theology of liberation. Granted, there is scarcely a theologian of liberation to be found who does not acknowledge a certain dependence of liberation theology on European theology, especially "political theology." But more importance is accorded to the theory of dependency, as developed by the social sciences in Latin America. This is evinced in the ready use of sociological concepts, like dependency, repression, liberation, imperialism, and class struggle, in theological writing.[5] Indeed, a certain antipathy for European theology is impossible to ignore, especially with regard to taking the concrete Latin American context seriously. Here we need to see some examples:

> It is unlikely that outside eyes, however expert—say those of European theologians—will be capable of analyzing these basic problems as they have emerged from our historical experience.[6]

Here [in the theology of liberation], evangelization and social commitment find their synthesis. . . . [This theology] is confronted with the pioneering task of integrating the destiny of Latin America into a single unity. This is where it bids European schools farewell. Here is where it is the first typically Latin American theology ever to have existed. The reasons are two: First, its content is Latin America's unique reality. Second, an analysis of this reality with the help of the social sciences pertains to its methodology—in fact is its point of departure.[7]

Elsewhere, the author of this latter citation goes on to identify the precise points of divergence between European and Latin American theology. Of course, Hugo Assmann also sees the points of convergence. Both, he says, proceed from the premise that Christ is active today. But, he adds, when one says that, one must go on to say just where, and for or against whom, this Christ is active. Then he says:

To my way of thinking it is precisely at this point that European "political theology" has begun to grow afraid of its own courage and has passed to vague niceties that fail to find their way to expression even in the scientific theological language and concepts already available (if imperfect) with respect to the conflictive gambits of power in history. They simply have not dared to continue their analysis of the historical mediations of the role of power.[8]

And elsewhere:

We believe that the theology of the rich world, as it is presented today, has amply forearmed itself with loopholes and excuses so as not to have to come to grips with this sort of problem [an analysis of the social environment]. Even in its (socially) most daring assertions, it has carefully staked out the limits of its competency and responsibility. It knows where its rights of interference end. Thus it has constructed for itself a more or less peaceable kingdom, in which it is possible to flirt with revolution at a distance and not get its hands dirty.[9]

One can also come at the question from a somewhat different viewpoint and reproach the churches of the rich world with too much concern with intrachurch affairs, so that worship becomes the central focus of everything while "social action" is like an appendage.[10]

When all is said and done, [the theology of the rich world] will never be accused of being a theology that has made any effort to be sensitive to the prime challenges of history.[11]

Enrique Dussel even sees European theologians in Latin America as called on the carpet by liberation theology's arrival on the scene. In fact he is much more emphatic than Assmann, and his recriminations ring like a prophet's:

> Latin America's prophetic faith today is coming to the discovery that it is dependent and alienated, and that this situation is the result of centuries of sin. This faith knows which way the idol lies, and which way instead the road to the liberation it must proclaim. Today's European theology can help in this task only very little if at all. Especially, the presence of European theologians in Latin America who neither know Latin America's situation nor understand its history and temperament, and who yet have the audacity, the presumption, to wish to propagate "Christian teaching" here today, can only be most corrupting and detrimental. We have simply to tell them that they are committing a basic methodological error.
>
> These theologians speak words and propound dilemmas that belong to Europe, not to Latin America. Let this be the last harvest of a pedagogical subjugation to which we must put an end once and for all. We beg the European theologians—our love for them as our brothers and sisters forbids us to name them—not to have the audacity to come to Latin America today to perpetrate the same errors, hundreds of years later (when their guilt will be infinitely greater), as the Conquistadors committed and Las Casas bitterly decried.[12]

José Comblin emphasizes the interlacing of the theology of liberation's Latin American commitment with a particular social option. He says that Latin American theology has managed to choose among three visions of church and world—that of the conservatives, that of the ideologues of developmentalism, and that of the revolutionaries. The adoption of this third vision implies a break with European theology, Comblin says. Then he goes on:

> That theology which trusts to the evolution of current Western society is also willing to endorse the good conscience of Europeans and North Americans, and consequently the prevailing structures.[13]

Latin American theologians participating in the 1973 conference of the World Council of Churches (May 1–4) drafted a compromise statement, which read, in part:

> Our efforts at dialogue are beset with a basic difficulty—basic and decisive for us as Latin Americans—consisting in the contradiction between oppressor and oppressed, between a developed world and the nations held in a state of underdevelopment.
>
> This earmark of our historical context and our historical experience, which up to a certain point consists of certain contradictions obtaining in

reality, today leaps received confessional boundaries, and is determinative for:

1. Our conception of Christianity's role today.

2. Our method of coming to grips with theological problems.

3. All the various particular questions that come up in theology—the understanding of the ecumenical movement, church membership, one's approach to the biblical proclamation, the indissolubility of the bond between faith and efficacious love, the relationship between profession of faith and political option, and so on.[14]

Finally, an assertion of Assmann's surely demonstrates the deadly earnestness of liberation theology's demand for a coming to grips with socio-political reality. Without such confrontation, Assmann argues, one's discourse risks pure garrulousness, or even blasphemy:

> This kind of thought is apparent in one book entitled *Christ Died Gratuitously*,[15] which shows a real lack of sensitivity to the harsh realism of the play of history. It demonstrates the alienating devices of those who try to reduce the historicity of faith to those "moments of gratuitousness" in which, supposedly, "one loves, without a thought for anything other than love." This romantic and a-historical ideology of gratuitousness, typical of affluent, one-dimensional societies, leaves the course of injustice in the world totally untouched and leads ultimately to a religion applicable only to leisure moments. To apply this sort of evasive gratuitousness to him who was condemned and put to death as a subversive rebel, stirring up trouble against the occupying power, is a real blasphemy against the Son of Man.[16]

A somewhat farther-reaching attempt to identify what is new in the theology of liberation is to be found in a seminar presentation that declares the necessity and possibility alike of a socio-cultural Latin American theology:

> 1. Latin American theology is not "part" of theology. It is an *entirely new and original sketch* or blueprint for theology.
>
> 2. It takes its point of departure from a new spiritual experience: the *political struggle* for liberation.
>
> 3. It has another point of departure, as well, one which European theology lacks: the *nonacceptance of current social reality,* which implies a praxis of liberation, and a rediscovery of the mystery of the Liberator-God as revealed in the gospel.
>
> 4. This praxis occasions a *crisis of faith,* issuing in a new faith experience and a new manner of its profession.
>
> 5. The subject, or agent, of this theology is not the individual theologizing person, but a collectivity—*the people*—from whose midst theology issues with its formulations.

6. Latin American theology is a prophetical theology. It interprets the faith anew, from a particular situation. And then, in its own way, it interprets this situation anew in the light of this faith.

7. Through their commitment to the people, and by their vital, living praxis, the theologians have a prophetical function: to express the theological creativity of that people.

8. Latin American theology is deeply *bound to tradition*. It recognizes historical experience as a basic theological locus, in which the interpretation of praxis and the collective memory of the people of God converge.[17]

Let us examine one last text, in which the characteristic thesis of the theology of liberation is set in conjunction with antecedent theological tradition.[18] In a context of Latin America's special role as a continent of broad Christian stamp, we read:

The theology of liberation is a specifically Latin American phenomenon. Its method has as its most recent forerunners the direction marked out by *Gaudium et Spes,* and the trail blazed by Medellín. What is peculiarly Latin American about the theology of liberation—apart from its methodology, which is perhaps not as unique as meets the eye—is that Latin America is the only continent of the Third World that is preponderantly Christian. This favors a Christian reflection on the inhumane situation in which the majority of Latin American believers live. It is these believers, reflecting on the manifold conditions of their unjust marginalization, dependency, and poverty, in the light of their faith, who are building this theology of liberation.[19]

This is not the place to try to solve the disputed question of liberation theology's methodology. Indeed, I see it as less than of paramount importance whether the commitment to a use of an analysis of the Latin American situation results from the method, or from the condition of Latin American Christians. In either case it is certain that a view of socio-political relationships sets the theological thought-process in motion, and that this is characteristic of the theology of liberation.[20] And so let us allow Juan Luis Segundo to have the last word, as we cite his *The Liberation of Theology,* where he is drawing up the balance sheet of liberation theology's first years. Here is how he ends his book:

Whether they are followed or not, the pathways opened up here lead into a long and unforeseeable future. The only thing that can be said for sure is that they take their cue from flesh-and-blood human beings who are struggling with mind and heart and hand to fashion the kingdom of God out of the human materials of our great but oppressed continent.[21]

The New Praxis as the Target

The Christian committed to liberation is attempting to bring a transforming and liberating praxis to bear on the unjust situation, and so do
away with it in favor of a new society and a new human being.[22]

This assertion, purporting to represent the position of Gustavo Gutiérrez,
implies: praxis is not only liberation theology's point of departure, in the
sense that it is analyzed in order to theologize, but constitutes its goal as
well.

Gutiérrez' observation that "theology *follows;* it is the second step,"[23]
has set this aspect in relief. The critique of liberation theology has placed
this notion under indictment (see chap. 3). By comparison, Gutiérrez's
preceding sentence has an altogether harmless ring: "[Faith] works through
a charity which is—at least ought to be—real charity, action, and commitment to the service of men."[24] Here no Christian theologian could object.
And yet, something surprising lurks within this latter statement as well. For
if you erect an analysis of the Latin American situation into the point of
departure for your theological reflection, you must not forget that this is an
analysis precisely of praxis. Now, notice, you have reversed the traditional
roles of theological reflection and praxis. Now praxis has snatched the primacy, for (1) your theology begins only as a critical reflection on praxis,[25]
and (2) the goal of the whole process is not a new theology but a new praxis.

Floristán puts it this way:

Theology unrelated to practice, theology that does not have praxis as its
point of departure in order indirectly or directly to return to it as its goal,
is irrelevant. And just the other way around, theology, in our understanding, is pastoral theology when it enjoys a basic relationship to a
reality-transforming praxis.[26]

And Galilea:

The central concern of the theology of liberation is to help enlighten and
drive forward the mission of Christians in Latin America.[27]

The implications of this emphasis on a new praxis are evident in assertions made by Gustavo Gutiérrez, as early as his foreword to *Signos de
Renovación,* in 1969—hence, shortly after Medellín:

But to stress the need for liberation . . . means that we see the ongoing
development of humanity in a particular perspective, and in terms of a
specific philosophy and theology of history. It means that we see it as a

process of human emancipation, aiming toward a society where men and women are truly free from servitude, and where they are the active shapers of their own destiny. Such a process does not lead us simply to a radical transformation of structures—to a revolution. It goes much further, implying the perduring creation of a wholly new way for men and women to be human.[28]

Here, in tension, as it were, with liberation theology's scientific claim, we have an example of the pathos of world transformation—just as characteristic (in most authors) of that theology as the scientific claim. José Porfirio Miranda even formulates it in a kind of credo:

A world of understanding, in which no human being exploits another, is *possible*. This is the belief that was reborn in Mexico in 1968, and will never be snuffed out again.[29]

And as one last example of this new consciousness:

But we know that we have taken up our stand on the further side of the modern, oppressive, European closed system. Our minds are set upon the liberation of the poor. We point toward the world—man of the future—man who shall be eternally free.[30]

But now, at least two questions are raised by this orientation of liberation theology toward new praxis: first, that of the theological basis of this new orientation; second, that of the relationship of a faith praxis with political praxis. Here too, we shall listen to some Latin American voices.

Theological Basis

Juan Carlos Scannone argues as follows:

Thus theology does not cease being theology. In fact, it is all the more theology for being appropriately historical and practical. For the *Theós* whose *lógos* it expresses (and this makes it theology) is the *God* of history, and the *Word* that articulates that history. He is the Word of God become flesh, who gave his life to liberate brothers and sisters.[31]

And so one part of the answer to our question (our first question) is posited in a theology of the incarnation. But side by side with this incarnation theology and its argumentation, there are other tasks our theologians take in order to establish a theological basis for their orientation to praxis. We now cite one of these. It will be understandable in the light of three presuppositions considered by one author to be key for his establishment of this theological basis: (1) A revolutionary situation obtains in Latin America;

(2) The church is not poor; it goes out to the poor; (3) The theology of liberation is not an idea which the church can contribute to the revolution: it is a particular way of living the faith.

Now for the theological foundation itself:

> What was this future, this promise of God's, made to human beings [in Abraham]?
>
> The promise is threefold: the land (Gen. 12), progeny (Gen. 15), and, finally, God (Gen. 17:17, Gal. 3:16).
>
> What does this mean?
>
> The answer is very simple. God is accessible to human beings only to the extent that God revolutionizes their situation, turns it upside-down. God gets them under way, dispatches them down the road to hope (land and progeny were hope par excellence in those days). Only in this terrestrial hope does God mediate ultimate hope.[32]

For another theologian, the theological basis for liberation theology's orientation toward praxis includes the bridging of the chasm between a purely secular understanding of liberation and a theology of purely religious orientation:

> That is, this theology is an attempt to make faith responsible for this world too—for this history of ours which so abundantly demonstrates the worldly content of religious experience. At the same time, the theology of liberation is an attempt to restore to secularized strivings for a liberated life—to restore to political life—roots in a religious transcendence, by demonstrating that the human experience of liberation is deprived of a very profound and important component, rich in problems, when the experience of liberation and the wish for it are compressed into a purely political dimension. The problem of the human being's deliverance is not to be found in a political context alone, but in the face of the fact of death, as well, and especially in the face of an inability to love, which is sin. This is why this theology speaks of "integral liberation."[33]

The Relationship Between a Faith Praxis and Political Praxis[34]

"Faith and the proclamation of the gospel have an essential relation to politics" is the lapidary pronouncement of the working paper of the third meeting of CELAM's Coordination Committee for Pastoral Theology.[35] To be sure, the assertion could be variously interpreted. What does this "relation" look like? What is meant by "politics"? These are the questions that often divide liberation theologians from one another. First let us cite Juan Carlos Scannone:

> For we believe that there is a genuine *historical unification* between a given basic political option and the theological virtue of love, even

though this love criticizes that option, liberates it, and transcends it.
Indeed, one might even speak of a *necessary connection* between the two,
if by "necessity" one does not mean a logical or dialectical necessity, but
the necessity proper to charity, which necessarily, in fear and trembling,
seeks out the most *efficacious* path, in order to serve the liberation of
one's brothers and sisters here and now. This love knows its own logic.[36]

Or, instead of a rather philosophical approach like this one, one may
employ direct political argumentation. Luís Alberto Gomez de Souza posits
connections between Latin America's political development and certain
theological positions: Christian Democracy corresponds rather to a
theology of development, while the more radical Christian groups, with
their more strongly developed sense of Latin American society's class structure, are sympathetic to the theology of liberation. And he continues:

> Just as the churches at first were influenced by the middle classes, whose
> avant-garde thinking had become radicalized, everything seems to point
> to a future for the theology of liberation in the struggles of the workers
> and peasants.[37]

Leonardo Boff envisages a common commitment of faith and political
activity. His concern is for the defeat of the driving forces of Western civilization that currently prevail: hegemony, profit, and exploitation.

> Any revolution which does not change the cultural ethos at the roots of
> our Western history will be at most a variation on a theme—never a real
> liberation.[38]

Enrique Dussel, as well, is wary of too simplistic an understanding of the
relationship between a faith praxis and a political one:

> The mistake is not in engaging in political activity, not even when this is
> all one does. The mistake is in thinking that Christian liberation is ex-
> hausted in the political-historical.[39]

And further on:

> Historical and eschatological liberation occur in a dialectical relation-
> ship—*never one without the other*. They condition one another. . . .
> An eschatological liberation without an historical one (a cultural, politi-
> cal, economic, etc., one) would be an angelic, disembodied, un-human
> liberation. Historical liberation without eschatological liberation would
> be atheism—the mythical absolutization of the relative—and would en-
> tail the human being's annihilation, for now his and her way would be

barred forever from an historical growth toward that total fulfillment that will never be totally reached in history.[40]

Finally, let us hear once more from Juan Luis Segundo, as he sets forth what he sees to be the common element in all liberation theology:

It is not easy to say what the exact content of the theology of liberation is for all the Christians involved in it. Certain basic points, however, are clearly shared by all. They would maintain that the longstanding stress on individual salvation in the next world represents a distortion of Jesus' message. He was concerned with man's full and integral liberation, a process which is already at work in history and which makes use of historical means. They would maintain that the church does not possess any sort of magical effectiveness where salvation is concerned but rather liberating factors in its faith and its liturgy; that the victory of the church must be viewed in functional terms rather than quantitative or numerical terms, insofar as the church's specific and proper means manage to exercise a truly powerful impact on human history. They would also maintain that there are not two separate orders—one being a supernatural order outside history and the other being a natural order inside history; that instead one and the same grace raises human beings to a supernatural level and provides them with the means they need to achieve their true destiny within one and the same historical process.[41]

Championship of the Cause of the Poor: Liberation Theology's Focal Point[42]

Anyone familiar with Latin America's manifold neocolonial dependency has learned to view the situation of the poor with new eyes. It is the very weakest who are offered in sacrifice in the worldwide "order" of injustice maintained by their fellow human beings—or rather by those of them who are wealthy.

And so in order to speak about "liberation," you have to speak about the liberation of the poor. Here again the theology of liberation moves ahead with what was begun in Medellín.[43]

Liberation theology has several different accents here: orientation to the example of Jesus (more on this in part 2), reference to the class society, and the reinterpretation of biblical texts.[44] Here again we shall cite individual testimonials, in order to round out the picture given us by Gutiérrez in his *A Theology of Liberation*.

Julio de Santa Ana says:

Whenever theology takes a prophetical stance, it has to take cognizance of sociological reflection. Similarly, the biblical proclamation leads us to a basic option for the poor.[45]

And Gutiérrez himself:

> Poverty—the fruit of social injustice, whose deepest roots are sin—is taken up not in order to erect it into an ideal of life, but in order to bear testimony to the evil it represents. Our sinful condition, and its consequences, were not assumed by Christ in order to idealize them, surely, but in order to redeem us from sinfulness, to battle human selfishness, to abolish all injustice and division among human beings, to suppress what divides us into rich and poor, exploiters and exploited.
>
> The witness to poverty, lived as an authentic imitation of Christ, instead of alienating us from the world, places us at the very heart of a situation of spoliation and oppression. From there it proclaims liberation and full communion with the Lord.[46]

Elsewhere Gutiérrez compares the church's option for its own poverty with Christ's incarnation, as it springs, he says, from the same motivation of love and solidarity.[47] He reproaches scientific exegesis with being an exegesis of the dominant class, and calls for a reinterpretation of the Bible from the viewpoint of the poor. Only thus, he says, can the Bible's own call for justice be implemented.[48]

One finds a similar line of thought in Luís Fernando Rivera. In commenting on the concept of *prosōpolēmpsía,* found in James 2:1, "making distinctions between classes of people," or what we call "human respect" or "acceptance of persons"—he states that

> the word usually translated as "acceptance of persons" would correspond today to acceptance of the principle that society is divided into classes.[49]

Here Fernando considers some Pauline expressions, then continues:

> Hence our text calls not only for the "respect that the poor deserve" (as it is titled in the [Spanish version of the] Jerusalem Bible),[50] but more: *it deduces from the Christian faith that the division and dismemberment of society into classes is forbidden.*[51]

We are, however, favored with no instructions as to how the prevailing distinction of classes is to be done away with.

Segundo Galilea brings a stronger spiritual emphasis to bear in his considerations on the poor and poverty.[52] Galilea defines poverty as, ultimately, powerlessness and lack of influence. Accordingly, he sees the church's commitment to the poor—in Jesus' footsteps, in his true discipleship—as consisting first and foremost in a renunciation of power and influence on the part of that church. This commitment must be made, however, not out of abstract ethical motives, but in order to serve the poor.

Chapter 3

Critical Inquiries into
the Theology of Liberation

After the merely supplementary considerations of the last sections there can be no question here of managing a comprehensive critique of the theology of liberation. Nor can we yield the floor to authors whose approaches we have not yet seen. Nevertheless we should like to call attention from the very outset to the fact that criticism of the theology of liberation is forthcoming from an extremely broad spectrum of viewpoints.[1]

First, there is the *critique from within*. Theologians like Assmann, Galilea, Gutiérrez, and Segundo know very well where questions are still open or where their own first approaches have not been thoroughgoing or where there are peculiarities in "rough drafts" stemming from their own subjective bent. Accordingly, they maintain an open, critical dialogue with one another. We have a good example in an assertion of Luís Alberto Gómez de Souza, to the effect that it is important to consider both the fortunes of liberation theology up to the present and its prospects for the future. Gómez seconds Gustavo Gutiérrez's demand that the theology of liberation be the product of historical praxis. Gómez says:

All this indicates the need of the theology of liberation not to live in the world of the utopias—the world of the great ideal images. It must be a theology of political action, but at the level of strategy and concrete tactics. It must not be a political theology in the general sense, as Metz's theology. This is relatively difficult for middle-class Christians, whose reflection tends to be abstract.[2]

But by far the bulk of the critique is *from without*—that is, coming from theologians who do not consider themselves liberation theologians.

The European critique occurs in pontifical pronouncements,[3] other Roman documents,[4] and the writings of private theologians.[5] None of this will concern us here.

The *Latin American critique* spans a broad spectrum in its own right, ranging from extreme aversion to critical sympathy. Here, first of all, there are two theologians whose position is not easy to categorize. The Argentinian bishop Eduardo Pironio, who was Secretary General of the Latin American Bishops' Conference during the preparation for the Medellín conference, considers himself a liberation theologian. But he is outspoken in his criticism of Hugo Assmann and Gustavo Gutiérrez on key points, and they in turn do not consider him a liberation theologian at all. On the other hand, another Argentinian, Protestant theologian José Míguez Bonino, prefers to speak of a "theology in a context of liberation" rather than of a theology of liberation, and was an early critic of the latter. Yet his actual position is very similar to liberation theology. We shall be hearing from them both.

There is also another difficulty that arises when we attempt to assess the Latin American critique from without: the difficulty presented by an occasional time lag between the appearance of an article in a Latin American periodical and its coming to the attention of theologians elsewhere. A good many criticisms emanating from Latin America have been valid when they were voiced on that continent, but by the time they were heard and evaluated elsewhere they were valid no longer. For example, Héctor Borrat wrote that the theology of liberation was received only in two areas of the Latin American church, the clerical, and the academic—and only by a minority of the representatives of these two groups.[6] This was indeed the case, as Borrat was writing; but it is no longer the case today.[7]

With these reservations, then, we shall now address ourselves to three intrinsically connected aspects of the Latin American critique of liberation theology "from without": (1) the critique of its adoption of Marxist, or Marxist-inspired, social analysis; (2) the critique of its actual concept of liberation; and (3) the critique of its presentation of the relationship between faith and politics.

The Adoption of Marxist Thinking

In the area of liberation theology's adoption of Marxist or Marxist-inspired thinking as a target of criticism by its adversaries, there are two points of particular importance to be considered. First is its adoption of the "theory of dependency," a theory stemming from the Marxist critique of imperialism. Second, there is the question whether it is even possible to adopt Marxist theory in part only—without adopting the whole.

Alfonso López Trujillo complains that, in the theology of liberation, dependency is seen as the *only* cause of the untoward circumstances obtaining in Latin America. He does not dispute the fact of dependency; he only laments that none but Marxist sociologists have concerned themselves with a theoretical explanation of it.[8] He rightly insists that if theology seeks to make use of sociological theories and their conclusions, it will have to keep abreast of any discussion and correction of these theories and conclusions that may take place within the discipline of sociology itself.[9]

But Lopez's more important objection is that one cannot adopt Marxist thinking without running the risk of having to adopt the whole system—including atheism, antireligion, and class struggle. Lopez Trujillo's critique is cautious, but dogged.[10]

Juan Gutiérrez Gonzalez's criticism along these lines is less guarded.[11] For him, atheism and Marxism are simply identical.[12] Hence any admission of truth anywhere in Marxism is a surrender of at least some part of theology. He concludes his considerations of Gustavo Gutiérrez's encounter with Marxist thought as follows:

> Hence one would have to say that instead of Marxism (that widespread Latin American phenomenon) being a factor in this "new way of doing theology," it is rather that the "new way of doing theology" is in the service of Marxism. Instead of "including Marxism," [liberation theology] is itself included by it [*comprehendido*]. Marxism has persuaded our author to do a Marxist rereading of the gospel and of the whole Bible.[13]

This sort of criticism can have the wholesome effect of keeping theologians of liberation alert to other viewpoints in Latin American theology. This will of course be very much in order for a theology which means to take its point of departure in concrete reality. After all, the theology of liberation claims to be a "conversion of theology." Surely, then, it will wish to keep its eye on the theologians to be converted—the theologians unfavorable to the theology of liberation.[14]

The Concept of Liberation

The theology of liberation is described as, and should indeed be, a theology of "that attitude and teaching of Christ that permits human beings to find ways of living their faith in conformity with their worth and character as persons redeemed."[15] The difference in the concepts of "liberation" of a Gustavo Gutiérrez and a Hugo Assmann, then, are not to be passed over lightly.

"Liberation" is a frequently occurring word and notion in the documents of Medellín.[16] And yet its origin is indisputably in the Marxist theory of dependency. Hence surely its content will have undergone some adaptation if it is taken over by the Latin American bishops in their explanations and reflections.

This adaptation and accommodation are most clearly signaled by the qualifications, "true," or "integral" in the bishops' documents. Thus we read of "true liberation," or "integral liberation."[17] But evidently these modifiers do not endow the concept with the last degree of conceptual precision, seeing that both the liberation theologians and their critics make use of it, and both the liberation theologians and their critics look upon themselves as authentic interpreters of Medellín. Eduardo Pironio, for example, emphasizes, first, that neither the essence of Christianity nor that of mission consists utterly and solely in liberation;[18] and, second, that liberation must begin from within persons.[19] Then he goes on:

> Thereby the notion of liberation emerges as one of Medellín's central ideas. Indeed it is the theological key to all the documents of that conference. But it is necessary to interpret it correctly—in its biblical richness, in its Paschal and eschatological content, in the total context of the demands of the gospel. Neither may we limit liberation to the naked sphere of the inner and the ultimate (grace and eschatology), nor may we reduce it to the purely historical and temporal.[20]

A little further on, Pironio says:

> The Christian meaning of liberation, as a liberation that is perfect, peaceful, and fruitful,[21] is manifested to us only in Christ and his Easter mystery.[22]

Gilberto Giménez presents his critique from another viewpoint. He observes that, owing to its philosophical dependency on Europe,[23] Latin America has never developed its own system of ethics. This, he says, has resulted in a partial occupation by the theology of liberation of the place that rightly belongs to ethics. Then he goes on:

> The absence of ethical reflection on the theme of liberation in the Latin American context has had extremely negative consequences. Thus for example the enormous delay in the development of an ethics of liberation, in comparison with the evolution of the theology of liberation, has had the practical result of allowing the latter disproportionately to usurp the inalienable functions of the former. Consequently, on the one hand the task of liberation as a worldwide task goes unrecognized; on the other hand faith is reduced to ethics, so that the theology of liberation is as it were utilized as an ideology in the service of the justification of revolutionary social change.[24]

Yet another definition of liberation, and freedom, is that of Javier Lozano. Lozano agrees with the theology of liberation that the latter is a part of theological reflection on church praxis. But he refuses to include an analysis of social reality in his definition of liberation theology. He opens his theological considerations with these words:

I understand human freedom as a consciousness that human beings have of themselves, and that is identified with their own existence. Freedom is the internal registration of a multiple openness, a multiplicity of "unfulfillednesses" that open up human beings and at the same time make them sensitive to whatever can fulfill these open, empty places. It is the discovery and awareness that all created fulfillments fall short of the mark, and thus it is a tendency toward the transcendent. It is a certain indifference vis-à-vis created means and modes of behavior, for the purpose of attaining the transcendent—that personal Transcendent who is the basis of liberation, inasmuch as he bestows the capacity of attaining himself as the ultimate agent of fulfillment, as he obviates, and helps his creatures to obviate, the existential obstacles to attaining to him in a personal relationship. Freedom is a reality that transforms human beings into Jesus Christ, who through his Pasch delivers them from the Devil, from sin, from the flesh, from death, and from the Law. Freedom is a merciful work of God, who in grace-ful wise bestows on human beings the gift of truth and the status of sons and daughters of God. It is a force that makes the human being a subject, not a product of the evolution of nature. It is a radical force that strikes root in the mystery of existence, and bestows on human beings ultimacy and eternity, in their individual histories and in salvation history. Freedom is a constant journey toward the plentitude of deliverance—a deliverance that will mean the eschatological assumption and exaltation of the human being.[25]

Faith and Politics[26]

Lamberto Schuurmann sums up the relationship between faith and politics as follows:

[Liberation theology] sees the liberating hand of Yahweh and of Jesus Christ in the liberation movements of the Third World.[27]

Here we have two basic tenets of the theology of liberation. First, profane history and salvation history go hand in hand. Second, faith calls for involvement in politics.[28]

But critics counsel caution. Virgilio Zea G. insists that liberation must begin within—in the deepest heart of a human being.

A continent seeking to be delivered from the structures of enslavement will first have to deliver human beings from the injustice that wells up out of their hearts . . . (cf. Matthew 23:23, 15:11). One would think Jesus had Latin American regimes in mind when he said that. Murder, graft, self-enrichment at the expense of misery for the worker, the torture and exploitation of the poor, all rise up out of the evil of the human heart, in socialist regimes as well as in capitalism.[29]

Eduardo Pironio is less sweeping in his assertions, but is more explicit in his hesitation about involvement in politics:

> We do not do liberation theology because we want to mix in politics. We do liberation theology because we . . . are ever more sensitive to the religious task of the church in its *totality*. The religious area, the faith, the gospel all have an essentially historical dimension, and accordingly embrace the human, the social, and the political.[30]

Melecio Picazo Gálvez is another author who speaks of the church's responsibility where exploitation is concerned.

> Real liberation will not be achieved with the mere cessation of oppression. It will be achieved only when the oppressor ceases to be an oppressor! That means that the church, in its attempt to liberate the oppressed, in virtue of its very mission may not be allowed to marginalize the oppressor.[31]

There is little doubt about José Míguez Bonino's solid background in Protestant tradition when—long before the advent of the theology of liberation, as it happens—he takes a quite different position from that theology, almost as if he were drawing up a kind of advance critique. This position of his is of interest in view of what we will consider in part 2 and we shall attempt to elucidate it here.

In his search for a biblical basis for political involvement, Míguez argues that the thinking of Jesus and of the sacred authors of the New Testament is eschatological. For them the end of the world is at hand. In principle, then, this world, which is in the power of the evil one, has already been overcome. The time remaining before the definitive manifestation of this victory, the Last Judgment, is God's "meantime"—the interval provided by God's forbearance for the spread of the gospel.

This is where the church discovers its own proper task. Only, the political involvement required on the part of the church is much broader today than ever before. It includes the battle for human rights, and the fight to vanquish misery and oppression in general. Now, then, a question arises: What may be the result of a like political commitment? And Míguez answers:

> Once again, we must emphasize that we may not look to him for a kingdom that will be the gradual metamorphosis of this world into the coming world. This world with its structures stands condemned, and is on the way to its dissolution. The notion of a constant and gradual transformation is radically excluded.[32]

Carlos Bravo, who recognizes not only negative but also positive facets of the theology of liberation, explains that Gustavo Gutiérrez has no intention of expounding a whole new theology, but is merely attempting to present new "perspectives."[33] Gutiérrez, says Bravo, introduces a new viewpoint, and an important one for the relationship between faith and politics:

Faith, and its exposition, theology, place the human being under the obligation of taking sides with other human beings. But neither faith nor theology exonerates human beings from the obligation to be responsible for their own decision-making.[34]

Chapter 4

New Political Situation, New Latin American Accent: A Theology of Captivity

In 1975, Mexico City saw a great theological congress. Its proceedings were published under the title, *Liberation and Captivity*.[1] This congress had set as its main goal a study of methodology in Latin American theology. Hence it could scarcely ignore the fact that since the time of the bishops' conference in Medellín in 1968 the Latin American political landscape had altered considerably. The democratically elected government of Chile had fallen to the military in 1973.[2] In Bolivia, reform-minded Torres had been ousted by reactionary General Banzer. In Uruguay, a reactionary military had seized power in a coup. In Argentina, since Juan Perón's death in April 1974, rumors were flying of an impending military takeover, which of course finally occurred only in 1976, but when it occurred it too was under a reactionary aegis. In Peru, where a reform-minded group of officers had seized power (under Alvarado) in 1968, in 1975 (under Bermúdez) the lofty goals of social revolution were already in difficulty.

All these political shifts held their consequences for the theology of liberation. And when we consider the additional circumstance that, as cited in the so-called Rockefeller Report,[3] groups within the Catholic church had now become the mouthpiece of social change in Latin America—that is, that the Catholic church was no longer playing its old role of bulwark of the status quo—it is scarcely occasion for astonishment that the "super-Catholics" of all continents suddenly lashed out against "Christians like that"—Christians who had grown aware of situations of social injustice and now were actively involved in work for social justice.[4]

Accordingly, Juan Luis Segundo distinguishes two stages in the development of the theology of liberation: (1) its *rise* (since around the time of Medellín), which on one hand was concerned with getting a project under way (*teología argente*, roughly, "theology on a white horse"), and yet was

32

still enmeshed in the self-produced trammels of snap judgments, jejune biblical hermeneutics (especially a too exclusive emphasis on the Exodus event), and an exaggerated aversion for European theology; and (2) *continuation today*—since about 1974 or 1975—a period marked by mounting experience and further development. At the same time, the possibility is envisaged of a reaction setting in further down the road, on grounds of allegations like those of the Rockefeller Report.[5]

Leonardo Boff characterizes the new situation in this way:

> With the installation of military regimes in many of the countries of Latin America, and in the face of the totalitarianism of the national security ideology, the tasks of the theology of liberation have basically changed. We must live and think from a situation of captivity. We must work out a genuine theology of captivity. This theology will not be a substitute for liberation theology—it will be new tactics, dictated by the repressive systems. Captivity shapes the greater horizon against which we must work and reflect on liberation.[6]

At the outset of this same article, Boff proposes that the essential traits of the theology of captivity will be the same as those of the theology of liberation.

> The theology of liberation and captivity, as it is articulated in Latin America, has no intention of being a theology of relationships, or genitives, as for example the theology of sin, of revolution, of secularization, of the religious life, and so on. That is, it has no intention of being just one theological theme among many. On the contrary, it intends to offer a comprehensive manner of articulating the task of understanding the faith in a church dedicated to praxis. It means to be a different way and manner of doing and thinking theology. This manner of doing and thinking embraces, and presupposes, a different manner of being, a different manner of living. This new manner of living is called captivity—liberation's antithesis.[7]

Pablo Richard gives a bit more attention to the background of the new situation. He sees the development of the political situation since 1968 as having traversed three stages: (1) the disappearance of the bourgeois classes; (2) the development of new forms of domination; (3) the strengthening of movements under way among workers and the masses.

Richard sees three different possibilities for the church's response to the new situation: (1) the church can adapt to the new forms of domination; (2) it can attempt to reconstruct the old relationships; (3) it can renounce the old forms, cease relying on the dominant sectors for support, and take sides with the oppressed.

Finally, Richard sees three active currents in theology: (1) the theology of captivity; (2) theological protest against the national security systems—commitment to human rights; (3) the theology of pastoral activity among the masses.

By way of cursory evaluation of these three currents, Richard says that the theology of captivity can scarcely pretend to be a new theology, but can only contribute to an awareness of the factual situation. After all, what praxis can it possibly undertake? He looks for more from the theological protest approach, but, he warns, this approach runs the risk of speaking rather too idealistically of "humanity" and "the people." Finally, in the theology of a popular pastoral praxis he sees an important new contribution (the discovery of the culture of the people), but here he thinks there is the danger that the actual class situation of the people may be overlooked.

All this leads Richard to conclude that the theology of liberation is irreplaceable. Far from having a successor, it must now be radicalized, and this in a twofold manner: in political praxis, and in the "claim of faith":

> The radicalization of the theology of liberation is possible only from this double, intrinsically interconnected, radicality of politics and faith. Ideological backsliding and the weakening of the faith condition each other mutually. The theology of liberation is militant, and believing. More than ever, we must strengthen and develop it today through the radicality of our revolutionary commitment, and of our faith in the resurrected Christ.[8]

Gustavo Gutiérrez draws two conclusions from the new situation. One affords us access to the significance of the reality with which we are faced. The other demonstrates that the old basic thesis of the theology of liberation still holds good.

> But in view of the political function these groups [those opposed to liberation theology] perform in today's society, and in the church in Latin America, one must realize that deeper things are at stake: life or death for countless Latin Americans, and the hope of a Christian community bearing witness to a God of liberation.[9]

And at the end of his study of "theology from the underside of history," Gutiérrez writes:

> What is primarily at issue is not a theology, but popular liberation. . . . In order to be a part of theology and a service to a concrete process of liberation, it has to be liberated—as do we also—from every restraint that impedes solidarity with the poor and exploited of this world.[10]

PART II

THE RETURN TO JESUS CHRIST IN THE THEOLOGY OF LIBERATION

Since the time of Hugo Assmann's statement in 1971 that the theology of liberation had no suitable Christology,[1] Christological and "Jesuological" reflection within that theology has grown by leaps and bounds.[2] As the theology of liberation began to see the light of day, in the context and aftermath of the Medellín Conference, it was the theme of the Exodus event that stood in the foreground of its biblical reflection.[3] Later the Exodus theme was joined by a Christological one. So, for example, Arnaldo Zenteno wrote, at the turn of the decade:

The Exile and Return are experiences of death and resurrection. They unveil the intentions of God (Isa. 53), and find their fulfillment in the New Testament. Christ is the living way to genuine holiness (John 14:6), but he is a way, a road, whose end we have not yet reached. For Paul, life in this mortal body is an exile (2 Cor. 5:6). For John, Christians are in the world, but not of it (John 17:16). God's holiness and truth must be our support, for God will surely lead us, through Christ, to our true country (1 Pet. 1:15).[4]

Zenteno draws the same parallel when referring to the New Testament conception of Jesus as the "new Moses" (alluding to Deut. 18:18), and this grounds his understanding of the redemption through Christ as the fulfillment of God's rescue plans for human beings, prefigured in the Exodus event.[5]

Juan Hernández Pico makes another connection, this time in the area of the faith experience.

This experience is articulated in various essential moments. *First*, it implies the profession of a Christian identity that accepts and assumes as its "first word" the word of summons and mission spoken by God from within the history of human beings. But his word is spoken not from within just any history at random, but specifically from within the history of an oppressed and abandoned people, whom God calls forth to a liberation and solidarity which will constitute them, creatively, as a people of God. This structure of the "first word," the revealing word of a God in history, flashes forth now in the model of Abraham, now in the model of Moses—both of them "Exodus models"—and then, despite all undue "spiritualization" of the gospel, achieves its culmination in the model of the historical Jesus, who is the model of the "new Exodus," open, once more, to the upbuilding of a free and united people of God.[6]

Thus the Exodus theme is salient even as Christology is introduced. But Christology in the theology of liberation did not stick there. Gradually there arose an independent and recognizable body of reflection that may finally be characterized and presented as liberation theology's "return to Jesus." This body of reflection calls for our investigation. We shall undertake that investigation in the pages that follow, in which we shall attempt to systematize some of the elements that the theology of liberation has developed in the area of Christology.

Chapter 5

Interest in Jesus[1]

Christ died so that we might know that not everything is permitted.
    But not any Christ. The Christ who cannot be co-opted by accommodationists and opportunists as the historical Jesus.[2]

Thus in this programmatic declaration, with which he concludes the one-page preface of his book *Being and the Messiah*, José Porfírio Miranda serves notice that his interest in Jesus is not historically conditioned, but is, in the broadest sense, political: not everything is permitted. His concern is to discover a pre-eminent, pure instance for study, so as to be able to take sides in a Latin American situation charged with conflict.

The time has come when all those who write or speak about Christ must also state whether they are struggling for the church or for Christianity. . . . Justice and exploitation are not . . . indistinguishable.[3]

And yet, in spite of his preface's assurances to the contrary, Miranda's book is not about Jesus. Rather it is a study in Johannine Christology, with the purpose of establishing a love of one's brothers and sisters (fraternal charity) as absolute demand, and realized eschatology as this demand's absolute perspective. Miranda makes it explicitly clear that the point of departure for his considerations is the situation he lives in, and that his purpose and goal is the renewal of praxis. Thus he demonstrates his endorsement of the basic aspirations of the theology of liberation.
    How do the other authors express an interest in Jesus and a Christology of liberation?

Hugo Assmann

Although he himself has developed no Christology,[4] Assmann explains why the theology of liberation must also do Christology. As part of that

37

explanation he makes a distinction between the intrinsic demands of scientific scholarship and the demands of praxis. He gives two principal reasons why it is necessary that liberation theologians give significant emphasis to Christology.

1. In view of his insistence upon an interdisciplinary approach to theology, as well as because, in his view, the ultimate root of political activity must be love, theology for Assmann will have the capability, and inalienable duty, of examining the basis of love.

To be sure, to Assmann's mind, all our committed contemporaries have something to say about love as the root of human political behavior:

> But there is a high point of love in the praxis of liberation: the capacity to give over one's life entirely for others; and this high point goes straight to the heart of liberation. *The symbol of its reality* (at once its symbol and its reality) *is the cross of Christ*.

The question is a radical one. What sense and meaning can it have to die for someone else? Assmann's view is that the theology of liberation can answer this question—in dialogue with all who are committed to liberation—for the theology of liberation can uncover the historical and political dimensions of the death of Jesus, and can learn to interpret this death as the radical praxis of liberation.[5]

2. But there is a practical reason, as well, why the theology of liberation should do Christology. The dialogue with non-Christians—with the "simple humanist"—pragmatically requires it. Assmann holds that the distinguishing characteristic of Christians is their greater commitment to liberation. And he explains:

> The Christian discovers Christ here and now, and clings fast to him— Christ present at this very moment in our sisters and brothers, especially the oppressed. This is what the expression, "the historical Christ" must come to mean, first and foremost, for Christians. That is, they must cling to the Christ present in current history, all the more so inasmuch as the discovery of this contemporaneity of Christ will call for a confrontation with Christ in his life and works of long ago. . . . Now a backward look into history acquires new meaning, as we cast our gaze back over two millennia of witness to liberation—liberation accomplished or slipped away, liberation hoped for or forgotten, liberation proclaimed and fundamentally accomplished in Christ. Now the task before us is to identify the Christ who effects human reconciliation in the "meantime" of the here and now with the Christ of long ago, the Christ who died and rose as the "man for others," thereby revealing the deepest mystery of humankind, the mystery of God himself in Christ, the basis and enablement of all human encounters that serve for mutual liberation.[6]

The first thing that strikes one is that Assmann's terminology is not characterized by the distinction between the historical Jesus and the Christ of proclamation and kerygma. For Assmann, "Jesus" and "Christ" are interchangeable terms. To this extent his Christology is identical with that of church tradition. Nor again is the fact that he simply presupposes this confession, this faith, and does not seek to explain or justify its origin anything new to Christology. What is new is that he only asks the Christological question after a contemporary situation has forced it upon him, and hence considers this retrospective inquiry as meaningful only insofar as it appears to him to be helpful for gaining control of the present situation. His interest is in Christians' collaboration in the liberation struggle of Latin America. The question of Jesus, or of Christianity, has meaning only in so far as it furthers this collaboration.

Gustavo Gutiérrez

Nor has Gustavo Gutiérrez developed his own Christology. But under the heading, "Jesus and the Political World,"[7] in which he goes back to an earlier article of his by the same title,[8] he makes it clear why he poses the question of Jesus. First, to be sure, it is striking that his subhead, "Christ the Liberator," occurs fifty pages earlier under another general heading.[9] Since Gutiérrez makes the terminological distinction between Jesus and Christ in these respective headings, it will be interesting to us to look into the material contained under each.

"Jesus and the Political World"

Gutiérrez's quest for Jesus, and especially for Jesus' attitude toward the political constellation of his own time, is conditioned and molded by the liberation movements in Latin America. That is, Gutiérrez seeks to answer the question of how a Christian should behave politically in Latin America and thinks we can learn something from Jesus' example. To be sure, Gutiérrez is aware of the risks of this approach:

> But [a serious reconsideration of the alleged apolitical attitude of Jesus] has to be undertaken with a respect for the historical Jesus, not forcing the facts in terms of our current concerns. If we wished to discover in Jesus the least characteristic of a contemporary political militant we would not only misrepresent his life and witness and demonstrate a lack of understanding on our part of politics in the present world; we would also deprive ourselves of what his life and witness have that is deep and universal and, therefore, valid and concrete for today's man.[10]

Here too a profession of faith in Jesus is presupposed, and the interest in the Jesus question is a practical one, just as with Assmann.

"Christ the Liberator"

This heading is ranged in the systematic part of Gutiérrez's book and within the chapter entitled "Liberation and Salvation." The author's point of departure is the interpretation of the global Latin American situation as a sinful one: sin is the name he gives to all recognizable factors of misery and exploitation. Christians have always known that their struggle is with sin. The discovery of the "political dimension of sin" leads to a new understanding of Christ's role in this struggle. The kingdom of God as gift, the death and resurrection of Christ as a fundamental liberation from all sin, and today's struggle for liberation are for Gutiérrez aspects of the same comprehensive liberation process.

> Those who reduce the work of salvation are . . . those who in order to protect salvation (or to protect their interests) lift salvation from the midst of history, where men and social classes struggle to liberate themselves from the slavery and oppression to which other men and social classes have subjected them. It is those who refuse to see that the salvation of Christ is a radical liberation from all misery, all despoliation, all alienation.[11]

Here, then, we have a matter of systematic interest. The gift of the kingdom of God, Gutiérrez holds, and the human struggle for liberation turn out to be intrinsically interrelated. Of course, Gutiérrez's practical interest—that of motivating Christians to become involved in the liberation of Latin America—is not to be overlooked.[12]

Segundo Galilea

The overriding preoccupation of this Chilean theologian, to whom Reinhard Frieling attributes a "perspicacious, carefully considered" Christology,[13] is the reorientation of Latin American spirituality. Galilea has observed that, for one group of Latin American Christians strongly committed to the struggle for liberation, prayer has receded into the background; indeed it may appear to them to be altogether superfluous. For another group, prayer is very much "front and center," while it is social involvement that is "writ small." Galilea insists that the specifically Christian contribution to Latin American liberation is, instead, the internal connection between "contemplation and commitment,"[14] and he elucidates his position by referring to the example of Jesus.

> Jesus' example is . . . instructive in the highest degree in spite of its uniqueness. . . . The contemplative's involvement with the poor and little ones can find concretization in two directions. The one leads to the direct political option. . . . The second option for involvement with the

"little ones" is only indirectly one of everyday political commitment. Directly, it is the option of Christian prophetism.[15]

A detailed presentation of Jesus' example, in his renunciation of power, violence, and marriage, is to be found in Galilea's article, "Powerlessness as Poverty and Prophetic Stance."[16]

Galilea takes a clear Christological position with respect to the Christ of faith and the Jesus of history, opting for the former, which, he says, has always held the primacy in good Catholic teaching.

Juan Luis Segundo

Segundo's main concern is to see the church of Latin America today forthrightly tackle the basic problem of whether the future of the continent ought to be determined by capitalism or by socialism.[17] Here he makes two presuppositions: (1) Religious institutions, including the church and theology, have only a relative, functional value vis-à-vis a human communion delivered from alienation. His reference here is to Mark 2:27: "The sabbath was made for man, not man for the sabbath." (2) Theology has the duty to call attention to all deviations on the part of the church from its original, basic orientation. Here, holds Segundo, it will be of value to refer to Jesus' confrontation with the theology of his own time. Segundo finds the latter conflict particularly clear-cut about the "way to make theology and about the instruments used by one camp or another in the theological task."[18] Prophetically—and "imprudently," Segundo remarks, with a side-swipe at European political theology—Jesus called healing simply "salvation" and liberation from creaturely ills "deliverance," when these favors remained ambiguous as to the future.[19]

One of the conclusions Segundo draws makes his main interest once more very clear:

> When the political theologians of Europe requires Latin Americans to put forward a project for a socialist society which will guarantee in advance that the evident defects of known socialist systems will be avoided, why do we not demand of Christ also that before telling a sick man who has been cured, "Your faith has saved you," he should give a guarantee that that cure will not be followed by even graver illnesses?[20]

Juan Hernández Pico

Hernández Pico's concern is for a new consciousness of the task and method of theology itself. Traditional theology has been too esoteric in its scientific approach to its material. It has done its work without contact with basic Christian living. As a result, theology's principal concern has been the maintenance of the ecclesiastical system. This is where a new consciousness of the task and method of theology steps forward, in reference to Jesus.

There is no legitimation for the ecclesiastical institution outside the gospel of Jesus Christ. Its deviation may never be allowed to go to the extreme of failing to transmit the good news of Jesus. This message—however obscurely it may be presented, however disincarnate it may be offered—is alive with the charismatic power of Jesus. There is but one gospel, and the Spirit keeps the memory of Jesus' disquieting message alive there. The revolutionary fact that God in Jesus did not choose the mighty of this world, the fact that the wisdom of God engaged in no dialogue with the wisdom of the dominators (1 Cor. 1–2), has occasioned the rise in Latin America (and not only here) of a new method of doing theology, based on a new way of understanding the theological function.[21]

Two Documents from Church Praxis

The following texts are not from scientific theological works, but they are evidently inspired by the theology of liberation. They make no ex professo appeal to that theology, but their method of argumentation makes it clear that they are going back to Jesus in an effort to acquire the thrust and stimulus they need for a renewal in the area of church praxis, in their respective Latin American contexts.

"A People on the Move"[22]

Jesus Christ was very courageous. His love for the oppressed was carried to its ultimate consequences. This love threatened the privileges of the powerful. And so the powerful nailed him to a cross and he died. But as God always wins out over evil, God gave a living Christ back to the people. God's people now set out on Christ's own road of love—and an oppressed people become the lords of history.[23]

"I Have Heard My People Crying"[24]

To be sure, it is not enough to diagnose these difficulties merely from a scientific knowledge of the situation. Christ has taught us by his example to live what he proclaimed. He preached a human communion of brothers and sisters, a love which all structures of society ought to inspire. Above all, he lived his own message of liberation, carrying it to its ultimate consequences. The mighty ones of his people saw in his message, and in the efficacious love with which he proclaimed it, a genuine danger for their economic, social, political, and religious interests, and they sentenced him to death. But his Spirit, active today as yesterday, restores his thrust to history, and manifests himself in the solidarity of those who fight for liberty in a spirit of truly light-bearing love for their oppressed sisters and brothers.[25]

Leonardo Boff

Leonardo Boff is the Brazilian theologian who produced the first cohesive Latin American Christology. His book's subtitle, in the second Spanish edition, reads: *Toward a Critical Christology for Our Times*. Any connection with the theology of liberation would seem at first glance to be in sole virtue of Christ's title of "Liberator." Neither Boff's chapter titles[26] nor his citations, which are almost all from European, mainly German, literature, indicate a typically Latin American Christology.[27] But Boff too has the Latin American situation in view, and directs his attention particularly to the role of the church. His purpose is to develop a new Christology, one that will call church praxis to account.

Latin American society is most afflicted by the problem of the marginalization of immense proportions of the population. The question cannot be posed merely within the dimensions of a personal conversion. There are structural evils that transcend individual ones. The church is, whether it likes it or not, involved in a context that transcends it. What will be its function? Shall it be oil or sand within the social mechanism? On the other hand, it ought not to create its own little world within the great world. It ought to participate, *critically*, in the global upsurge of liberation that Latin American society is undergoing. Like Jesus, it ought to give special attention to the nobodies and those without a voice. It ought to accentuate particularly the secular and liberating dimensions contained in the message of Christ. It should emphasize the future that he promises for this world, a world in which the future kingdom is growing between the wheat and the cockle, not for a few privileged people, but for all.[28]

It is easy to see that Boff is less concerned than his peers with a study of Jesus for the sake of a social critique. His primary interest in Jesus is for the sake of a critique of the church, which, he says, must now seek a new role in a Latin American reality that is undergoing such transformation. The thirst for liberation, which Boff understands as liberation from all forms of alienation, and which he says is surging like a wave across the whole of Latin America, has become the hermeneutical key for the return to Jesus.

The Churches in Latin America have been on the side of the holders of power and therefore on the side of the oppressors. At the same time there is the new hermeneutic possibility, revealing liberating aspects of Christ which would otherwise have remained concealed. In every century Christians have read texts concerning the Kingdom of God, Jesus' conflict with the Pharisees, and the text of Luke 23:2 about Jesus subverting the people. But their situation has not allowed them to hear the political echoes of these words. Today, for many Christians of Latin America these texts have acquired an immediate political and existential significance. Their concentration on the liberating aspect has resulted in a new image of Jesus Christ and enormous possibilities for the praxis of liberation.[29]

Jon Sobrino

Sobrino opens his consideration of the renewed interest in the historical Jesus with a reference to José Porfirio Miranda (see our note 2, above). Unlike many of his colleagues, Sobrino shows no interest in the topical value of a return to Jesus Christ in general. He consciously distinguishes between the historical Jesus and the Christ of faith. He is struck by the intensifying desire of liberation theologians to return to Jesus, and he says:

Latin American bishops have not hesitated to invoke that figure [of the historical Jesus] at the Synod of Bishops in Rome. This interest is not merely exegetical or historical. Latin Americans are not interested solely in ascertaining the historical facts. They regard the historical Jesus as the most satisfactory theological focus for all the different themes in liberation theology.[30]

For Sobrino, the question of the interest in Jesus is only part of the question of interest in theology.[31] He finds the specific difference of Latin American theology vis-à-vis European theology to be the following:

In the face of the liberating movement of the Enlightenment, [Latin American theology] spontaneously orientates itself toward the challenge presupposed by the Second Enlightenment: the liberating function of knowledge does not reside in its capacity to explain an existing reality, nor again to lend meaning to a faith threatened by this reality, but in its capacity to transform a reality, and thereby lend it meaning at last, and in this manner to recover the lost or threatened meaning of faith.[32]

A little further on, he adds:

Latin American theology asks not only what the intention of the theologian is in doing theology, but what also the actual benefits, the actual consequences to society, of that theology are.[33]

Only now, then, do we see why Sobrino's orientation in Christology is more toward the historical Jesus than the Christ of faith:

We can gain access to the Christ of faith, the resurrected Lord, through some sort of direct intentional act: e.g., a profession of faith, a doxology, a prayer, or cultic worship. However, we cannot gain access to the historical Jesus that way, as the Gospels make clear. We gain access to him only through a specific kind of praxis, which the Gospels describe as the "following of Jesus," or "discipleship."[34]

Javier Jiménez Limón

Jiménez Limón makes no new contribution to Christology as far as content is concerned. What he brings to bear on the topic is a consideration of a special aspect of Christology which we shall take up more in detail below: the problem of Jesus' attitude toward power.[35]
His article begins:

My position is that, from a Latin American viewpoint, one of the most urgent, and at the same time most difficult, theological tasks of the present day is the formulation of a theology of power. Its urgency arises principally from the Christian ethical imperative efficaciously to combat stupendous forces of oppression. The difficulty lies mainly in the tendency to enlist Christian statements about power in the service of a "demobilizing ideology"—or simply reject them as themselves "ideological," in favor of a kind of direct political pragmatism. Perhaps the tension between the two citations from Paul on our title page ["The kingdom of God is not just words, it is power"—1 Cor. 4:20; and "God's weakness is stronger than human strength"—1 Cor. 1:25] will serve to demonstrate that the urgency and complexity of the subject of power are nothing new, but that they reside in the extraordinary nature of the force with which God has demonstrated his power in the history of Jesus.[36]

One has to say that we are confronted, in the structure of Jiménez's argumentation—position of the question, reference to the current situation, reference to tradition, attempt at a synthesis—with a theological approach that is altogether traditional. In the actual execution of the task he sets himself in this structure, however, there are two points that are typically Latin American. First, Jiménez's reference to the current situation is drawn up not mainly along rational lines, but existential ones—lines of personal commitment. Second, he has a clear political position of his own. Thus we note that it is only after these two points have been clearly made, in the elaboration of the earlier elements in his traditional-looking structure, that he approaches Jesus for the purpose of shedding light on these same two matters.

Ignacio Ellacuría

Ellacuría teaches theology in the same university as Jon Sobrino (Universidad Centroamericana José Simeón Cañas, in San Salvador). He has writ-

ten a book entitled *Teología política*—in English, *Freedom Made Flesh*.[37]
For Ellacuría the theological problem of consuming interest is that of the
relationship between profane history and salvation history. "What does
salvation history have to do with salvation in history?" he asks.[38]

In order to answer this question, Ellacuría looks into the matter of the
return to Jesus, the new interest in Jesus. Then he attempts to work out an
explanation of the relationship between the gospel and the mission of the
church. Finally, he speaks of the consequences of all this for the Latin
American church.[39]

At the outset of his investigation of the return to Jesus, Ellacuría writes:

> To determine the nature and extent of salvation in history within salva-
> tion history, we must center our reflection on Jesus himself, who brings
> salvation history to its culmination. The thrust and import of this
> culmination is certainly historical; in other words, it comes from and
> moves towards something. At the same time Jesus is clearly an indispen-
> sable key to the whole process and somehow a definitive element in this
> coming from and moving towards. Thus the prophecy of the Old Testa-
> ment, for example, takes on its full ascendant import only in terms of
> what Jesus himself represents. By the same token the meaning of Jesus
> himself would escape us if we disregarded the history of prophecy.
>
> There is no lack of difficulties in trying to explore Jesus' prophetic
> mission. A study of the political character of Jesus' mission would cer-
> tainly provide us with a sound orientation for determining how much
> salvation in history plays a role in the full picture of salvation history.
> But the political character of his mission is already clouded and obscured
> in the New Testament version of his life. It continues to be obscured in
> the course of centuries by both the classic and the less classic readings of
> the New Testament. The classic readings suffer from an ignorance of
> exegesis and history; the lesser readings suffer from a mere desire to con-
> tinue what has been said before.
>
> The political character of his mission is also obscured by the ahistor-
> ical cast of various traditional christologies, which do not take Jesus'
> historical life very seriously in trying to construct themselves. This brings
> us up against a preliminary problem that we must discuss a bit: What can
> a christology be? What should it be?[40]

One's first impression is that Ellacuría's theological interest in a study of
Jesus is theoretical. This impression, however, is not borne out in the rest of
the book. The purpose of looking into the question of Jesus is not to shed
light on a theological discussion but to show the direction the Latin American Church ought to take in its current praxis. Ellacuría invites the reader:
"Let us analyze the prophetic style of Jesus more in detail, since it has a
major role in giving shape and form to the prophetic aspect of the
Church."[41] Hence with Ellacuría as well, a practical interest stands behind
his theoretical concerns.

Eduardo Pironio

Pironio, an Argentinian born in Italy, was Secretary General of the Latin American Bishops' Conference at the time of Medellín and exerted a telling influence on the course of that meeting. He has emphasized in many ways that it is the key word, "liberation" that will unlock an understanding of Medellín's conclusions. As a bishop he became very involved in the discussion of the theology of liberation that ensued upon the Medellín conference and made no attempt to conceal the fact that his episcopal viewpoint was of great importance for his reflection—as for instance in his introductory reflections to the minutes of the CELAM meetings, *Liberation: Conversations in CELAM.*[42] It is the episcopal stance from which he seeks, among other things, a revitalization of church activity through a consideration of the liberating activity of Jesus. "Liberation," he says, "is something that is actualized in time, and something that the church, which continues the liberating mission of Jesus, must be about the business of actualizing."[43]

But Pironio is concerned to underplay the political implications of the concept of liberation and accentuates the "religious" moment of Jesus' mission:

> The subject of liberation must be approached in the integral context of salvation history and the essentially religious mission of the church. Like Christ, the church is sent "to bring the good news to the poor, to proclaim liberty to captives, . . . to set the downtrodden free" (Luke 4:18). It is concerned with the good news of the kingdom (Matt. 9:35) and the freedom of the Spirit (2 Cor. 3:17). The road to change ever passes by way of the inner demands of the Beatitudes of the Gospel (Matt. 5:3–11).[44]

One cannot simply reject out of hand the impression that Pironio's interests, while couched in the language of liberation theology, are none the less primarily in the ecclesial, or religious, area.

> The reason why we are interested in the liberation of human beings is that we are interested ultimately in God and the liberating deed of Jesus Christ.[45]

Synopsis

All our theologians have one thing in common. Their interest in going back to Jesus is not a theoretical one. They make their Christological study neither as pure historians and exegetes, nor as systematic theologians. Their interest in Jesus is practical. They find themselves in a most tense situation of social, political, and economic extremity, and this situation appears to them as the result not of the ineluctable human lot, but of the action of contingent external forces.

Hence they begin to reflect in a new way on the role of Christian faith. In doing so they by no means question the standpoint of that faith: rather they reinforce it. Faith in Jesus Christ is the firm foundation on which they stand. But their concrete situation has opened their eyes to a new view of the person of Jesus. In a word, they have discovered the political dimension of Jesus' life and mission, and consequently of our faith in him. When they come to the question of just how this dimension ought to come to expression in the present situation of Christians in Latin America, differences appear. One group of theologians is primarily interested in a change in political and social relationships, and thereupon of course in the church's cooperation in bringing these changes about. Another group, however, is primarily concerned with changing the church, and only ulteriorly with a new order in politics and society.[46] The unexpressed, basic principle underlying the interests of both groups, however, is that what Jesus wills is good for human beings.[47]

Chapter 6

Going Back to Jesus

At the risk of oversimplification, we might venture to say: Liberal
theology's interest in Jesus was historical, with dogmatic implications; post-
Bultmannian theology's interest in Jesus lies along the lines of systematic
theology; and liberation theology's interest in Jesus is in the area of
praxis.

Hence it will come as no surprise if, in the argumentation of liberation
theologians who treat of New Testament assertions about Jesus, little importance is attributed to the distinction often so meticulously drawn in
European exegesis and theology between the *ipsissima verba Jesu* and the
words of the primitive Christian community. Our liberation theologians do
distinguish between the New Testament presentation of Jesus' words and
deeds in the framework of his life, and its presentation of his resurrection.
But even here the line drawn is not between historically verifiable assertions
and statements belonging to a profession of faith, but between "Jesuological" and "Christological" assertions of the New Testament with respect to
their relevance for certain aspects of the social situations in which Christians today seek to live their faith as a liberation praxis.

Particularly suggestive reflections along these lines are offered by the
writers of the statement "Biblia y la liberación de los pueblos":

> The Bible is the record of certain decisive moments in history in which
> the face of God and human destiny have been revealed. Now, they have
> been revealed there not as something that always existed and is just now
> coming to light, but as something new, something just now arising. The
> word becomes flesh. Jesus goes about doing good. Jesus comes to serve.
> Jesus suffers capital punishment. God does not abandon Jesus. Jesus
> rises from the dead and gives us his Spirit. We must live by doing the
> truth. . . . It is nonsense to ask what Jesus did in his lifetime in order to
> copy it today. This literal way of believing is not the Christian way of
> believing. The letter kills. It is the Spirit that gives life.[1]

It will become evident in the course of our investigation that the theology of liberation prefers certain New Testament passages to others. Further, our theologians often clearly borrow their selection and interpretation of these texts from one another.[2] Hence we shall divide our treatment here not by theologian but by material, and we shall cite differences among theologians only when they differ from one another in their interpretations of the same text.

The "Political Jesus"[3]

The task of drawing near to the human Jesus of Nazareth, in whom God became flesh, is becoming an ever more urgent one.[4]

But when one "draws near to Jesus" one discovers the political dimension of his activity. It is fairly simple to lay this discovery out in theoretical fashion, almost in thesis form, and this is what we shall do first, before undertaking a consideration of our theologians' various concrete approaches in their mutual dependency.

Like Gustavo Gutiérrez, Segundo Galilea places the accent on a recovery of a Christology of the incarnation. His purpose, to be sure, is to afford Christians involved in the Latin American liberation process, who lack a political Christology, the opportunity to orientate their involvement on the model of Jesus' political involvement. For Galilea—and here he relies on the work of Martin Hengel and Oscar Cullmann—it is clear that various attempts to see Jesus either as simply unpolitical (as an Essene) or, at the other end of the spectrum, as a revolutionary (a Zealot) have now splintered on the rocks of objectivity. Jesus was a person of his time, and thus part of the social, religious, and political movements of Palestine. He was surrounded by conflicts. His story shows his inability to avoid conflict with the religious and political authorities of his day. So says Galilea, referring to Luke 23:2–5 and John 19:12.

In order authentically to place Jesus' mission within the situation of his time, we must relate the mystery of the incarnation to this case.[5]

Samuel Ruiz García, too, holds the historical circumstances of Jesus' activity to be of great importance for an answer to today's urgent questions.

The best thing to do is to ask theology and exegesis what Jesus tells us about these problems [of violence, unity, and peace]. A satisfactory answer will not be forthcoming from a theology reluctant to ascribe meaning to the concrete historical life, passion, and death of Christ. We can look for an answer only from a theology whose exegetical infrastructure keeps its eye on Jesus and his actual historical context. If Jesus' politics had been one of "Don't get your hands dirty," he would not have died on the cross.[6]

Juan Luis Segundo takes something of another tack, asserting that the mistake we have been making in assessing Jesus' attitude toward politics has been to identify the decisive political quantity in Jesus' Palestine as the Roman Empire. No, Segundo insists, it was the Jewish theocracy. And of course there can be no question about Jesus' decided opposition to the Jewish theocracy.[7]

Four Areas

Coming down to particulars, we can distinguish four different areas in which a discovery of the "political Jesus" has been taking place: (1) the new assessment of the prophetic element in Jesus' life and teaching; (2) the new assessment of the relationship of individuals and structures; (3) the new attention to Jesus's praxis; and (4) the new considerations of the relationship between biblical tradition and revolution.

THE PROPHETICAL ELEMENT IN JESUS' LIFE AND ACTIVITY

In the platform of the Argentinian movement, Priests for the Third World, we read:

Christ unites in his person the prophet and the priest. But the priest is subordinate to the prophet. All the pictures of Jesus drawn by all the evangelists show him first and foremost as the prophet. His activity is not a "sacral" one, shut up within the Temple and its precinct and unfolding within the context of public worship. Jesus' activity takes place in the realm of the "profane." His precursor is a prophet, John the Baptist. And like the prophets of the Old Testament, he strides forth to meet the priests, colliding with the established powers.

He gives public worship a new meaning, by practicing a duty and a justice that find their culmination in love. Before you bring your gift to the altar, you must solve the problems you have with your brother. Jesus approves the behavior of the Samaritan who "becomes involved" with the one in need, and condemns that of the priest and Levite who stroll by unconcerned.[8]

Via this interpretation of the prophetic element, the authors seek to restore to Argentinian Christians, especially to priests, their rightful role as prophets.

Segundo Galilea is of the same mind. He sees two possibilities for arousing Latin American Christians from a consideration of Jesus to Christian praxis. They may be moved either to direct political praxis or to prophetic pastoral involvement. Both ways are expressions of committed love. They are not opposed. They belong together. Both are nurtured by Jesus' encounter with the poor. To be sure, the former alternative, that of direct political praxis as an expression of Christian love, is in Galilea's view of things modeled rather on the example of Moses, while the latter, that of prophetic pastoral involvement, is inspired by Jesus' example directly. But Jesus' prophetic proclamation and message have precisely a social and political content, inasmuch as they expose the injustices and inhumanity of the prevailing social system. And they thereby provide an orientation for Christian commitment to the poor.[9]

Elsewhere, Galilea summarizes his position on Jesus and politics in five theses:

1. In virtue of the incarnation, and of the historical nature of his mission, Jesus was part of the society of Israel, its political tensions and its power conflicts. His trial and death are political facts.

2. On the other hand, Jesus neither claimed to be nor behaved as a revolutionary or as a political leader. His message contains neither a program nor a strategy for political liberation. Jesus essentially proclaimed the Kingdom of God as a religious and pastoral message.[10]

3. Nevertheless, in his religious and pastoral message, Jesus generated a dynamism of socio-political change, for his time and for all history to come.[11]

Galilea elucidates this third thesis with argumentation to the effect that the Christian proclamation stands in opposition on nonconformism to any society or politics, sheerly on principle[12]—just because it seeks to change human beings and society. After all, the gospel contains values of justice and freedom, and all systems call these values into question.

In this same sense, Christ's activity, too, is political. For, in its consequences, it veers into the realm of political society and produces changes in political societies. . . . The proclamation of the kingdom constitutes the implantation in history, once and for all, of a principle of freedom and social critique, both as promise and as denunciation.[13]

The next thesis runs:

4. The political consequences of Jesus' message in the society of his time are due to the fact that that message relativized Roman totalitarianism and called the poor to the kingdom, to the universal consciousness that it created in the disciples, and to the proclamation of the specific values of the Beatitudes.[14]

This assertion, too, is accompanied by an explanation, which reads, in part:

> Without offering a model for a better society, or any concrete program
> of liberation, Jesus creates a movement for freedom and community that
> we encounter at the origin of so many later social changes.[15]

Finally:

> 5. In his conflicts with the established powers of his time, Jesus as-
> sumed a pastoral and prophetical stance. This led him to renounce all use
> of temporal power and every form of violence.[16]

Now Galilea proceeds to the pastoral conclusion which he says is to be
drawn from all these theses taken together! Jesus' behavior was charismatic, as can be seen from his renunciation of political power and violence
alike; both of these renunciations are now to be brought to fulfillment by
charismatic persons in the church; neither, however, is binding on all Christians.

> The proclamation of a society of equals, of sisters and brothers, "has a
> name" today. It corresponds to historical undertakings, and precise
> political programs, whose ideals—a society in solidarity, a community of
> brothers and sisters without special privileges—are but the socio-political
> translation of the call to the poor to come share the kingdom.[17]

Thus Galilea sees Jesus as the inspiration for our own political behavior.
But he says nothing about how the politics inspired by Jesus ought to look.
He has no specifics to offer regarding goals or principles for the removal of
injustice and poverty, the effecting of a community of brothers and sisters,
and so on.

The inner unity that obtains between religious renewal and social im-
provement is a characteristic of Jesus' proclamation for Gustavo Gutiérrez,
as well. Jesus is in the great prophetic tradition, says Gutiérrez, the tradition
that subordinates sacrifice to mercy and acknowledges authentic divine
worship only where social justice prevails. Ineluctably, the prophets injected themselves into political conflicts. Not that we are thereby afforded
pretext for thrusting the individual and religious facets of Jesus' message
into the background, in favor of too exclusive an emphasis on the political
facet. Here is what Gutiérrez says:

> What then are we to think of Jesus' attitude in these matters? The facts
> we have recalled vigorously ratify what we know of the universality and
> totality of his work. This universality and totality touch the very heart of
> political behavior, giving it its true dimension and depth. Misery and

social injustice reveal "a sinful situation," a disintegration of brotherhood and communion; by freeing us from sin, Jesus attacks the roots of
an unjust order. For Jesus, the liberation of the Jewish people was only
one aspect of a universal, permanent revolution. Far from showing no
interest in this liberation, Jesus rather placed it on a deeper level, with
far-reaching consequences.[18]

This argumentation leaves open the question of the relationship between
deliverance from sin and the suppression of injustice. The political aspect of
Jesus' life and work is not clarified by its relegation to a "deeper level."

Hugo Assmann lays emphasis on Jesus as the culmination of the historicity of God. But it is the task of prophets to keep watch over our consciousness of that historicity—and thereby to indicate a direction for the
prophetic attitude of the church as a whole. Says Assmann:

> The originality of Judeo-Christianity when compared with other reli-
> gions resides above all in the historicization of the experience of the en-
> counter with God, and hence in the historicization of salvation itself. The
> culmination of this historicization is the incarnation of God in Jesus of
> Nazareth.
>
> The human being's salvation does not proceed via a noncosmic, non-
> historical relationship with the divinity in a vertical dimension. All essen-
> tial biblical categories have to do with changing history—to moving
> history forward. Everything is orientated toward exodus, toward emer-
> gence into the light of the promises, toward leaving one's land, towards
> messianism, and so on. Today we would say it was a long story of dis-
> placed persons. This is the framework of the mission of Abraham and
> the mission of Moses. This is the basic theme insisted on by the prophets.
> The importance of the themes of desert and exile are here, as well.
> Whenever the people of Israel fell into the temptation to "install them-
> selves" (even in those days, the establishment sought to legitimate itself
> by the elaborate beauty of its public worship and fidelity to tradition),
> the prophets arrived on the scene to place things in their proper perspec-
> tive of Israel's destined journey down the pathways of history.[19]

As yet Assmann proposes no concretization of Jesus' prophetic role. His
line of thought runs: commencement in the prophets, culmination of the
prophet-model in Jesus—and now return to Jesus in the present situation of
commencement, of new beginnings, in Latin America. Assmann's conception of the incarnation as the culmination of God's injection into history
evinces his starting point: a Christological profession of faith.

INDIVIDUAL CONVERSION AND ALTERATION OF STRUCTURES

For Gustavo Gutiérrez, a key to the interpretation of Jesus' political
stance will be found in a new assessment of the relationship between indi-

vidual conversion and the alteration of structures. (To be sure, Gutiérrez has already developed this line of thinking without reference to Jesus—having stated that Latin American Christians are slowly coming to the realization that the question, What is the good of changing the structures without a change in the human heart? is a specious one: conversion of the individual also depends on a change of structures.[20]) Gutiérrez takes issue with Oscar Cullmann's thesis that Christian political involvement does not flow from Jesus' proclamation but from despair of the imminent coming of the kingdom of God. No, Gutiérrez insists, the intention to alter structures was an integral component of Jesus' general aim. His call for personal conversion is not to be understood as an alternative to structural change, but rather as an alternative to formalistic worship, and this is why Jesus' proclamation includes a concern for social structures. "The life and preaching of Jesus postulate the unceasing search for a new kind of man in a qualitatively different society."[21]

HUMANE VS. "PHARISAICAL" THEOLOGY

Juan Luis Segundo plots the political dimension of Christian faith by observing Jesus' praxis. It is true that Segundo also argues from Jesus' theology, as the New Testament presents it in contradistinction to that of the Pharisees. Here, according to Segundo, one can see the internal connection between Christian theology and political questioning and position-taking. But ultimately it is Jesus' actual praxis that tips the balance.[22] Referring to Mark 3:1-6, Segundo asserts that Jesus' adversaries were confounded because they attempted to deal with him on purely theological grounds—which was precisely how Jesus refused to argue.

> To their surprise . . . Jesus rejects the possibility of forming any concrete judgment on the initial basis of theology or its realm of competence. One cannot begin with certitudes deduced from revelation: that is his response to them, embodied in the question for which they had no answer. It seems to be a purely human question in which the Sabbath is no different from any other day of the week: "Is it permitted *to do good* or *to do evil* on the Sabbath?" The Pharisees were prepared to answer a different question—an abstract, formal question of classic theology which took account of only the Sabbath itself, not human beings: "Is it permitted to do *anything at all* on the Sabbath?" Faced with Jesus' question, they have no theological criterion whatever and so they have nothing to say at all. Jesus' question points up a level that is prior to any and all theological questions, a level where human beings make their most critical and decisive options, i.e., the heart.[23]

And a little later, referring to Mark 3:23-28, Segundo says:

> Jesus reformulates the question or the problem on the only level where it can find a positive answer: in terms of what is good for people. For all

practical purposes, his response can be paraphrased as follows: it really doesn't matter who liberates them so long as they are really and effectively liberated. Why? Because it is God who is directly or indirectly behind any and all liberation. . . . The ultimate criterion in Jesus' theology is the remedy brought to some sort of human suffering, however temporary and provisional that remedy may be.[24]

Finally, a propos of the synoptic "Beelzebul pericopes" (Luke 11:14-16, paralleling Matthew 16:2-4 and Mark 8:11-13), Segundo says that here, as well, Jesus refuses to be measured by purely theological yardsticks, inasmuch as "he tries to show [the Pharisees] that they must leave room and openness in their theology for the relative, provisional, uncertain nature of criteria that human beings actually use to direct their lives in history when they are open to what is going on around them."[25] Segundo continues his discussion of the confrontation between Jesus and the Pharisees:

> But Jesus goes even further here and accuses them of being *hypocrites*. Today we would not dare to go so far. At most we might accuse theology of being too academic. But Jesus goes one step further, and that further step is typically *political*. If the Pharisees do in fact know very well how to find historical direction within a context of uncertainty, their quest for some theological authority is not prompted by any overwhelming anxiety in the face of events. It is prompted by their intention to impose on other people a kind of authority from which there is no appeal. That authority ranges from the realm of religion itself to the whole socio-political structure of Israel, which is determined far more by them than it is by the Romans (see Matt. 23:4-7).
>
> The other very different possibility, which might seem more logical but in fact is much more difficult in such matters, would be to place theology and its certitudes in the service of human beings who are scanning the complex signs of the times and trying to use them to find out how to love more and more, how to love better and better, and how to make a commitment to that sort of love.[26]

Then Segundo summarizes:

> There is no unbridgeable gap between the Church and politics, as Pharisaical theology claims. There is an intimate tie-up between the realm of human sensitivity and political commitment on the one hand, and theological reflection on the other hand. Recognition of that tie-up is an essential precondition for any theological methodology that purports to imitate the liberating creativity of Jesus' own methodology.[27]

Jesus is political, then, in Segundo's understanding, not by virtue of having undertaken any determinate political activity, but because he strove for the ultimate goal of all political activity: the betterment of the human condition. Hence, given the fact that, in his time, this goal was being proclaimed by religious institutions, Jesus saw his task as one of opposition to these institutions, whereby he could unmask their inhumanity. For Segundo it is of secondary importance whether Jesus' praxis be labeled political or theological. In either case he will measure it by the primary yardstick of humanity, healing, and liberation.

REVOLUTION AND BIBLICAL TRADITION

José Comblin develops his concept of a "political Jesus" on grounds of an affinity he discerns between the theme of revolution and the themes of biblical tradition. Comblin appeals, then, to "the revolutionary themes of Christianity,"[28] which he handles in two series: "New World" (subtitles: "Newness," "Promise," "Hope," "Freedom," "Covenant," "Spirit"); and "Transformation" (subtitles: "Judgment of God," "Kingdom of God," "Conversion," "Love," "Party of the Poor," "Death and Resurrection," "The Form the Church Takes").

In the section entitled "Freedom" Comblin says, in part:

> The New Testament is clearer still. Jesus' struggle with the Pharisees is a struggle to win back justice. Jesus was sentenced to death because he sought to replace a religion of servitude and obedience with a religion of love. The Sermon on the Mount is the Christian Declaration of Independence.[29]

And in "Death and Resurrection":

> The crucifixion is the judgment of God, the transformation, the fall of the rich, and the end of the old world. The resurrection is God's victory, the triumph of the poor, the realization of the promises, hope, love in action, the freedom of the daughters and sons of God, and the new people of the Covenant of peace and justice.[30]

It should not be overlooked that Comblin takes concepts that are provocative, "red flag" notions in Latin America, and considers them to arise from the New Testament. It is understandable, then, that for him there is nothing in contemporary thinking more suitable, more "analogous," for summarizing what Christians and the church have to say today than the concept of "revolution."[31]

Following these general remarks,[32] Comblin once more considers the words and works of Jesus. Modern men and women are weary of words, he says. They yearn to know what Jesus' deeds mean, in the hope of finding orientation for their own behavior.

> In order to arrive at a correct assessment of Jesus' deeds, we must take into account the Redeemer's consciousness of his role. Of course, then,

even without plunging into the chaos of the classical question of Jesus'
self-consciousness, we can posit that Jesus was indeed aware of the tremendous scope of his deeds. Surely he must have had a clear notion that
he stood at the midpoint in the divine plan for history, and knew that his
deeds were destined for a universal effect—correcting, of course, for the
limited notion of universality that people of his time could have. In these
circumstances, it would be altogether unthinkable that Jesus would have
become a member of a particular, limited group—that he would have
become a Qumran monk, or a doctor of the Law, and have to submit to
the rules of one of these callings. This could have been all very respect-
able in itself, but it would have been limiting everything right from the
start. Could a Qumran monk, for instance, have been able to accomplish
deeds of universal value?—works which in their turn would set other
works afoot that would have a universal effect, decisive for the course of
history?

Jesus' deeds have an extraordinary character. No one can pierce the
sense of history as Jesus can. Others of his time are confined to a limited
situation. Jesus was never a tax-collector, for instance. Hence neither did
he teach us how one should conduct oneself as a tax-collector. And so
forth and so on. Jesus' deeds cannot be imitated. They are invested
with universality, they look to a universal effectiveness. One can indeed
imitate a certain style, a certain spirit. What really is called for is to in-
corporate oneself into Jesus' work by taking up this or another particular role in that work, rather than to hope actually to imitate his
deeds.

From the fact that Jesus was not a Zealot the conclusion cannot immediately be drawn that a Christian is never allowed to participate in a revolutionary movement. To be sure, Jesus could not have sought such a role
for himself. It would have been too confining. It would have had no
relationship to his principal task. He must save his strength for the deeds
which, on a higher and more universal plane, would have an infinitely
more important and more decisive effect on the future history of humanity than the futile strivings of a few Jewish bands to break free of Roman domination. Not everyone is capable of deeds that are decisive for
the whole of history. On the other hand it is entirely possible that, for
the poor Jewish fellow who day after day had to bring the Roman
commandos the people's taxes, the only choice was to become a Zealot.

To be sure, we may not simply isolate the peculiarity of these or those
words or acts of Jesus, and then posit a comparison between this peculiarity and the peculiarity of some behavior in some other historical context. This is not what is meant by taking one's point of departure in the
deeds of Jesus.

Still another consideration puts us on our guard. Jesus must surely have been altogether conscious of the effects his works and attitudes would have in the future, at least in their main outlines. Therefore he must have indirectly approved the foreseeable effects of his life and work. For example, Jesus must have foreseen the persecutions to which his disciples would be subjected. Indeed, on many occasions he expressly showed that he did. Then must he not also have discerned, at least vaguely, that his proclamation of freedom would evoke tensions and oppositions—reactions whose violence would become uncontrollable? The history of Christianity is full of wars and revolutions, all done in the name of Christianity. Well, does this not all spring from the very nature of the Gospel itself? Are these inevitable consequences of the proclamation of freedom not all part and parcel of the history of Christianity itself? If we take Jesus "at his word," must we not be willing to face the risk of having to use violence as an ineluctable consequence of that word?[33]

Comblin recalls comparable antecedents in other revolutions. No revolutionary wants violence for violence' sake. The glorification of violence is the badge of fascism. Revolutionaries foresee moments of violence, to be sure, but their aim is not violence, but liberty.[34]

This consideration of Comblin's presupposes two others: the universality of Jesus' proclamation, and freedom as its inmost essence. To Comblin's view, Jesus is political to the extent that these two moments necessarily imply political behavior, or at least occasion it in others. But he also makes these implications explicit in Jesus' public work and mission. He bases his explication on four circumstances which, he says, even the most critical of contemporary exegetes cannot call into question: (1) Jesus sought conflict with the Pharisees; (2) he forthrightly took sides with the poor; (3) he was sentenced to death because he came into conflict with the great, dominant parties of the Jewish people; and (4) his sentence was only handed down after a public trial at the hands of the Roman authorities.

We should note that Comblin is less concerned with the historicity of these events, which he presupposes, than with their significance.[35] Here again a longer excerpt will afford insight into his argumentation.

1. Jesus rose up against the Law of Moses (as the Pharisees understood it), the letter of the Law, a religion of prescriptions and commandments, the hypocrisy of outward observance, a system of apartheid between Jew and Gentile, the attitude that non-Jews were untouchable, and so on. He sought to liberate his disciples from the yoke of this religious system.

What does this mean?

In order to understand his attitude here, we must consider its context. Obviously the context is that of the history of Israel. It would be impossible to understand Jesus' attitudes without recalling that he is a Jew, and that all his deeds necessarily have the history of Israel as their background. Our point of departure must therefore be that Jesus thought as an Israelite.

Now, like any other child of Israel, Jesus is first of all a rebel against everything Gentile. He is the scion of those Israelites who, thanks to the power of God, were delivered from the slavery, the corruption, and the idolatry of the land of Egypt—which represented the whole rest of the world. Israel as such is a people of rebels. The entire history of the Jewish people is but one expression of the Exodus after another.

Historically, the religious system of the Pharisees arises out of the comprehensive Jewish system, where the outcry against the Gentile world surges up from vast depths indeed. But the outcry is not for a transformation of society—in this case, the society of the Roman Empire. These rebels demonstrate their nonconformism by living apart. Their behavior is typical of a sect (in Ernst Troeltsch's sense), and Pharisaism is a system of constraint calculated to guarantee the loyalty of the sect to its own sort of outcry.

What does Jesus have in mind when he deprives the religious system of its native vigor? In the eyes of the Pharisees he is simply acting unconscionably. He is imperiling Israel's spiritual and social lines of defense. He is setting about the dismantlement of the dams protecting Israel from the world of the Gentiles. Is Jesus unaware of the danger posed by the Gentile world? We cannot hypothesize that he wishes to betray Israel and deliver his people up to the attacks of the Gentiles by breaking their power of resistance. Then what does he have in mind?

Jesus is well aware of his Gentile surroundings. And he is in no way opposed to the outcry of Israel. But he seeks to direct that outcry elsewhere. Instead of keeping Israel locked up in a closet of self-defense, he seeks to lead Israel out into the midst of the Gentiles. Not that he wants to make Gentiles of his disciples. On the contrary, he wants to make disciples of the Gentiles—foolishness, of course, in the eyes of the Jews.

Jesus cannot be deceiving himself about the resistance the biblical proclamation will meet in the Gentile world. He cannot be assuming that the journeys of his disciples out into the corruption of the Roman world will be nice and comfortable, or that his teachings will be received with enthusiasm by the dominant sectors of society. His intention is to unleash the explosive force of Jewish prophetism, the forces of the mighty roar that lies slumbering in the Old Testament—release these forces from their isolation and imprisonment and give them back to the world. Obviously he foresaw that contact between the Hebrew roar and the structures of the Roman world would provoke collisions. The first result of the first contacts are the frightened, exaggerated view of things we have in the Book of Revelation. The leaven is beginning to work in the paste of the Roman world.

The Pharisees are harder on the world of the Gentiles than Jesus is.

They seek to protect themselves from it. Jesus explains to the Israelites how he trusts them. He considers them capable of going out and facing the world without falling apart or being corrupted. His tactics consist in letting his disciples out of the closet they have been kept in to keep them from getting dirty. He demonstrates an extraordinary confidence in the strength his people will have at their disposal in the battle against the Gentile world. Jesus has to be sure of himself, and he has to be sure he can provide his disciples with a personal, interior armament that will enable them to stand fast in the midst of the temptations of a corrupt society. Not only does he consider them capable of preserving the roaring heritage of their forebears, he considers them capable of successfully matching it against the might of the empire.

Jesus' behavior vis-à-vis Pharisaism—imprudent and headstrong at best, if indeed not simply illusory—becomes understandable only in view of his intent to prepare human beings for confrontation with the Gentiles, confrontation with the world. And so he has to liberate his disciples from the need to seek their self-defense in isolation, introspection, and observance of the Law—all the things that enable the ''just'' to identify themselves with themselves and set up their defenses accordingly. Jesus believes that his followers can do without all that—that not only will they not succumb to the world, they will change it.

Jewish politics was basically sectarian and nonrevolutionary—something like Pentecostalism today. Jesus' attitude, on the contrary, is profoundly revolutionary. To take people steeped in the Old Testament and send them forth into the midst of a pagan society means a fermentation process, with persecutions, collisions, and revolutions. Or at the very least it means constant ongoing protest at the heart of the Roman world.

The Zealots' project, compared with this one, is extremely conservative. What were the Zealots after? They sought to insure complete political independence for Israel. They sought to isolate the Jews from their neighbors even more radically than they already were. They sought to bring about an extreme Judaism, an extreme isolationism. Jesus sought the exact opposite. Jesus had no intention of leaving the world to itself by erecting a wall no one could climb. Jesus wanted to transport the Jews right into the midst of the pagan world. The Zealots were no more revolutionary than today's Pentecostalists. The one who wanted revolution in the Roman world is Jesus. To have followed the Zealots would have been to step backward into the past. The Zealots had not the least intention of changing the Roman Empire.

2. Jesus moves among the poor and seeks his followers among them. When he accepts the rich, he removes them from their milieu. It would be superfluous to point out that Jesus' attachment to poverty is not a matter of enthusiasm. It is no more from enthusiasm than it is from ''populism''[36] that Jesus is a simple artisan and forms his church of simple people. It is a matter of political realism. It would have been ridiculous, of

course, to count on the great ones of Israel to be sent as his disciples to take the Roman world, the universe of that time, by storm. The united strength of all the great of Israel could not have done the battle forces of the empire the slightest harm. This is clear from what happened A.D. 67–70.

But the culture of the Pharisees and the doctors of the Law presented the most serious obstacles. In order to penetrate Roman culture, one would have to begin with people who were not too marked by that Jewish culture, people relatively free from hard and fast characteristics of that culture. A Jew who had been schooled by the doctors of the Law could never have made people overlook his origin. Only the poor could have mingled with the poor of the empire. It would have been unimaginable for Jewish rabbis and Greek philosophers to have come together in a single church. It is eminently imaginable, on the other hand, for there to have been a church in some quarter of the city of Rome that joined Jewish immigrants, simple artisans of the people, and other immigrants from all parts of the world.

But one must hypothesize an extraordinary spiritual self-awareness in these poor in order for them to be able to survive in their new homeland. Jesus bestows upon these poor, who have no cultural solidity, an interior security—a force of conviction, of transformation and conversion—that will move forward under its own power.

Jesus' poor, however, are not chosen from among slaves. Let us take note of that. They are the progeny of the Hebrews who struck a covenant at the foot of Mount Sinai, who know the laws concerning justice, and who feel themselves to be free and equal with everyone else. The Law forbids a Hebrew to hold another Hebrew as slave. Slaves never stage a revolution. They can murder their masters or run away, but that is all they can do. Revolutions are made by poor people filled with the spirit of freedom. Were someone to send the poor of Israel forth into the world, insuring their spiritual identity and endurance and preventing them from living in isolation from their neighbors, such a one would have sown the seeds of revolution in the world.

How can Jesus not have known and willed this, at least in its broad outlines? Unless we wish to paint ourselves a picture of a Jesus dedicated only to the interior life and the conversion of internal attitudes, there is no escaping the fact that he must indeed have known and willed what he was actually bringing about.

3. Jesus awakened messianic hopes. At the same time he rejected any messianic role the masses ever wanted to lay on his shoulders. Here is another area the New Testament specialists have left unexamined. How is this to be explained? It is hard to believe that Jesus would have cited Old Testament texts and accomplished messianic deeds and not foreseen the effect this would have on the multitudes. It is hard to believe that the reaction of the crowds surprised him, so that he finally saw that he

had been acting foolishly and must forthwith correct his behavior.

We believe that Jesus was very well aware of the kind of reactions that his manner of speaking and acting would provoke. If he aroused messianic hopes for justice and peace on this earth, it must have had a meaning in his plan. Otherwise he would have kept hands off, and all his difficulties would have vanished. All he would have had to do was to keep to a yearning for heaven, and the Wisdom tradition, and cite only authors who limited themselves to this yearning and this tradition.

There is an element of perduring value in the messianic hopes. It should have been easy to foresee that this element would call established societies into constant question once it was injected into the machinery of those societies. The New Testament texts which have preserved the messianic sense of Jesus' preaching are obscure, and it is their obscurity that is so pregnant with meaning. It would have been so easy to get rid of them completely!

But Jesus renounces power in order to mobilize and implement messianism's true content. Is this not precisely keeping hopes alive and issuing an invitation to seek to overthrow political power without availing oneself of political power? Once abroad in the Roman Empire, Christians will not forget their hopes for a more just world. But they will not think its attainment possible through seizing power.

4. Jesus' Death. The problem with Jesus' death is the ease with which he could have avoided it. Why would anyone in his position head straight for Jerusalem, challenge all the authorities of Israel, and deepen the suspicion of the Romans? Why does he not stay in the background, training his disciples in some out-of-the-way spot, and await better days for his reappearance on the public scene?

For the Jesus of the holy cards, of course, this is no problem. He went up to Jerusalem because he had to die, and he had to die to pay for the sins of humankind. Human circumstances had nothing to do with it. Everything is guided by the hand of God. Pilate, the Pharisees, and Jesus are but marionettes who carry out what stands written in the Prophets. All this is occurring outside human history and dispenses with any connection with the occurrences, or powers, of this world.

This is the problem we want to pose the exegetes. By conceiving Jesus' execution in this manner, do we not diminish his humanity? Are we not making it a holy-picture humanity, wafting above the earth like a painting in a church?

If on the other hand we seek to identify the human aspect of the death of Jesus, we can begin by examining its observable historical effects. Jesus' death established a deep cleft between his disciples and official Judaism. Now that they had seen this, the disciples knew they could never count on the Jewish system again. They were conscious of being free now of every obligation in its regard. They felt themselves definitively cut off, liberated, from the "yoke of the Law"—delivered from strict ties to the country and the tradition of the Jews. They were outlaws now: this death drove them out of the old Israel. In view of this new situation, they must now summon all their strength, be willing to renounce all aid and assistance, and live their lives isolated and shunned, free of the past, and free of every bond and tie with the present.

After Jesus' death his disciples feel driven toward the Gentiles. They have ceased to see in the "heathen" a sinful fall, a castastrophe, a waste. Now they see them as the open door to the future. They see them as the new Israel. We might say that what Paul writes of the reconciliation of Jews and Gentiles with each other and with God is historically as well as politically true:

> This was to create one single New Man in himself out of the two of them and by restoring peace through the cross, to unite them both in a single Body and reconcile them with God. In his own person he killed the hostility [Eph. 2:15-16].

Had Jesus died a natural death, at peace with the world, his disciples would have stayed in Palestine, enjoying the same respect and attention commanded by other sects the authorities tolerated, or like the monks of Qumran. Thus a definitive, unsurpassable fait accompli was necessary in order to generate an irrevocably new situation from the old one.

Humanly speaking such a death is only understandable from the intention to cause a rift in Israel that could never be spanned, and thus oblige the Christians to turn to the Roman Empire. Now they *must* break out of the narrow walls of that fortress that was Old Testament Israel.

Jesus' own testimony before the Roman authorities points to a new way of behaving. That new way is to face up to the empire. It will no longer do to live in a corner—on the margins of the world's great events. Jesus faced up to Caesar's lieutenant. His disciples will feel challenged to do the same. These considerations in no way cancel traditional interpretations of Jesus' death, which ascribe it to the causality of things invisible. On the contrary, they complement them by subjoining the human causes involved.

The effect of Jesus' death can be seen in the Book of Revelation. It is easy to see how conscious the Christians are of forming a new Israel and breaking off from the old one, how they are taking a new position vis-à-vis the structures of Roman society—vis-à-vis the universe.

What is unclear in Revelation are the results of this new attitude. But the political significance of Jesus' death and proclamation is perfectly clear. The Christians have decided to strike no compromise whatever with the sin of this world, or to commit their virtue to the patronage of an order that stands under curse and condemnation. This must be taken into account when we seek to grasp why Jesus behaved as he did, as well as in what true imitation of him consists.[37]

Not every point of Comblin's argumentation is altogether clear. Is Jesus' universalism adequately demonstrable from his actual words? What is the precise nature of his "revolutionary leaven"? Can one legitimately draw conclusions from the effects of Jesus' death about his own intentions concerning that death? Still, Comblin does, we must admit, present us with a political profile of Jesus that can be captured in crisp, key concepts like universality, ongoing revolution, authentic synthesis of the prophets' legacy, Exodus-consciousness, strategic orientation to the poor.

Or we might put it this way: Jesus has taken the political elasticity inherent in the liberation movement of the Exodus and the critique of the prophets and made it the launching pad for a more just world, by internationalizing the spirit of rebellion against injustice—whether that spirit originally manifested itself against the injustice of the Egyptian pharaohs or against the heirs of David in Samaria or Jerusalem—and channeling it toward rebellion against any and every form of injustice on the face of the earth (at that time, the *orbs terrarum*, the ring of lands surrounding the Mediterranean—the Roman Empire). He did so by taking sides with those particular poor who were ready and willing not only to transform their own personal lot, but also to have their aspirations or freedom and justice become the model for a new world. The death of Jesus is, first of all, documentation of the mortal danger of this enterprise of transformation. But it also catapulted the disciples headlong into the accomplishment of that enterprise.

When we attempt to draw comparisons among the various political interpretations of Jesus' words and behavior, there is one basic item that leaps out at us from them all: the desire inspired by Christian faith to go and build a more just world. The Latin American situation's challenge to Christians with their eyes open plays a role of varying importance in all these expositions of the words and works of Jesus' public life. Here we have both a strong point and a weak point in these characterizations. The rediscovery of the power of the Jesus-tradition for the humanization of the world, for the concretization of theological tradition in the service of justice and peace, is counterbalanced with a management of the historical details of Jesus' life and the gospel tradition that is rather too little secured—too bound up with a particular situation.

But let us now pass to a consideration of some of the particular aspects of the political interpretation of Jesus.

The Inaugural Sermon: Luke 4:16–30

Among the arguments advanced by the Argentinian movement, Priests for the Third World, in support of its option for socialism is an appeal to Luke 4:18: " . . . to set the downtrodden free."[38] The theology of liberation handles the Lucan pericope as a key locus for a Latin American understanding of Jesus' proclamation.

Eduardo Pironio uses Luke 4:18 to demonstrate both the "essentially religious mission of the church"[39] and its obligation not to "calm the oppressed—lull them to sleep, lull them into an acceptance of their condition of servitude, abandon them to their own resignation,"[40] which of course can only mean that the church has an obligation to awaken the political consciousness of the oppressed.

For Ignacio Ellacuría this passage means that Jesus is not merely to be placed in the line of the prophets generally, but precisely in the line of the prophets as conscious of their political mission. Ellacuría posits an internal connection between this text and Matthew 25:31–46—about what the Son of Man shall say to those on his right and on his left—and thus claims to demonstrate "the crucial character of these . . . texts in determining the mission of Jesus and of those Christians who seek to follow him."[41]

Leonardo Boff considers Luke 4:18–19 a kind of synthesis of Jesus' proclamation of the kingdom of God. He connects it with Mark 1:15 ("the kingdom of God is close at hand. Repent, and believe the Good News"), and uses it to elucidate the Jesuological utopia, shall we say, in which all alienation is overcome and all evil destroyed.[42]

Jon Sobrino sees Luke 4:16–19 as the expression of Jesus' concept of his own liberating activity, as well as of the "partisan nature," or partiality, of God's love.[43]

For Hugo Assmann, Jesus' inaugural sermon in Nazareth demonstrates that Christian faith means conversion to the activity of God in history. The conversion to God's lordship for which Jesus calls in the exordium of his sermon is thereupon exemplified in the liberation of captives. This indicates that the good news means conversion to a project of transforming history by taking one's fellow human beings seriously.[44]

Gustavo Gutiérrez takes Luke 4:16–21 as justification for the contemporary interpretation of the kingdom of God as concern for the poor:

> [Jesus] is proclaiming a kingdom of justice and liberation, to be established in favor of the poor, the oppressed, and the marginalized of history.[45]

A booklet published in 1968 by the Instituto de Reflexión y Orientación Ideológica, *El Congreso Eucarístico de Colombia y la lucha de clases* (The Eucharistic Congress in Colombia and the Class Struggle) is more a piece of emphatic indoctrination than an essay in theology, but it is an early example of the appeal to Luke 4:17–21:

> In this situation of a prevailing dialectical struggle, Jesus refuses to take a position of hypocritical neutrality. He exercises his power of option— and makes the poor his life's addressees.[46]

Even one of liberation theology's principal critics, Alfonso López Trujillo, concludes from Jesus' inaugural sermon in Nazareth that Christ is here presenting himself as the fulfillment of the Old Testament promises and as the liberator.[47] He does not, however, specify just what he means by this. Elsewhere López says that Christians may understand the liberation Jesus proclaims as secularization, provided they do not renounce God in the process, but, on the contrary, use the concept to "work out his ultimate identity."[48]

Our theologians' manifold appeal to Jesus' inaugural sermon in Nazareth really offers very little in the way of a thread of consistency. One is, however, struck by the nearly universal reference to Isaiah 61:1 (which the Lucan text quotes), with its key words, "poor," "liberty," and "captives." There is no room for doubt that it is a heightened awareness of the social situation of the overwhelming majority of the Latin American population that has led to the discovery of the importance of this pericope.[49]

The Sermon on the Mount: The Beatitudes

In May 1973, six bishops of the west-central region of Brazil[50] published a pastoral letter in which they draw a detailed picture of the economic situation in their part of the country and inquire into its causes. This letter provoked the reaction of the cardinal archbishop of Porto Allegre, Alfredo Vincente Scherer, who on June 15 delivered a radio address, "Why It Is Not the Business of the Church to Take a Position on Government Economics."[51] Then this broadcast was rebutted by one of the authors of the pastoral letter, Bishop Fernando Gomes Dos Santos, of Goiânia, with "Why the Church Has the Right to Take a Position on Government Economics."[52]

Gomes says, in part:

> Christians, at least, are obligated by the prophetical thrust of the gospel. Right from the start, the prophets condemned all manner of oppression and injustice. Now, Jesus Christ is the prophets' synthesis and culmination. He preached and established a new social order, and its Magna Carta is the Beatitudes. Surely here is the One who came to redeem and deliver the people.[53]

The Beatitudes, then, are understood as the basic law of a just social order, and precisely because they go back to Jesus Christ. In other words, what is basic is the Christological thesis—but this is also precisely what furnishes a lever for responsible Christian behavior in today's politics.

Juan Luis Segundo holds a similar thesis. Taking issue with declarations by Uruguayan and Chilean bishops for the 1975 holy year, he takes up the Beatitudes and finds two vectors of force: (1) God's plan for the world has not been realized in the present order of things; and (2) Christians must take sides with those whom Jesus assures of God's "recompense." Hence, according to Segundo, reconciliation must be taken as an eschatological concept, and therefore reconciliation is falsified wherever it is utilized as a slogan to promote a specious, sham unity and peace in a situation of real social contradictions. The road to eschatological reconciliation, Segundo says, passes necessarily by way of the discovery of the actual obstacles to genuine reconciliation in the present.[54]

The key to Segundo's argumentation is the factual social situation. By going back to the New Testament tradition one can develop a set of critical guidelines for the political behavior of the Church.

Héctor Borrat also examines the political implications of the Beatitudes but he draws different conclusions.[55] He begins by observing that in the ancient Greek vernacular, beatitudes were "everyday little good-luck wishes," and that in the Old Testament they were also "everyday little good-luck wishes," but that there they included "fear of the Lord," and could even include reference to suffering. Then in the New Testament, on the contrary, it is the poor, the hungry, the weeping, and the persecuted who are proclaimed "blessed"—people who had *bad* luck every day. This paradox, for Borrat, can be understood only in view of Christ: "The 'cross' of the Beatitudes is participation in the cross of Christ."[56] And a little further on:

> The paradox of the Beatitudes—this call to rejoice, in the midst of afflic-
> tion, in the promised kingdom—is a magnified image of the paradox of
> the servant who is master, the defendant who is judge, Jesus crucified
> who rises again, Jesus who is absent and yet on his way back in the Pa-
> rousia. Jesus' resurrection was the first historical expression of this tran-
> sition from cross to kingdom—the kingdom promised to those the
> Beatitudes declare "blessed." With Easter, history turns the corner and
> promises these suffering "blessed" ones that Jesus is coming back. Eas-
> ter is his return in anticipation.[57]

This sounds entirely traditional. But then Borrat addresses the question of the meaning of the Beatitudes for social change.[58] What he has to say about the poor and the persecuted merits our special attention.

On the poor:

> The sharp contrast between the Beatitudes and the Woes in Luke—
> Blessed the poor! Woe to the rich!—is sufficient to enable us to expound
> the problem right from the text of the Gospel itself. There are poor be-
> cause there are rich. There are rich because there are poor. The poor
> march to the cross (and hence to the kingdom); the rich thrust the cross
> aside (and hence will be condemned by God's judgment).[59]

And a few pages later:

> All the Beatitudes form a unity. *The poor are those who show mercy*,
> who behave like people helping others in a storm, who bring peace to

everyone around them. *They are the political poor.* It is not just suffering, it is conduct, too, that is at the basis of this Beatitude. It is not
enough to suffer. One must effect changes. One must show mercy, in
order to build peace for justice' sake. One must get involved in politics.[60]

And on the persecuted:

When those persecuted for justice' sake are Christians, this Beatitude not
only provides a stronger thrust to hasten their commitment to social
change, it invests this commitment with a deeper, lasting meaning by
incorporating it into the oikonomia of the kingdom—the kingdom that
already basks in the Easter light, but teeters on the brink of the all-
transforming Parousia.[61]

And later on:

The contribution to social change made by those who are persecuted for
justice' sake is neither measurable, nor even demonstrable, from a purely
worldly viewpoint. For the recipients of the promise of the kingdom, its
efficacy is sure.[62]

Borrat, then, approaches the Beatitudes from two directions. First, the
social situation in Latin America is such that "there are poor because there
are rich." This means a challenge to get involved in politics. Here the poor
become the agents of a movement to establish social justice, and the Beatitudes provide the thrust.

His other approach is from the direction of faith. Faith teaches us that
the definitive kingdom of God transcends the mere machinations of human
beings, and validates the place poverty and suffering have in this world.
Here, the Beatitudes give this faith its meaning.[63]

For Jon Sobrino, the Beatitudes are the basis for the "partisan nature,"
or partiality, of God's love: God loves the poor and the "little ones" first
and foremost. Hence the Beatitudes also transmit to us the notion Jesus
himself had of this God he called "Father."[64]

Segundo Galilea appeals to the Beatitudes to demonstrate that Christ is
basically someone who is politically dissatisfied. He is a "leaven of transformation in a society bent on self-exaltation."[65] One of Galilea's principles
is that the Beatitudes are part of the Promises, and that therefore they enjoy
an incipient reality now, in history, but are to reach their perfection only in
the Parousia. In this perspective, the Christian is a priori open to any
change at all; but he or she "relativizes" politics, prevailing politics as well
as political change—while of course appreciating that any progress is a step
in the fulfillment of the Promises.[66] Galilea is especially concerned to attract
a great number of Christians to political involvement by emphasizing the

spiritual side of the Christian faith as well, which he describes as a "spirituality of liberation."[67]

Jesus and the Poor

One could well say that the core of all Latin American theology is the subject of Jesus and the poor. Indeed this is the basic interest not only of the theology of liberation, but of its adversaries as well, for they too proceed on the assumption that it will be the Latin American church's relationship with the poor that will decide its credibility and hence its destiny. This, all agree, will be the touchstone of the genuity of the church's witness to Jesus. Thus throughout the entire spectrum of Latin American theological publications we find sociological and political analyses of the situation of the poor. Here we shall treat one aspect of the question only: the extent to which Jesus' relationship with the poor is seen as part of his political conduct.

A strong passage from the minutes of a meeting held by a Catholic labor organization, the Catholic Action Labor Movement, lets us have a taste of how theological reflection can influence church praxis:

> The church must become incarnate in this reality of people who suffer, this reality of the very poorest, as Christ did. Christ chose to:
>
> > Be born in a manger . . .
> > of a mother who was lowly . . .
> > preach to the poor . . .
> > live as one of them, with nowhere to lay his head . . .
> > and take apostles from among the people, fisherfolk.
>
> In no other way will it be possible to develop a pastoral ministry among the working classes with the goals of the workers' struggle in view.[68]

Texts of this kind, whether in official Church documents or in those of unofficial groups, come within the purview of the theology of liberation very often, if only to differ with it at times. They argue neither exegetically nor theologically, but they do appeal to Jesus' relationship to the poor as exemplary, or orientating, for the conduct of Christians, or the church, in Latin America. They reflect the Latin American situation, but they also handle New Testament texts, or Jesus' life and work, in a characteristic way. Let us examine some of them.

A "Pastoral Letter of the Cuban Bishops," under date of April 10, 1969, says:

> As we seek the welfare of our people, in fidelity to the service of the very poorest according to the commandment of Christ and the recently pro-

claimed commitment of Medellín, *we denounce this unjust situation of
the blockade.*[69]

Even with all the rhetoric, it is easy to see that there is no divorcing the appeal to Jesus' commitment to the poor from the rest of the statement. It is
the poor who are decisive. The appeal to Jesus has the nature of a legitimat-
ing and motivating reference.

Three separate Chilean documents broaden the field of vision. Dated
April 1969, an open letter from two hundred Catholics to the archbishop of
Santiago, complains of political abuses in Chile:[70]

> When one is striving for revolutionary changes, and seeks to liberate the
> people, one cannot recognize a "people's government" that oppresses
> the poor. Jesus does not want slavery for the people, he wants liberation.
> Thus those "servants of the people" who transform themselves into the
> people's executioners divest themselves of any authority or legitimacy.[71]

"Jesus," here, is not much more than a buzz word. He comes up in the
argumentation, to be sure; but the danger of tendentiousness is very great.
Still, we see the social situation forcing the church to take a position.

In 1971, the Chilean bishops, partly because of growing pressure from the
Christian left,[72] published a declaration to the effect that the church cannot
come out for any particular group, since that would mean it was against the
others.

> But still less can it abandon those groups accused of being made up of
> sinners. Jesus himself rejected a like proposition, and said he had ac-
> tually come for sinners—since "it is not those who are well who need the
> doctor" (Luke 5:31). Hence the Church cannot *opt*—for one human
> group over another—rather it must *decide*—for those for whom Jesus
> himself "decided": for the *whole* people, who in this case are all the
> Chilean people together, whom Jesus has called to conversion to the
> status of *people of God* through their acceptance of his gospel. . . . Of
> course, this does not prevent the church from *preferring*—decidedly, and
> with a whole heart, just like Jesus Christ himself—and consecrating itself
> to the sevice of those whom he preferred and who always shall be his: the
> suffering, the poor, and the abandoned. . . . But this by no means im-
> plies identifying Christ with a particular social class or political group.[73]

One discerns the bishops' disinclination to identify the "poor" in the
biblical sense with the members of the Chilean lower classes. They seem
willing to identify the rich with sinners—perhaps on the basis of statements
made by Medellín; but in no way do they thereupon conclude that the
Church ought to break with the rich. Unlike the authors of the letter cited

immediately above, the bishops recognize that the rich, too, as sinners, are capable of being converted, and this is the point on which they most explicitly appeal to the teaching of Christ.[74]

The document "The Kingdom of God Suffers Violence (Matthew 11:12) and in Chile. . ." appeared in November 1973, two months after the coup. Its authors are various Christian groups. It was never published. Here under the subhead "Time of Conversion" we read:

> Evangelization never cripples or paralyzes. Quite the contrary. It penetrates the heart, and produces conversion—deep, radical change. The word of the Lord is cutting. It glosses over nothing, defends nothing. The hand of the Lord transforms our life and goals. It has no intention of leaving us satisfied with the powers that be or of allowing us to feel very secure. Jesus takes up the cry of John the Baptist, who calls out in the wasteland: Be converted! Don't do that anymore! Don't stay in sin! Your life must change! For the kingdom of God is near (cf. Matt. 3:1–2). John the Baptist refuses to "talk through his hat." He speaks out loud and clear: "Even now the ax is laid to the roots of the trees, so that any tree which fails to produce good fruit will be cut down and thrown on the fire" (Matt. 3:10). And the people of those days, like the faithful today, ask, "What must we do, then?" (Luke 3:10). Conversion means changing ourselves, to the point that we are willing to share the goods of this earth. Then equality will reign. Jesus demands of holders of public office that they refrain from making use of people as if they were things. And to the military he says: "No intimidation! No extortion! Be content with your pay!" (Luke 3:13–14).
>
> And so the gospel calls for a concrete change in each and all—not only in our personal state, but in our relationship to others. This change will presage the coming of the kingdom of equality and justice. Sin, lurking deep in the heart of everyone, expresses itself in social injustices. There is a great deal of sin in all of us—not only in the great exploiters. Our commitment may seem very evangelical and generous. But we have committed a great sin of omission. There is much we have *not* done, both for the liberation of a poor people, and from the point of view of fidelity to God. Now is the time for conversion. Our witness today must not repeat the inconsistencies and errors of yesterday. We are all responsible for the total oppression in which our people languish. One cannot blame everything on "the others"—those who have done nothing, or those who have done something but not the right thing, or the middle class, or the imperialists. We are each and every one of us to blame for the evil and sin that crush and oppress our people. We have not persevered; we have not carried our commitment through to the end. We have lacked courage, organization, combat discipline, analyses of reality, and spirituality.[75]

This document, too, cites our Lucan passage (if not always altogether accurately), and what is most striking is its definition of the poor, to whom the first Beatitude says the kingdom of God belongs. The poor are defined as the exploited and oppressed, and since this equivalency has Jesus for its surety, it stands up even when generals have staged a coup. Now the question in the minds of all may be who is at fault for the way things have worked out politically in Chile; but the New Testament goes right on providing the ideological basis for Christian cooperation in the building of this kingdom of equality and justice.[76]

Equally ideological, if less concrete from a political standpoint, is the volume we have cited, *The Eucharistic Congress in Colombia and the Class Struggle*.[77] The situation of people in Latin America, especially the poor, now has to answer to God's commitment to those poor, as expressed in Old and New Testament alike.

> With the coming of Christ, God's option for the poor, his alliance with them, reaches its culmination. Abandoned by all—including himself— Jesus offers himself as God's perfect sacrifice. For he is the sacrifice of a God who is love. Christ is the human being of unconditional love.

In the life and preaching of Christ, as the first Christian communities grasped it and expressed it, we find an essential element for the solution of our problem. The gospel presents Christ as someone who actualizes his basic attitude of being-for-others in two dimensions: one is what Paul Ricoeur calls the "short-span relationship," which consists in the concretization of love on an interpersonal level. We see this on page after page of the Gospels when we read of Jesus' exemplary encounters in the area of friendship with his sisters and brothers. His boundless sensitivity, his intuitive grasp of things, his ability to put himself in another's place, his proclamation, his readiness to forgive, his measureless giving, his loyalty to friends, his reverence for others—all enter into his so very human encounter with other people. And in our opinion the passages in the Gospels where Jesus speaks of turning the other cheek, or of loving our enemies, are part of this dimension of being-for-others.

The second dimension, which Ricoeur calls "long-span relationships," places Christ in contact with people in their cultural and socio-economic structures. Here, in the midst of a society built on a dialectical struggle between master and slave, Christ lives his unconditional being-for-others by clearly, unambiguously opting for those on the underside of the dialectic. This is the sense in which Christ's love is political: that it is the love of the God of Israel, who comes to full historical actualization in Jesus. And this is the key to the famous dilemma with which Jesus confronts us—and obliges us to make a choice: "You cannot be the slave both of God and of money" (Matt. 6:24). Being "God's slave" means serving God's plan, and God's plan from the beginning has been the challenge to live in the dialectical tension between possession and anticipation of his kingdom on earth. Thus one's personal life plans must make room for humanity.

Being the slave of money, then, gives one's individual life a direction contrary to God's plan for humanity. Those who serve money plan their lives with others in such a way as to satisfy their thirst for happiness with possessions—and with lordship over those others.

At the heart of this option, at the core of politics, where the decision is made how the organization of society will be directed, we find violent traits assumed by the love of Christ in certain of its expressions and challenges:

1. The peace and freedom that Christ wishes to effectuate, from among the poor, come necessarily by way of division and struggle. [Here follow quotations of Luke 12:51–53 and Matt. 12:30.]

2. Jesus not only takes sides with the poor, he battles the rich, and curses those who base their lives on having rather than being. [Luke 6:24–26 is quoted.]

3. This fundamental choice and decision yields a new criterion for the evaluation of action and praxis, and presents a violent paradox. [Luke 9:24–25 and Matt. 20:25–28 are quoted.]

4. Jesus introduces a violent breach with the ritualistic piety of his time. God is not to be worshiped in the temple, but "in spirit and truth" (John 4:23). What is essential in the actualization of this new spirit is active, effective love for others. The exemplar of this new order of piety and religion is not a priest or a doctor of the law, but a Samaritan (Luke 10:29–37).

Here occurs the subhead "A New People Celebrates a New Passover," under which we read:

On the basis of the call to transform this love of neighbor into action, and inject itself into the slave-master dialectic, which love must do if it is to be authentic, Christ seeks to call together a new people. This people can only be the people of the poor—a people without spatial, historical, or racial boundaries, a people that lives among all nationalities, that moves en masse, that lives in the midst of all nations with their social and political "orders" of established disorder down through history. This people will arise in every age, for in every age there are people of the liberation and the Exodus. This people is that part of humanity whose destiny is emigrations without number—new historical departures that bring humanity even closer to mature, definitive liberation. This is why Christ left them the Supper of the New Passover, before he took the step forward from slavery to freedom in his own person. For the Eucharist is the repast that signifies a willingness to start out for a new country of justice, a new community of brothers and sisters, even when it costs one one's life.[78]

Here is another text which begins with a profession of faith in Jesus. In Jesus, God's plan for history beomes visible. The Christological slogan,

"Jesus, God's unconditional love," is in the first instance neither concrete nor political. Its political aspect surfaces only in the "second dimension," in the transformation of love into structures of interpersonal obligation—in commitment to the poor, who in the society of that time were the equivalent of slaves (*pace* Comblin).

The business of politics often involves the use of violence. Our text— more rhetorically than analytically, it is true—adduces certain characteristics of "violence" in the effect Jesus has on the destiny of the church as a "people of the poor." The step taken by the primitive church toward the internationalization of the Christian faith is transferred to the potential unification of the poor of all lands. This "Poor of the world, unite!" is of course distinguishable from its prototype, "Workers of the world, unite!" by virtue of the spiritual background these poor possess in Christ, whose passage to the eschatological was by way of death.

Our final sample of these rather more prophetical than argumentational approaches will be a passage from Helder Camara's *Race Against Time*. Camara offers the following specific example of how a return to Jesus can demand reform in the praxis of the church where the poor are concerned.

> Even where the house of God is concerned, the moment has come to review the problem of its construction. Without doubt, we shall always make ours the words of Solomon on the consecration of the Temple of Jerusalem and we shall always keep present the word of Christ to Judas in defense of Magdalen. But in a world where two-thirds of the people are in a state of underdevelopment and hunger, how can we squander huge sums on the construction of temples of stone, forgetting the living Christ, who is present in the person of the poor? And when shall we come to understand that in too sumptuous churches the poor have not the courage to enter and feel at home?[79]

Here we have a line of argumentation that will be taken up in our next section, in an appeal to the Parable of the Last Judgment, Matthew 25:31–46.

But there are also more strongly polemical examples of the appeal to Jesus' behavior toward the poor as part of his political commitment. We have seen something of this above, in Julio de Santa Ana.[80] Following that passage, Santa Ana says:

> Here Christ's example [in turning to the poor] speaks for itself. Jesus assumed all the consequences of the sinful human condition (cf. Phil. 2:5–8), and while rich, became poor out of love for others, so that "you might become rich through his poverty" [*sic*] (2 Cor. 8:9).[81]

Here we have two citations together from the Pauline corpus, which is not much used in liberation theology. Poverty is conceived of as a result of the sinful human condition, but at the same time is basically overcome by the salvific deed of Christ. The thought itself is scarcely original. But Santa Ana places a special accent on poverty as an indicator of the human need for salvation. The use of Christ's turning to the poor as an example of authentic Christian behavior is altogether in the line of argumentation of Philippians 2:5-11.

Raúl Vidales draws conclusions from Jesus' attitude toward the poor for the pastoral character of theology today. These consequences simply void all theology, he says. Under the heading, "Social Appropriation of the Gospel by the Poor," Vidales writes:

> We know that one of the most shocking situations Jesus had to face was precisely the manipulation and captivity to which scripture and the authentic Mosaic tradition had been reduced by the dominant classes of his time—the sacerdotal and lay-bourgeois aristocracy. Confronted with this de facto situation, Jesus focuses in on the messianic "signs of the time," the messianic signs of the salvation he bears. And the most profound and characteristic trait of that salvation is rooted precisely in the proclamation of the good news to the poor (Matt. 11:5 and parallels; Luke 7:22). Now, the poor are none other than the "tax collectors," the "prostitutes," the "sinners," the "gluttons and drunkards," those "who labor and are overburdened," the famished crowds, and so on (Mark 2:16; cf. Matt. 11:19, 28, 21:31-32; Luke 15:1-2, 7:34, 18:11).
>
> Most significantly, Jesus calls his followers "poor ones," as well— "little ones," "least," "mere children" (Mark 9:42; Matt. 10:42, 25:40-45, 11:25-28; and parallels).
>
> The expropriation of the good news by the poor by wresting it from the hands of the rich, then, meant running the radical risk inherent in Jesus' message. Consequently, the acceptance and implementation of that message by the poor will be its most subversive characteristic. Jesus' historical offer of liberation to the poor became highly dangerous, and he himself warned of the danger when he called those who were not scandalized by it "blessed."
>
> An evangelization of liberation implies the specific intent to tear the gospel out of the hands of the dominant classes and deliver it to its privileged addressees—the poor of our continent and the whole world. Through these poor, the gospel of freedom acquires its genuine dimension of universality, becoming a shout raised by all the exploited of the world and dinning in the ears of their exploiters. We know that ultimately the struggle is not among nations, but social classes. This is why Jesus' message, in its original content, means revolutionary subversion.[82]

In the conclusion of Vidales's article the same thought is resumed in a broader context:

The echo awakened by Jesus' proclamation of the good news to the poor was a torrent of indignation, especially from the priestly aristocracy of the Pharisees (Luke 12:53–54, 15:2, 16:14; Matt. 12:11, 11:19 and parallels; Luke 7:24–25; Mark 2:7, 2:16). Their reaction is scarcely surprising, in view of the fact that this proclamation not only contradicted all the rules of piety prevailing at that time, but, on a deeper level, attacked the interests of the dominant classes.

Further: by Jesus' own testimony, the Father's love is directed particularly to the undervalued, the "lost," sons and daughters of Israel (Matt. 10:6, 15:24; Luke 19:10, cf. 15:6, 8, 24). Thus the occasion for scandal consists precisely in the proclamation of the good news to the poor (Matthew 11:6 and parallels), and not primarily in Jesus' call to repentance. Along the same lines, Jesus' response to this scandal is almost obsessive: God is love, and he reveals himself in his limitless mercy toward the "least" ones (Matt. 20:1–15; Luke 15:4–10, 18:1–8, 9:14, 15:19, 24). We cannot help but be struck by Jesus' "scandalous conduct" in finding this love of the Father only in circumstances of servitude—which is where his mission was to be accomplished.

Confronted with this message, human beings are split into two camps (Mark 4:11, Matt. 10:13–15). This polarizing reaction pertains to the very essence of the good news. Thus the pre-Paschal scandal was precisely in the common board Jesus made with the poor and with "sinners" (Matt. 11:19 and parallels, Luke 7:34, Mark 2:16 and parallels). The post-Paschal scandal will be the ignominious death of Jesus on the cross—the consequence of his concrete struggle in history.

What differentiates Jesus from all the separatist movements and tendencies of his time is precisely his message of the universality and "unconditionality" of love (Matt. 23:37 and parallels, Luke 13:34; cf. Matt. 22:14). The God that Jesus reveals is the Father of the poor, the little ones, those of no value. He is not a neutral God. Even his messenger, Jesus, is one of them (John 1:14). Further, those who open themselves up to God's initiative verify the essential characteristic of this new people: the condition of sons and daughters of God. This means walking in a world of gratuity, of grace (Matt. 18:3). This condition of "filiation" pierces Christian experience. It is the gladness of being human and comports a certitude that translates into rebellion—a struggle for the effective construction of a world of brothers and sisters.

Love for one's sisters and brothers, especially for the "least" of them, is the quintessence of the gospel (Mark 12:28–34, Matt. 7:12), and its measure is Jesus' own concrete, historical activity, culminating in the total gift of his life. Hence the central law of this "new people" is revolutionary love, which means a limitless capacity for gift (Matt. 5:28–44 and parallels, 13:44, 5:44; Luke 7:36–50, 10:25 and parallels), promptitude and alacrity in service (Mark 10:42–45 and parallels; Luke 22:24–27), and works of love of every sort (Matt. 25:31–46), including even love of ones enemies (Matt. 5:44 and parallels; Luke 6:27–32). But the most intimate characteristic of Christian love is not its radicalism, its heroism, its loftiness, its rigor—but its new motive: the gratuity of the love that comes to us from the Father. This is love born of liberty and freedom, and it generates more freedom (Luke 7:36–50, 19:1–10). That is why it is revolutionary in history.

The practice of Christian love to the hilt—to the point of laying down one's life, in liberty and for the sake of liberty—fecundates history itself, and situates the new human being and his and her new society within the realm of things possible.[83]

Vidales develops the political aspect of Jesus' life and work by taking today's concepts of "dominating" and "repressed" groups and applying them to the social situation in Palestine in the time of Jesus. In the class struggle of those days, Jesus took sides with the oppressed—or the exploited, as they are also called. "Poor," in this analysis, functions as a generic concept for various groups which, in various ways, shapes, and forms, stood in conflict with a (broadened) concept of the "Judaism" of that time. Jesus' disciples, too, are subsumed under the concept of "the poor." Jesus brings these poor the good tidings, and thereby takes the first step toward the overthrow of this society. In his footsteps, the church of Latin America today is challenged to transmit these same good tidings to the poor of Latin America, so that the social injustices prevailing there can be overcome.

When Vidales comes to the conclusion of his article, he goes further. He cuts through his theological framework and posits that, in this praxis of Jesus and Christians after him, the love of God is brought to actualization. Now he speaks not only of liberation, but of freedom too: he is constrained to, by his position that the origin of the whole liberation process is in God, and God's gratuitous and gracious turning to human beings. Jesus' political commitment is a concretization of this gracious condescension of God. Jesus' turning to the poor testifies to God's partiality for the little ones of the earth.

Segundo Galilea takes a different approach in characterizing the poor. He begins by remarking the difficulty of identifying just who the "poor" are, all the different "poor" down through the course of the ages. But he finally gathers all types and categories under one basic concept—which, he holds, reveals the cause of poverty in Latin America today:

The poor are those who have no power or influence in their own behalf. They are thrust aside by the "great" whenever there is question of decision-making or power structures. The poor are basically the powerless.[84]

Citing Philippians 2:5–11, Galilea sees Jesus' powerlessness as his essential note and reduces his kenosis to three traits of his praxis: renunciation of political power, renunciation of violence, and renunciation of marriage.[85] By becoming poor, Jesus laid the foundations of a new world in which poverty would be the earmark of the new human being.

Already we see that Galilea ascribes a spiritual component to poverty. And he writes:

> As founder of a religious movement that sought to alter human beings and their society from the ground up, it would have been easy for Jesus to raise himself to temporal or political lordship. Evidently the temptation to political power dogged his steps in the troubled Palestine of his day (Matt. 4:8), and he had to resist it inwardly (in the temptation in the wasteland) as well as outwardly (in the face of the importunities of the multitude, John 6:15, and even before the Romans, John 18:33-40). His freedom to criticize the religious or political system (Matt. 11:8, Luke 13:32, 22:25, 11:37-54) is in proportion to his renunciation of power.
>
> Like all renunciation for the sake of the good news of the kingdom, Jesus' renunciation of power is creative. Jesus effects new forms of socio-political, or revolutionary, transformation. In proclaiming an ethics and religion based not on the legalism of the Torah but on love for and imitation of the Father, he prepares the collapse of the established religion of Israel. In calling for a comprehensive equality and communion of brothers and sisters, in which the magic spell of each and every system and ideology of lordship will be broken, Jesus radically threatens the power of Roman imperialism, and thereby as well the basic principle of all totalitarianism, for he introduces the great creative principle of all liberating revolution. In calling the poor and "little ones" to his kingdom and assigning them a privileged place in it (Matt. 25:31-41, Luke 14:21), he creates a conscious, mighty thrust that will determine the course of history.[86]

For Galilea, poverty is not just something suffered in society. That is, it is not just an evil to be overcome. Poverty can be voluntary. It can be something positive, something to strive for. Galilea is most concerned to identify the biblical group of the "poor," who of course are Jesus' preferred addressees, not only in terms of a social class, but also in terms of a basic spiritual mentality. The poor person is the person who allows himself or herself to be taken into the renewal movement which Jesus is promoting. That movement is a move away from, and critical of, prevailing political praxis, today as in the time of Jesus. Hence it renounces the use of power. Poverty is powerlessness, but it is not powerlessness undergone or suffered. It is voluntary powerlessness. And so Galilea describes the church's call to follow Jesus under the heading, "Poverty of the Church as Renunciation of Power."[87]

Elsewhere, Galilea seeks to place Jesus' preferential choice for the poor in a perspective of his universal call to conversion. He organizes his thought in seven points.

1. Jesus' first purpose is to seek sinners. His call is basically a call for their conversion, and his laying down his life is unto the forgiveness of sins. This is the perspective in which the concepts of poor, rich, poverty, and liberation must be viewed.

2. Together with this search for sinners, we find Jesus' preference for the poor. He makes an "option" for them. In fact, for Jesus the liberation of the poor is a sign of the presence of the kingdom, a sign that the actual forgiveness of sins is under way.

3. We must somehow find who the "poor" and "sinners" are, in social and public categories, in the various moments of history. We are not suggesting that this identification exhausts these concepts, either biblically or theologically; but there is no escaping their incarnation in actual people, and it is a necessary historical imperative to identify them if we hope to be able to direct the mission of Christians as it should be directed.

4. Today, "sinners," sociologically speaking, are identifiable as those who use and abuse might and power, in particular the power of money, which works such exploitation and torment. This tie-up is not the only modern form of sin, nor is it the only biblical form of sin. But it is a "sign of the times" in the Third World, especially in Latin America.

5. A condition for the conversion and forgiveness of sins of the rich and the mighty, in the language of the Bible, is "poverty of spirit." For them, liberation means a new attitude toward the poor, and the ability to imitate the poor.

6. Poverty of spirit is the locus of reconciliation of rich and poor. It is the attitude which renders possible the liberation of the mighty and the rich themselves.

7. Evangelization will always be the search for sinners and the sign of preference for the poor. Evangelization is liberating the poor. It calls them to the freedom of the Kingdom, with all the social, cultural, and political consequences of this freedom. On the other side of the coin, the evangelization of the rich points the way to their liberation, by challenging them to imitate the poor and put themselves at the service of their historical liberation.[88]

These theses also clarify what Galilea by no means intends to say: (1) that the poor to whom Jesus addresses himself by preference are identical with the members of the underclasses of today's Latin America; (2) that wealth is in no way a determinant of salvation; (3) that the Christian faith justifies unjust social structures. Galilea's positive declarations are less precise than this. Especially, it is unclear what "poverty in spirit"—to be striven for by rich and poor—means for the poor. Without this precision, of course, it is unclear what the rich are to do in order to imitate the poor, as Galilea says they must.

Our last witness will be Gustavo Gutiérrez, who has a number of different things to say about Jesus' attitude toward the poor, and the consequences to be drawn from this attitude. In the foreword to the volume of documentation *Signos de Liberación,* he characterizes the current pastoral change of direction in this way: Formerly, when persons were in need of help, they were expected to turn to the church. Today the pastoral team heads for the streets, factories, and slums to see who needs help. This new pastoral stance alters the world of church ministry, particularly in the new perception of the poor in their concrete situation. Further, the experience of this new tack leads to the discovery that, in the gospel, it is the poor person who is our neighbor par excellence.[89] Elsewhere Gutiérrez elaborates on the primacy he gives to praxis:

> The praxis of liberation must lead one to become poor with the poor. For the Christian committed to it, this will be a way of identifying oneself with Christ, who came into the world to proclaim the Gospel to the poor and liberate the oppressed. Evangelical poverty thus began to be lived as an act of liberation and love towards the poor of this world, as solidarity with them and protest against the poverty in which they live; as identification with the interests of the oppressed classes and a rejection of the exploitation of which they are the victims. If the ultimate cause of the exploitation and alienation of man is egotism, the underlying motive of voluntary poverty is love for one's neighbor. Poverty—the results of social injustice, which has its deepest roots in sin—is accepted, not in order to make it an ideal of life, but in order to witness to the evil it represents. The condition of the sinner, and its consequences, were accepted by Christ, not to idealize them, but out of love and solidarity with men, and to redeem them from sin; to fight against human egotism and abolish all injustice and division among men.[90]

His argumentation elsewhere is similar:

> The nub, the nucleus, of the biblical message, we have said, is in the relationship between God and the poor. Jesus Christ is precisely *God become poor.* This was the human life he took—a poor life. And this is the life in and by which we recognize him as Son of his Father.
> He was poor indeed. He was born into a social milieu characterized by poverty. He chose to live with the poor. He addressed his gospel by preference to the poor. He lashed out with invective against the rich who oppressed the poor and despised them. And before the Father, he was poor in spirit.[91]

Gutiérrez puts stronger emphasis on the social components of poverty than does Galilea, hence also on the importance of overcoming them as the goal to be kept in view. Poverty and sin go together. Jesus' becoming poor is to be understood soteriologically and not only as an example to be followed.

Consequently, struggle against exploitation and solidarity with the poor are identifying characteristics of the redeemed. Gutiérrez is far removed from any "spiritual" one-sidedness. He views Jesus' life-situation in the light of that of the majority of Latin American Christians. Their situation is a repetition of his, and his life is the theological model for theirs. We might call Gutiérrez's argumentation a "soteriological typology," in which he does justice to the traditional emphasis on Christ's work of salvation, while at the same time emphasizing the special challenge to Latin American Christians that springs from the situation in which they live.

The Parable of the Last Judgment: Matthew 25:31-46

The appeal to the Parable of the Last Judgment runs along the same lines of argumentation. We find this appeal scattered throughout a great number of texts calling for a renewal of church praxis. It is principally invoked, however, in a discussion of the relationship of orthodoxy to "orthopraxis." Gustavo Gutiérrez, for example, devotes a rather long section to it.[92] First he attempts to demonstrate that the "least of my brethren" are *all* the needy. Then he outlines the following "teachings" of the passage:

> We wish to emphasize three points: the stress on communion and brotherhood as the ultimate meaning of human life; the insistence on a love which is manifested in concrete actions, with "doing" being favored over simple "knowing"; and the revelation of the human mediation necessary to reach the Lord.[93]

This exposition is a key part of Gutiérrez's development of the notion of the unity of redemption and liberation, and it appeals to the person of Jesus only indirectly.

Segundo Galilea, whose special interest in a spirituality of liberation we have already remarked, sees in Matthew 25:31-46 a model for *active contemplation*.[94] Every Christian, runs Galilea's thesis, if he or she is not to "lose Christ," must be a contemplative. However, one can be a contemplative in two different ways. One can encounter the person of Jesus himself, or one can encounter Christ in one's brothers and sisters, especially in the "least" of these. Galilea places a Latin American accent on his thinking here when he says:

> The experience of Jesus in the service of our brothers and sisters also gives a whole social dimension to Christian consciousness, thus transcending any purely individualistic and private consciousness as well as any contemplation with "Platonic" tendencies. It gives to brotherly and sisterly love a social and collective dimension, insofar as the "little ones" are in Latin America not only individual persons but also—and above all—human groupings, neglected subcultures, social classes or sectors.

. . . There is in them a collective presence of Jesus, the experience of which is truly a contemplative act.[95]

If there is a collective presence of Jesus, then there must be a collective encounter with him as well—or in the language of the parable, a collective feeding of the hungry, and so on. Perhaps Galilea did not wish to come right out and say it, but the logical consequence of a collective presence of Jesus will of course be political conduct calculated to influence the lot of the collectivity. Indirectly, but ineluctably, the parable summons us to a Christologically based political involvement.

Pedro Negre Rigol has suggestions to make for how pastoral commitment today can avoid the extremes both of an exaggerated individualism and a pure orientation toward the masses. He bases his recommendations on our parable in Matthew 25:31–46:

> But an integral witness [i.e., one which avoids both extremes] feels Christ's compassion for the masses and makes them into individual persons.
>   "Neighbor," therefore, is both a quantitative and a qualitative concept. Christ and his humanity revealed themselves more strongly in those who are prevented from living, in the oppressed.[96]

Without expressly citing the Matthean parable, Negre's treatment applies the affinity and sympathy of Christ the judge for his "least brethren" and sisters to the social situation of the poor in Latin America. Here too we have a thought with political consequences which the author fails to make explicit.

Raúl Vidales sees in this parable a prototype of Jesus' own praxis, which obligates Christians to "go and do likewise." Under the heading "The Practice of 'Mercy Without Limit,' " Vidales says:

> In the context of Palestine's slavery, hunger, and misery, the evangelizing activity of Jesus is defined essentially as "the practice of mercy without limit." His teachings make this very clear, especially in the parables. Thus the parables of the Last Judgment (Matthew 25) and the Good Samaritan (Luke 10) are a synthesis of his approach.
>   To respond to the concrete, actual anguish of one's neediest sisters and brothers is the principle of liberation and justice in their fullest sense. "The just" are precisely those who "hunger and thirst for justice," who become efficaciously involved with the hungry, the thirsty, the cold, the lonely, the sick, and the oppressed. Correlatively, "the unjust" are not only those who commit injustice, but also those who are indifferent to oppression. The same undercurrent is present in the Parable of the Good Samaritan, where sentence of condemnation is passed not only upon the brigands who have committed the aggression, but also, and more

directly, against those who, while believing in the liberation message of Israelite religion, "pass by," without "getting involved" with the victim lying by the wayside. This is the way in which Jesus' practice of mercy without limit makes the dawn of deliverance for the poor something concrete and believable and explicates the transforming might of solidarity and commitment in love.[97]

What is striking here is the juxtaposition of the concepts of mercy, liberation, and justice. Surely mercy and justice could have been seen as antitheses rather than as belonging together. But for Vidales mercy is the principle of liberation and justice. This is a new accent. No political dimension is expressly referred to, it is true, but the emphasis on active involvement and the reference to oppression (which is not the subject of the parable, of course) oblige us to conclude that Vidales is at least on the way to a political understanding of mercy. For Vidales too, then, the parable is a prototype of Jesus' own praxis.[98]

José María Casabó Suque cites the parable of Matthew 25:31–46 in a discussion of the relationship between Christ's salvific deed and today's Christian cooperation in redemption. His thinking, which has areas of contiguity with that of Gustavo Gutiérrez, is partly a function of the distinction between (1) a unique, basic redemption-and-liberation through Christ, whose fulfillment is still to come, and (2) the ever-new attempt of Christians to effectuate this redemption-and-liberation. Casabó writes:

Redemption extends not only to souls, but to whole human beings. Victory over all evil—sin, suffering, servitude, and death—is total only in salvation's eschatological moment. But the redemption already being accomplished in the heart of the human being is possessed of a radial energy and thrusts outward to liberation from evil in all areas. Even now salvation seeks to suppress evil in all its forms.

Christ's deeds work outside from within. God's pedagogy in the Old Testament, as we have observed, God's revelation of salvation, began with external reality, with social and political servitude, and worked down to the deeper, causal reality: sin. Christ's procedure is just the contrary. He works his redemption on this deepest level, the level of sin; then from there he moves up to all the other levels.

And he involves human beings in this process. As the human being participates in the work of creation . . . so he and she participate in liberation from evil. To be sure, their participation does not take place at the inmost core, that of redemption from sin, for only God can redeem from sin. Human beings' participation takes place in the battle for the suppression of all manner of other evils, which follow and accompany sin. Their mission, through which they "fill up what is wanting" to the liberating deed of God, is to be equal to the battle.

Jesus makes it very clear how we ought to conduct ourselves. We are to love our neighbors as ourselves, will their good, and do for them what we would have done for us—hence, deliver them from all evil, not just from spiritual evil. Insofar as we can, we are to deliver them from every kind of misery, repression, and suffering: hunger, thirst, disease, nakedness, poverty, injury, captivity, and so on (Matt. 25:35–37, Luke 10:29–37, 1 John 3:17, etc.). Here Jesus provides us with the basic orientation, but the forms of activity appropriate for each age are to be determined by human beings themselves. And the social dimension may by no means be overlooked when the choice is being made. We must include it too if our love is to be genuine and effective.

The liberating power of Christ works on in history. Its full effectiveness will appear only in the eschaton, but in the "meantime" it must be brought into play against the various forms of oppression that ever appear in the various situations of history.[99]

Here the Parable of the Last Judgment is invoked only for its list of examples to be followed in Christian behavior. But the emphasis on this list is a mere guideline, to be specified and concretized anew in every new situation, and the further emphasis on the social dimension leaves ample room for a political implementation of the basic Christian obligation of love.

Héctor Borrat's reaction shows that he has familiarized himself with a number of explanations of this parable which argue principally from the identity of Christ the judge with his "least" brothers and which thereby develop a particular Christology. He warns against an exclusive concentration on Matthew 25:31–46, because, he holds, an identification of Christ with each and every one of the poor entails a loss of what is specific in the Christian thesis.[100]

A like reproach of "horizontalism" in the political mission of the church is rebuffed by Ignacio Ellacuría, and precisely a propos of the Parable of the Last Judgment. He extracts from our Matthean passage two arguments for the political and social dimension of Jesus' life and work:

1. The judgment refers to the immediate material needs of human beings.
2. The succor we proffer these needy is proffered for the Son of Man.

And yet there is no particular indication of this in the concrete circumstances in which the succor is forthcoming. That is, the judgment, the sentence of the judge, is based on no supernatural, cultic, or religious standard. It is simply Jesus' own attitude, Jesus own commitment. And it obliges the church to go and do likewise.[101] In other words, Jesus' own standard is altogether "horizontal."

Jesus and the Zealots

The question of Jesus' relationship to the Zealots has received thorough consideration at the hands of European exegetes.[102] Hence we are not surprised to find authors like Brandon, Cullmann, and Hengel cited by many

Latin American authors who deal with the subject. But in spite of their dependence on the historical investigation conducted in Europe, Latin American authors bring a new emphasis to the presentation and evaluation of the problem. It will be to our purpose, then, in connection with the question of interest in Jesus, to observe some of the traits of the Latin American presentation and evaluation.

Briefly put, the praxis of the Latin American church must take its orientation from the praxis of Jesus. Hence the burning question: Can Jesus' praxis be described as political praxis? An investigation into the relationship of Jesus to the Zealots will serve to clarify this question.

For Gustavo Gutiérrez, Jesus' relationship to the Zealots is but one of three aspects of his attitude toward the "political world."[103] On one hand, Jesus has a certain affinity and sympathy for the Zealots. At least "Simon the Zealot," and perhaps also Judas Iscariot, Peter, and the Sons of Zebedee belonged to this group. Further, the notion of the imminence of the kingdom of God, the question of Jesus' own role at its coming, Jesus' attitude toward Jews who are in the service of the Romans, the cleansing of the temple, and the triumphal entry into Jerusalem, all place Jesus in some proximity to the Zealots and their interests. "For these reasons, Jesus and his disciples were often related to the Zealots," observes Gutiérrez.[104]

On the other hand, over against these rather general points of affinity between Jesus and the Zealots—whose political relevancy is scarcely unambiguous in any case—Gutiérrez details a series of clear differences between them. Jesus thought universally; the Zealots thought nationally. Jesus saw the coming of the kingdom as a gift to be received; the Zealots looked upon it as a task to be accomplished by their own efforts. Jesus did not fight injustice and exploitation directly, but laid the axe to their root.[105] The balance sheet, according to Gutiérrez, is drawn up of pretty much equal columns. "It is not enough . . . to say that Jesus was not a Zealot. . . . Jesus' posture precludes all oversimplification."[106]

Ignacio Ellacuría's argumentation is clearer-cut. His consideration of the Zealot question is ranged under the head, "Part One, The Political Character of Jesus' Mission."[107] He emphasizes first that Jesus begins his public life at a time when the Jewish people were politicized in the highest degree. The fact that Jesus was executed as a political subversive, together with sporadic references in the New Testament tradition to efforts to confer a political role upon him (John 6:15, Matt. 21:14-16), show that Jesus can de facto be looked upon as a political messiah. (Whether he be rightly or wrongly so considered is not to the point.) Further, holds Ellacuría, Jesus himself is not altogether beyond suspicion:

Jesus gave the impression that he was the awaited Messiah. The Messiah had a clearly political dimension; Jesus tried to transcend this impression but did not evade it. This is a key point in our present study here: Despite the ambiguities surrounding his lifestyle, Jesus chose that lifestyle and no other. It is a theological datum of the greatest importance.[108]

Ellacuría characterizes Jesus' messianic consciousness as unambiguously in the line of the politico-religious tradition of his people and the hope they held of a new kingdom. This is where the temptation to a false messianism becomes the decisive temptation of Jesus' life. Ellacuría finds Jesus under its assault on three occasions: in the temptation in the wilderness (Matt. 4:1–11, Luke 4:1–13); in the temptation in the neighborhood of Caesarea Philippi (Mark 8:27–33, Matt. 16:13–23); and in the temptation on the Mount of Olives, on the occasion of his arrest.

> These three temptations indicate that the purely political dimension was never far from Jesus' mind. He got beyond it, but it was the great temptation of his life. However, he did not go to the other extreme. He never gave up the political "bite" of his salvation message.[109]

But now Ellacuría contrasts Jesus' political mission with the political activity of the Zealots. He begins, to be sure, by listing the elements that betoken a certain sympathy and affinity between Jesus and the Zealots: The Gospels record no single word of his against them. The apostles are considered by Gamaliel to be of the same category as Theudas and Judas the Zealot (Acts 5:37). Like the Zealots, Jesus ranges the tax-collectors with "sinners." He mocks the mighty (Luke 22:25). He opposes religious leaders who oppress and exploit the people. He counsels, on one occasion, the acquisition of a sword (Luke 22:35–38)—while later renouncing its use in his own behalf (Luke 22:50–51). He drives the merchants from the temple— although, remarkably, he does not direct this action against the Romans, which of course is what a Zealot would have been inclined to do.

Against this background of similarities, the differences between Jesus and the Zealots are easier to grasp. Jesus shares the Zealots' active hope for the kingdom of God, but not their extreme religious nationalism.

> In his preaching he favored the concept of the poor and poverty over the concept of the Jew and Jewishness. In other words he gave preference to a humanistic, social concept over a politico-religious concept. He ultimately took a stance in line with the universalism of the prophets and pushed that line of thinking further ahead.[110]

Another, more important, difference is that Jesus does not share the Zealots "immediatist religiosity."

> He rejected their overly simplistic religious formulation in which the kingdom of God in this world was equated with a political theocratic kingdom. In the theological realm this immediatist religiosity leads to an all too ready identification of the kingdom of God with a worldly political kingdom. In the socio-political realm it leads to a religious fanaticism.[111]

Interestingly, Ellacuría proposes the Chalcedonian formula of the immixture and indivisibility of the two natures in Christ as a guideline in these matters.

Ellacuría sees a further difference between Jesus and the Zealots in their methods of action. While the decisive means for the Zealots, in the tradition of the Maccabees, is armed force, for Jesus what tips the scales is the power of denunciation by the Word.

As examples of logia in which Jesus is probably clarifying his position vis-à-vis the Zealots, Ellacuría proposes Matthew 5:39, 11:12; John 10:8; Luke 23:28–30. Precisely because Jesus does partially share the Zealots' goals and aims, it is quite difficult for him to divorce himself from them in people's minds, and so it is as a Zealot that he met his death.[112]

Summarizing, Ellacuría says:

> Jesus worked to transform a politicized religion into a political faith. He did not give up the idea of saving humanity, but he was interested in the full and total dimensions of human salvation. From salvation in history one must move on to a meta-historical salvation. Proclamation of this meta-historical salvation will help human beings to see what authentic salvation in history should be, just as authentic salvation in history will be the one and only valid sign, comprehensible to human beings, of what meta-historical salvation means.[113]

Thus Ellacuría seeks to steer a safe course between two dangers. The first danger is to see Jesus' praxis as purely political. The second is to rob it of its political dimension altogether and call it purely religious.

On the specific question of the use of violence, Ellacuría strongly emphasizes the subjective character of Jesus' decision on the Mount of Olives to renounce armed resistance.

Altogether it is indisputable for Ellacuría that Jesus participated in the public life of his people—that he was not exclusively concerned with matters of religious interiority. The question of the Zealots helps to clarify the profile of this participation.

Jon Sobrino, who handles Jesus' relationship with the Zealots in connection with his death, comes very close to Ellacuría in his historical considerations. But he extracts a different element of theological meaning from them.[114]

> Jesus does not disagree basically with the Zealots on the idea that there must be some historical and socio-political mediation of the kingdom of God. That is why he could be, and in fact was, identified as a Zealot. But Jesus was not a Zealot because his conception of God was very different from theirs. What history tells us is not that Jesus was apolitical but that he offered a new alternative to Zealotism. Yet his alternative also had political implications and repercussions. Jesus' crucifixion was not due

to a misunderstanding because he was undermining the very foundations of the political view held by the Roman Empire and the rulers in society. Historically speaking, then, we can say that Jesus' death was occasioned by his work on behalf of God's kingdom, which symbolized a particular form of societal life for human beings.

These historical observations must be pushed further with more strictly theological reflections. Jesus did not calculate that the kingdom would come in accordance with some neat scheme or law, as other groups did. The rabbis urged asceticism and fulfillment of the law, advocates of apocalypticism urged close attention to the signs of the times, and the Zealots favored armed insurrection.

According to Jesus, however, God's coming was an act of grace. He did not espouse religious nationalism or political theocratism. The basic temptation facing him and others was the temptation to establish God's kingdom through the use of political power. The only true power in Jesus' eyes was the power embodied in truth and love. That is why he broke down the old dichotomy between friend and enemy, calling for pardon and love of enemy rather than vengeance.

His theological critique of the Roman Empire was much more radical. Jesus thoroughly desacralized the concept of power. The power of the Roman Empire and its organized realm, which had turned the Mediterranean into a Roman lake and produced the *pax romana*, was not divine. The emperor, who stood as the visible embodiment of that power, was not God.

It is here that we confront the real issue: What sort of power is it that really and truly renders the deity present?[115]

In thus focusing the question of Jesus' relation to the Zealots within the context of the question of the very nature of God, Sobrino loses interest in a more closely political description of Jesus' alternative to Zealotism. Sobrino is most persuasive. But one desiderates more concretion.

Leonardo Boff opens his considerations here by positing that Jesus, the Zealots, and indeed other Jewish groups, had one thing in common: they all looked for the coming of the kingdom of God. And this common interest constitutes common testimony "to the ultimate meaning of the world and its radical perfectibility to be realized by God and only by God."[116] But unlike others, Jesus knows no national frontiers of this kingdom. "He never said a word about rebellion against the Romans, nor did he ever allude to the restoration of the Davidic king."[117] True, a political messianism was a real temptation for Jesus. But he overcame it.

He is indeed the Messiah-Christ, but not one of a political nature. His kingdom cannot be particularized and reduced to a part of reality, such as politics. He came to heal all reality in all its dimensions, cosmic, human, social. The great drama of the life of Christ was to try to take the ideological content out of the words "kingdom of God" and make the people and his disciples comprehend that he signified something much more profound, namely, that he demands a conversion of persons and a radical transformation of the human world; that he demands a love of friends and enemies alike and the overcoming of all elements inimical to God and humankind.[118]

Thus Boff takes a far less political view of Jesus' relationship to the Zealots than do the other authors we have considered. He stresses the "apolitical" nature of Jesus' mission. It must be said, however, that Boff defines the political very differently from Ellacuría. For Boff the political is a mere part of reality, a mere part of the world of the person, of the "human world," of the global reality of life that constitutes the object of Jesus' driving concern. For Ellacuría, on the other hand, anything that pertains in any way to the public area, to human interrelationships, whether among individuals or among groups—provided it be in this public area—is "political."

Raúl Vidales sums up his considerations on "Jesus and the Zelotic Movement" with the assertion that it is more important to discover the basis of the revolutionary dimension of Jesus' historical activity and proclamation than to know whether he happened to be a Zealot or not.[119] The reason he considers the latter question to be of lesser importance is, he says, that it brings nothing to an understanding of Jesus' radicalism.

Like other authors, Vidales first lists the indicators that Jesus might have been a Zealot; next he describes direct political messianism as a temptation Jesus had to undergo; then he goes on:

> Thus we can pose the following question. Must we assume that Jesus excluded the Zealots as outlaws, as an element that was irreconcilable with his proclamation and the establishment of the kingdom? Had he then decided for a plan and strategy that cut him off from the plan and strategy of the Zelotic groups? A simple answer does not seem possible. Whether we say yes or no, we shall have to nuance our answer at once. We know that Jesus' attitude toward these groups was not the same as his attitude toward the Sadducees or Pharisees. In any case, a correct understanding of the situation will demand that we keep in view that Jesus' historical activity could not proceed simply and solely from considerations of the value of what was new in his proclamation. He had to have a plan that would actually work—and workability is a product not only of one's goal, but of the complexity of historical mediations. Opportunity and feasibility necessarily determine strategy, if one is to have a strategy that will work. Thus we are brought to a consideration of the power of the impoverished as Jesus' point of departure.[120]

Now Vidales goes on to point out that the Zealots were not a unified group: one wing saw its purpose more as doing direct battle with the Romans, while another looked for confrontation with the mighty ones of Palestine.[121] Then he offers a brief characterization of social relationships in the Palestine of Jesus' time, where there was a new, impoverished rural proletariat (who were unaware, however, of their condition). He continues:

> In view of all this, Jesus' historical response becomes much more difficult. All too obviously, his proclamation is going to have to be carried out in this historical situation of conflict. The paths to the realization of the kingdom continue to be imbedded in the means of establishing a new society, a new human being, and a free order that comes closer and closer to his original plan.[122]

Confrontation with the occupying Roman power, then, Vidales insists, became a burning problem not only for a Zealot, but for any Jew who shared the messianic expectations. But Jesus was such a one. And so:

> Altogether aware of what he is about, Jesus seizes the opportunity which represents, in the faith of his people, the "fullness of time"—the long-awaited moment of deliverance. There can be no doubt that Jesus shared the sufferings of his people as could only that minority who were heirs to the hope of the messianic liberation (Luke 6:24).
> But in order to understand the originality of Jesus' activity, we must place ourselves in the perspective of the exercise of his messianism and the establishment of the kingdom. Here we must deal with the parables that reflect the class struggle of Jesus' time (Luke 6:24, 12:16, 16:19). The very recognition of this situation, let alone its confrontation, is dangerous. But the true revolutionary measure of Jesus' dynamics is in the fact that his messianism has no touch with a paternalistic approach to the problems caused by the unjust system. Instead he calls human beings to consciousness and responsibility, challenging them to plan out an effective historical action that will transform slavery into freedom—and thus move closer to his own original plan. His words against injustice, hatred, lying, selfishness, and the like cannot be relegated to the private sphere of the individual. No, they find their true resonance in the building of the new people of God.[123]

Thus, to Vidales's view, Jesus is no whit less political than the Zealots—and his call for the conversion of the individual is part of an overall political concept. (This is just the reverse of Boff's idea.) The concrete means to the realization of this overall concept are rooted, for Jesus as for the Zealots, in the historical situation. They will depend on what was actually possible there and then. Vidales's actual description of this concrete step is, unfortunately, somewhat colorless. Other than the protest of the kingdom and prophetic words, Vidales does not actually point to anything typical of Jesus.

Segundo Galilea clarifies the difference between Jesus and the Zealots by means of an example. The fact that the authorities released Barabbas instead of Jesus, he says, shows that in their eyes Jesus was more dangerous than a revolutionary—that his proclamation was more subversive than political incitement.

> From a reading of Jesus' life that takes into account the political context in which it was lived, it is clear that that life is the inspiration and model for all Christians who are involved in liberation more in prophetic ways than in political ones.[124]

Once more we note Galilea's concern for the spiritual.

To conclude this part of our study, let us see what Enrique Maza has to say about Jesus' messianism. After a very brief introductory remark to the effect that one difference between Jesus and the Zealots was that Jesus was not an anti-Roman extremist,[125] Maza takes up the thread again and goes into a little more detail:

> Jesus' messianism, in a class social structure ruled by the controllers of the economic, juridical, political, and ideological apparatus, consists in the challenge to share, to give. It is the challenge to distribute bread to all, when bread is a privilege of money, with which it can be bought, and money is a privilege of the rich, who have the means of making it. Consequently, Jesus' messianism means the overthrow of the class system—the system of economic value and exchange value in which things and persons are measured by what they cost.[126]

And a little further on, Maza adds:

> The ideologization of this class system entails a typical piety, based on a magical conception in which mysterious powers of the Beyond, good and evil spirits, and cosmic forces have a meaning for human deeds. Deeds must conform to these magical elements, and even imitate them. Conformity with the natural order is of the utmost importance. . . . Human conduct is regulated by prohibitions and ritual observances. Much attention is paid to externals—what I eat, what I touch, the people I meet, the things I see. Sin seems to arise from contact. So there are ritual purifications for this impure contact, and the ritually pure priestly caste owes all its importance and all its hegemony to its total control of other people's purity.
>
> To this conception of religion as imposed by the system, Jesus opposes one of social relationships among human beings. He proposes the necessity of a just social order, based on giving, receiving, and sharing, and on renunciation in order to share with those who have nothing. Injustice consists in hoarding, in the practice of miserliness for one's own advantage. Giving is life. Retaining is death. Giving is justice and giving is love.

Retaining is the denial of love, and hence, sin. The class system is institutionalized, justified retention. It is injustice masquerading as social order. It is the sin of the world.

Messianism is the overthrow of the sin of the world. The following of Jesus and the recognition of his messianism means taking a position against the class system and for the system of equality, for a reconciled humanity, for a society of brothers and sisters. Discipleship consists in just social relationships. There shall be no poor among you. You shall not exploit your neighbor. You shall distribute your goods to the poor. You shall respect your brother's and sister's good name. You shall not bear evil tales, you shall do nothing evil, you shall wish no one evil. You shall go in search of the one who has nothing and offer bread, water, clothing, society, health, and freedom. And love. And you will create justice and establish peace. For the only possible representation of God—in whose image you have been created—is the power that sets God's people free. It is possible to suppress social injustice, for injustice depends on relationships among human beings. Injustice is not something given in nature. Its source is the human being. Its remedy is the human being. Its healing is possible.

Against a closed, institutionalized system based on receiving, Jesus pits a subversive social system that sets the exploitation of human beings by human beings head over heels.[127]

Maza groups institution and class society on the one side, and Jesus with his call for a society of sisters and brothers on the other, in sharp opposition. It is precisely because Jesus sees his demands as political (without being exhausted in the political, to be sure)[128] that he is destined for destruction. The institution cannot want what Jesus wants, when it itself is being called into question.

In view of his thesis, it is not surprising that Maza scarcely touches the question of whether Jesus was more against the Roman Empire or the Jewish state. What is primary is his opposition to the institution, as such. And so Maza can quickly pass from a description of Jesus' position to its demands on his disciples. His anti-institutional mind-set naturally dispenses him from the obligation of identifying political programs or strategies as means to the implementation of moral demands. Thus although Maza states that Jesus' messianism was political, Maza's argument actually shows that it was largely prophetical.

Jesus' Way to Death

We have already begun to develop certain aspects of Jesus' trial and execution in the section just concluded, "Jesus and the Zealots." As some of our Latin American authors show by their argumentation, there is an intimate connection between Jesus' relationship with the Zealots, and his trial and death. Further, our confidence in the legitimacy of dealing with elements from the various moments of Jesus' life by substantial connection rather than by chronology is bolstered by the fact that most liberation theologians are less interested in the exact timetable of the life of Jesus than in the political implications of his life and work taken as a unit.

The "Galilean Crisis"

In the framework of his Christology of discipleship, Jon Sobrino comes to speak of the "Galilean crisis." A new situation has arisen, and Jesus' faith has undergone a change. His self-understanding, as well as his conduct, are different now.[129] How did this come about? What has happened? Jesus' certitude of the imminence of the kingdom of God has been shattered. The masses have heard him out. to be sure, but they have not become his disciples. The effect of this experience on Jesus is a new orientation, whose development we can discern in stages:

> In the first stage, logically at least, Jesus' demands proceed from the same conception of the kingdom of God as was present in the Old Testament. In the second stage, however, they begin to proceed more from the person of Jesus himself, and his destiny.[130]

Correlatively, Jesus' faith, in the first part of his public life, means a radical confidence in God and cooperation with God in the proclamation of the kingdom; in the second stage, Jesus' disappointment and scandal causes his faith to take on the nature of a "hope against hope." Hence for Christians who seek to model their own faith on Jesus' faith, two aspects of that faith now come to light: on one hand, Jesus is the way to the known God (stage one); on the other, he is the sole way to *come* to know God (stage two).[131] The Galilean crisis has deepened Jesus' understanding of God. In the first stage this understanding expresses itself primarily in Jesus' dedication through activity; in the second stage what is demanded of him is the sacrifice of his ideas, his concept of God, and his whole person.

> After the Galilean crisis Jesus enters into the unknown, into the area of that which is no longer under his control. In this sense the crisis is a condition of his ability to radicalize and concretize his relationship with his Father in trust and obedience.[132]

But we must not overlook a third and final stage. The crisis has been occasioned by external conflict, arising out of Jesus' opposition to the unlawful holders of religious, economic, and political power. This conflict has a profound theological meaning:

> At the same time, Jesus' path puts the genuine divinity of God "on trial." For what is at issue is (1) whether the true essence of God has been

expressed in the factual religious situation, and (2) whether the true power of God has been expressed in the prevailing political power structure.[133]

Sobrino does not investigate the historical side of the "Galilean crisis."[134] He is more concerned with systematic conclusions he draws from his historical observations: namely, the changes in the course of Jesus' life, and the consequences for Christians today who interpret their lives as a following of Jesus of Nazareth.

Jesus' Trial

Leonardo Boff's presentation of Jesus' trial puts special emphasis on two points.[135] First, the occasion of the death sentence handed down by the supreme council is Jesus' blasphemy. Jesus has the notion that, now that he is here, the kingdom of God is inaugurated. Second, Pilate's own sentence is nothing but a ratification of that of the Sanhedrin.

Boff concludes that the original indictment is religious, and that it has only been transformed into a political one in order to obtain more surely Pilate's ratification of Jesus' condemnation. Boff does not explictly consider Jesus' liberation proclamation in his discussion of Jesus' trial.

Jon Sobrino, as well, observes that Jesus was condemned for blasphemy. The fact, however, interests Sobrino less than the causes.[136] Sobrino finds these causes in the attitude adopted by Jesus toward the official Jewish religion of his time. He describes Jesus as a nonconformist, a liberal, when it comes to religion. He finds examples of Jesus' criticism of official religion in Mark 2:27 and 7:21. "Some people assumed that ritual and cult were automatically justified because they expressed due reverence to God; Jesus felt that they, too, had certain limits."[137]

But Sobrino detects a still deeper conflict between Jesus and official religion where a concept of God and the way to God are concerned.

> In religion as it actually presented itself to his eyes, Jesus saw a scheme whereby people responded to God through the fulfillment of certain obligations. God was pictured as distinct from human beings and greater than they, but he also stood in some sort of continuity with them. In philosophical terms the continuity lay in the fact that God explained the world; in religious terms the continuity lay in the fact that God stood surety for the established order. Insofar as access to God was concerned, there were privileged locales for it: the temple and cultic worship. Jesus noted that human beings were only too happy to accept such a scheme and enter into it. Despite its demands and obligations, it offered some ultimate feeling of security; it could also be manipulated in such a way that one need not heed the pleas of the oppressed. Such a religious scheme offers immunization against the deity since it clearly defines and

circumscribes God's demands. It also leaves room for casuistry designed to justify oppressive situations.

By immersing himself in this situation, Jesus *necessarily* introduced conflict into the heart of his life. If incarnation means accepting and then reacting to a given situation, then Jesus' polemics with the religious authorities were not just a didactic exercise; they flowed naturally from the inner dynamism of the incarnation. Jesus presented people with a God who stands in complete contradiction to the existing religious situation. His God is distinct from, and greater than, the God of the Pharisees. On the horizontal level Jesus expands the locale of our access to God enormously, no longer maintaining the temple as the privileged place of such access. In Jesus' eyes the privileged locale of access to God is people themselves. More specifically, it is the person who is poor, who has been forced into impoverishment.[138]

Sobrino continues:

The greater God proclaimed by Jesus is also described in terms of the vertical dimension. The reign of God draws near as a grace, not as a matter of justice related to people's good works. Here we find something completely new in Jesus' preaching. It has no parallel in the preaching of John the Baptist, in rabbinic tradition, or in the prophetic and apocalyptic tradition outside Jesus. Paradoxically enough, it is this teaching of God's kingdom as grace that proves to be the major obstacle for accepting Jesus. Jesus unmasks the effort of "religious" people to ensure themselves against God. If God's approach is an act of grace, then no human disposition can force his coming. God does not aim primarily to recompense people according to their works but rather to re-create the situation of every human being. It is a wholly gratuitous action, and the "religious" person feels insecure in the face of such a God. It is those who are legally "just" that cannot accept a "greater" God, a God of surprises; it is sinners and nonreligious people who are willing to put their hope in such a God.

Jesus' polemical discussions with the Pharisees can be understood only against that backdrop. It is the radical difference in their two viewpoints that explains the tragic end of Jesus. . . . Jesus died because he chose to bear faithful witness to God right to the end. . . .[139]

For Sobrino, Jesus' trial is a résumé of all his life and work. The basic conflict he sought to wage with the Judaism of his time comes out into the open—for at the heart of this juridical process is the question of the correct concept of God.

Ignacio Ellacuría deals extensively with the drama of Jesus before Pilate in its Johannine presentation (John 18:33–40), for he is still working with Jesus' "political profile."[140] First he observes that Jesus holds absolutely fast to the easily misunderstood concept of "kingdom." Obviously he could have left it to one side had he wished to avoid all appearance of political intent. Next, Ellacuría takes the "not of this world" qualification (John 18:36) in conjunction with its apodosis—"my men would have fought"— and concludes that Jesus is speaking of a kingdom having no governmental organization because it refuses to rely on the military.

As for a positive characterization of this kingdom, Ellacuría focuses upon Jesus' purpose to "bear witness to the truth" (John 18:37), which he interprets as follows:

(1) The truth of which he speaks here is not some speculative, non-operational truth; it is an efficacious and total truth. It is the truth about the world—what it is, what it should be, and what is going to take place in it. (2) Jesus upholds the judicial and dominating character of his mission and truth, even vis-à-vis the world insofar as it gives configuration to human existence. (3) From within the context of this total truth one must be a proclaimer and doer of truth, seeking to gain dominion over evil. The world is already being judged, and Christian history should help to move this judgment along towards its consummation. (4) The effect and impact of this truth is liberty. It is a truth that sets human beings free. (5) One must belong to this truth in order to be able to hear it. One must do this truth in order to be able to receive it in full clarity and plenitude.[141]

Obviously Pilate comes to realize that Jesus' struggle is not directly with Roman interests, so he offers his release. The fact that the chief priests (and of course the people, urged on by the priests) prefer Barabbas is, once more, evidence that in the eyes of the clergy Jesus was more dangerous than a Zealot: he threatened to destroy the social-, religious-, and political structures, whose guardians were the priests. Ellacuría attempts to explain the fact that the people sided with them by suggesting that Jesus' political position no longer appeared to the people as holding more promise than that of Barabbas and the Zealots.

The chief priests, on the other hand, feared Jesus. Jesus was more interested in the direct socio-religious repression to which the people were subject than he was in the struggle with the Romans. Hence the clergy actually indicted Jesus before Pilate on religious grounds. He made himself the "Son of God." The political overtones of this title are not lost on Ellacuría, and he cites the fear the chief priests must have felt at the realization that Jesus' claim of special access to God meant their theocracy was now headed for ruin. Hence Ellacuría also finds it appropriate that the "greater guilt" for Jesus' death is assigned to the Jewish leaders (John 19:11).[142]

In all this, Ellacuría holds, Jesus' "political profile" becomes even clearer. Pilate does not condemn Jesus because he finds him guilty of rebellion against the Roman political power. Pilate is pushed to this sentence by the representatives of Jewish theocracy, who feel threatened by Jesus. The political order of Judea, under the leadership of the Sanhedrin, was directly bound up with the faith of Yahweh. Jesus' new style of liberating discourse about God calls the established order into question. The vested representatives of this God-given order, orientated to the Law of Moses, must eliminate this person who speaks of God in a new, benign manner. Jesus, then, is just as political as the chief priests. For him, as well, faith in God—the manner in which one has access to God—is directly linked to the lifestyle of the human being in the political order.

Excursus: The Use of Violence

Here, we think, will be the proper place to take up the question of the use of violence. We shall not, however, attempt an investigation of how this question is dealt with in liberation theology across the board. We shall treat only of those aspects of violence that our liberation theologians discuss in connection with their appeal to the words and works of Jesus.

The theology of liberation exhibits a variety of positions on the question of Jesus and the use of violence. There are those who propound nonviolence as the Christian way par excellence. Here it is the Sermon on the Mount, with its call for love of one's enemies, that is cited. On the other side are those who appeal to the impossibility of Christian neutrality in the prevailing atmosphere of political tension in Latin America and hold that violence is the only effective means of resolving this tension in favor of the kingdom. Then of course Jesus' polemics, or the cleansing of the temple, are invoked. Let us hear from some of our authors on this question.

Segundo Galilea sees Jesus' revolutionary quality precisely in his renunciation of power, hence also of violence. Galilea's argumentation, which takes its point of departure from Philippians 2:6–8, underscores the creative character of Jesus' renunciation: Galilea sees a power in Jesus that transcends any official power of politics.

> Like all renunciation for the sake of the good news of the kingdom, Jesus' renunciation of power is creative. Jesus effects new forms of socio-political, or revolutionary, transformation. In proclaiming an ethics and religion based not on the legalism of the Torah but on love for and imitation of the Father, he prepares the collapse of the established religion of Israel. In calling for a comprehensive equality and communion of brothers and sisters, in which the magic spell of each and every system and ideology of lordship will be broken, Jesus radically threatens the power of Roman imperialism, and thereby as well the basic principle of all totalitarianism, for he introduces the great creative principle of all liberating revolution. In calling the poor and "little ones" to his kingdom and assigning them a privileged place in it (Matt. 25:31–41, Luke 14:21), he creates a conscious, mighty thrust that will determine the course of history.[1]

Likewise Samuel Ruiz García sees a power operative in Jesus that transcends the polarity of violence and nonviolence. He looks on Jesus' life, taken as a whole, as clearly a life full of conflict.[2]

Ruiz observes that Jesus, without being a violent revolutionary himself, does not hesitate to provoke violence on the part of his adversaries. Jesus is well aware of the consequences his conduct will have, including the political ones. But violence is not his goal.

A passionate love, and a yearning for the welfare of human beings bring Jesus to defy the violence that his conduct has provoked. The force of this love is the spirit of the resurrection. This force—gift and giving, through the risen Jesus Christ—establishes new, fruitful possibilities in human beings. It is more than a no to violence as a direct actualization of the kingdom.[3]

Even more vigorous is Eduardo Pironio's rejection of the attempt to legitimate the use of violence through an appeal to Jesus.

The way to liberation is the way of Christ: generous self-giving, even unto death on a cross. The only blood that may be spilled is his, "for the life of the world" (John 6:51). Liberation does not call for violence. On the contrary, the only violence employed by liberation is that of the kingdom, and of the perfect practice of the Beatitudes.[4]

In both writers, one desiderates a more precise description of the concepts "force" or "violence," when used in an affirmative construction. An ambiguous application of the concept of violence can be very confusing.

Nor does José María Casabó Suque altogether elude the difficulty when he writes:

Meekness, love, forgiveness, weakness-and-strength, the battle with evil by means of the mighty spiritual arms of the kingdom that grows and takes shape imperceptibly—this seems to be the New Testament doctrine concerning violence. There is a violence against which Jesus speaks out, and of which he refuses to make use—and there is a "holy" violence, which never constrains another. Jesus calls, proclaims, and accuses. But he never constrains others, or uses violence with them to force them to accept him. He relies on no earthly power, and no force of arms. On this level, he is strikingly nonviolent. His power lies elsewhere. And there can be no doubt of the enormously revolutionary character of his work and his teaching.[5]

One feels that what our authors have in mind is the question of the legitimacy of the use of violence by Latin American Christians in the struggle for liberation. But their reference to Jesus' nonviolence (or "special kind of violence'') is direct and exclusive, without any further examination of the relationships obtaining in Latin American reality.

Here José Míguez Bonino attempts a different thesis.[6] Míguez inquires into the role of Christians in the class struggle, where he is sure that only "God's comfort and God's demand in Jesus Christ" have anything to offer toward a solution of the violence question where Christians are concerned. But he does not directly conclude from the words or deeds of Jesus to the proper conduct of Latin American Christians today. He argues from the fact of an ongoing class struggle—which he describes as the contradiction between the interests of the dominant class, ever seeking to maintain the prevailing economic system, and the efforts of the oppressed to obtain a more just economic configuration.

A love whose desire is the kingdom, holds Míguez, cannot but take sides in a like conflict. A general call for nonviolence is nothing but camouflaged sides-taking with the established powers. "Reconciliation, in the Bible, does not mean conflicts and contradictions are ignored and brushed aside. It means they are efficaciously eliminated."[7] Then he says:

> The ideological appropriation of the Christian doctrine of reconciliation by the liberal capitalist system for the purpose of hushing up the brutal fact of class, of imperialistic exploitation, and of conflict is one of the great heresies of our time, if not indeed the greatest of all.[8]

Continuing, Míguez Bonino asks whether after all Christ is not the prototype and model for all-embracing love and nonviolence.

His answer stresses two points. First, Christ's love includes condemnation, criticism, opposition, and refusal (for instance where the Pharisees, or Herod, are concerned). Second, there can be no doubt that Jesus took sides with the poor and oppressed.

> If a Christian hopes to follow Christ in such a way that his or her decision for nonviolence will be credible, then that decision must be taken along clear and unambiguous lines of subversion of the oppressive order. We see many instances of so-called "Christian" nonviolence that leave this earmark of authenticity open to a good deal of doubt.[9]

Míguez bases Jesus' renunciation of political power on his consciousness of being the servant of God. Jesus had no aversion for politics as such, but he refused to interpret his role in categories of political power.

> The anointed of God is not sent to transpose human political struggle to the plane of God's omnipotence. He is sent to identify with the powerlessness of the oppressed. Renunciation of force means for Jesus renunciation of the use of divine power to regulate human affairs.[10]

The conclusion to be drawn by Christians is, first, they are to identify with the oppressed; second, they are to battle for justice with the arms of reason. Christian politics has no specific form. Consequently:

> [The discussion of the legitimacy of the use of violence] can be meaningful only as a discussion of the *forms of violence,* and of the conditions of violence in our concrete situation. We must ask who is applying these forms of violence, who has to suffer them, what the goal of these forms is, and how this goal is or is not being attained.[11]

To be sure, Míguez avers, nonviolent action is as appropriate for the Christian conscience as is the revolutionary purpose itself. But still:

> Nonviolence must ask itself the cost to human beings in terms of love and suffering, in terms of crippling frustration, dehumanization, and the emergence of a slave mentality. . . . Naturally, Christians in the struggle for liberation will bear witness to their faith, and to the ultimate goal of revolution, with full attention to the price of violence, and in the conscientious avoidance of all glorification of destruction, hatred, and revenge. They will seek to render the battle more humane; nor will they forget that, after the battle, reconciliation and reconstruction must follow. But they must not allow Christian scruples to stand in the way of a clear assessment of the situation. Still less may they abide by reactionary rules of the game and underestimate the intent of those who are reaping the profits of the system of violence that *already* obtains—thereby weakening the determination of the oppressed in their fight for liberation—with sentimental, however well-meant, pseudo-Christian clichés and slogans.[12]

In contrast with the authors we have cited above, Míguez Bonino's main concern is not the principle of violence, but its concrete context in the area of social relationships. Christian behavior is not simply a matter of logical deduction. It must be the result of a rational effort to find the "best way."

A modest contribution to the thesis that it is theologically impossible to conclude directly to Christian obligations today—in the matter of nonviolence, for example—from the words and works of Jesus is offered by Juan Luis Segundo.[13] He holds—in a context of the theologoumenon of Jesus' sinlessness—that, if we intend to take Jesus' humanity seriously, we shall have to admit that Jesus must have been subject to the "law of the limitations of human capabilities" (*economía de la energía*). As examples he cites Jesus' behavior after the arrest of John the Baptist, his limitation of his mission to a summons to Israel in the spirit of Jewish nationalism, and the collapse of the dialogue with the Pharisees. These modes of conduct— an effect of the law of limited capabilities—by standards of absolute nonviolence, contain a measure of violence (refusal of solidarity, prejudice against foreigners, and a neglect of individuals in favor of their incorporation into the group). Segundo draws the conclusion:

> Only idealistic oversimplification of Jesus' real attitudes can paint a picture of him as a human being dedicated to limitless love without a trace of resistance or violence.[14]

Clearly, then, for today's Christians as well, in their engagement in the struggle for liberation, there can be no absolute criteria for the use or renunciation of violence. They must themselves decide, according to the concrete circumstances in which they find themselves.

Thus the appeal to Jesus serves both the justification and the renunciation of the use of violence on the part of Christians engaged in the struggle for liberation—and even supports a position of basic aversion for the use of violence, with a margin for its legitimacy in individual cases, as for example when great violence is being brought to bear in the repression of the masses (cf. Medellín documents, vol. 2, pp. 34–36).[15]

Chapter 7

Jesus' Death and Resurrection

Leonardo Boff declares that the Latin American Christology of liberation gives the historical Jesus precedence over the Christ of faith.[1] It could
seem inappropriate, then, to treat of Jesus' death and resurrection in one
and the same chapter. But, as we shall see in the course of our exposition,
Boff's distinction between the historical Jesus and the Christ of faith is not
the same as that of classical European exegesis. For one thing, his Christ of
faith is more a Christ of post–New Testament theology. For another, his
attribution of precedence to the historical Jesus is in the order of the precedence of praxis to theory. The resurrection will actually be the cornerstone
of the precedence of praxis.

An article by Ignacio Ellacuría, in which he discusses an essay by Boff,
will help to clarify these relationships. Ellacuría summarizes and analyzes
Boff's position:

> Jesus Christ's liberation is not so much a doctrine to be proclaimed as a
> praxis to be carried out. In order to discover this doctrine and this prac-
> tice today, one must, to be sure, examine the words and deeds of Jesus
> with intent to discover their abiding content—but one must do so in a
> precise, exegetically sound fashion that will burst through the framework
> of Jesus' historical life and work and see a transcendent meaning in
> them. Of course the intent will not be to lose ourselves in this meaning,
> but to afford it incarnation in a new historical situation. Jesus' universal-
> ity and transcendence are comprehensive, of course, but they must be
> mediated and rendered visible in concrete steps of liberation. "Christ
> himself translated this universal liberation into practice by implementing
> a concrete approach to liberalism within his particular situation. We
> must do the same if Christ's liberation is to become meaningful in our
> own lives."

Boff, then, sets himself a double methodological task: "First, we must
show how Christ's liberation was a concrete liberation for the world with
which he had to deal. . . . Second, we must then try to discern in that

concrete liberation a dimension that transcends that particular historical embodiment of liberation, a dimension that has to do with us in our present and different situation in history."[2]

Now, Boff himself says, with respect to his methodology, that the resurrection of Jesus is profoundly bound up with his life, death, and proclamation of the kingdom of God.[3] Jesus' death and resurrection may legitimately be treated together, then, as Christological points of reference for liberation theology, in one and the same chapter. (We shall, however, consider them under separate heads—even while finding that quite a number of our theologians will be citing them in the same breath.)

Jesus' Death

Jesus' Death as Seal on His Life

A great many theological declarations on the part of our theologians tend to view Jesus' death as a seal set on his life in some way. Here, as often enough elsewhere, we find brief programmatic slogans and inspirational passages to be more common than attempts at exegetical or systematic reflection.

Thus for example we read in the booklet, *The Eucharistic Congress in Colombia and the Class Struggle* (1968):

> In this Latin America of our time, this continent that burns for acts more than goals, the redeeming deed of Camilo, together with those of so many others who have "laid down their lives for their friends" in the mountains—those mountains that are like a new Calvary—show us a new way of celebrating the Eucharist, and give us a glimpse of what the international congress of the future will be like. Then all the liberated peoples of the world will convene, not speaking much of Christ or of his Eucharist, but they will be very serious about his story and about actualizing its meaning: the equality of all men and women, all comrades together on this earth.[4]

Without so stating explicitly, this passage ascribes to Jesus' death the nature of a sign of hope, which Christians today may read in the deed of discipleship of Camilo Torres.

A 1970 pastoral letter of the archbishop of Montevideo, Uruguay, cites the duty of the Church to contribute to the comprehensive liberation of the human being, as well as the opposition that the church will meet in its proclamation. The letter sums up the interpretation of Jesus' death presented in the Letter to the Hebrews, then continues:

> But this doctrine grows out of concrete historical premises, which have themselves occurred in a concrete historical context. Jesus was sentenced

to death because he opposed a sinful situation, and because he did not hesitate to name those who had caused this situation. They did not execute him because he spoke of the lilies of the field and the birds of the sky, but because he cried out: "Woe to you, scribes and Pharisees!"[5]

Jesus' death is presented here as a consequence of his fearless commitment to liberation. Thereby it is also a prototype for the conduct of the Latin American church.

The connection between Jesus' commitment and church policy today is even clearer in the final document of the first congress of Christians for Socialism, held in Santiago de Chile in 1972. There we read:

> Christ has given us an example. He wishes to teach us to apply what he proclaims to real life. Christ preached brotherly/sisterly humaneness and love, and willed that these should mark all social structures. But above all he actually lived his own proclamation of liberation, right to its ultimate consequences.[6]

For Alejandro Cussiánovich the key to an understanding of the death of Jesus is the traditional formula, "deliverance from sin." Sin, holds Cussiánovich, basing himself on Medellín's doctrine, resides in unjust structures, and this gives Jesus' death its political note.

> Christ dies to deliver us from the sin that lies at the root of an unjust, exploitative order. But his death is not just a religious event. Jesus dies at the hands of the political power which is oppressing the Jewish people. The high council of the Sanhedrin had reasons of a religious nature, to be sure, for condemning a person who claimed to be the Son of God. But it had political reasons as well. Jesus' teaching and his influence over the people called into question the situation of privilege and power enjoyed by the great ones of the Jewish people. The Jews' political motives were then joined by those of the Roman authority, for whom a person claiming to be the Messiah, and king of the Jews, was certainly a threat and a danger.[7]

Another thesis concerning Jesus' condemnation and death is proposed by Bruno Renaud. Renaud argues out of a two-natures Christology, while at the same time seeking to do justice to Jesus' historical acts.

> Jesus Christ "pitched his tent among us" (John 1:14 in the Greek text) because the *whole human being* longs for salvation. . . . The whole human being yearned for salvation or liberation:
> —In his and her conscience, which was particularly repressed by the Pharisees.
> —In his and her political freedom, which was particularly repressed by the Romans. . . .

On the one hand it is clear that Jesus was concerned categorically to exclude and reject all superfluous confusion of competencies. . . . On the other hand, and by no means secondarily, Jesus committed himself fully and wholeheartedly to the human plane of existence.

Furthermore, Jesus did not have first to seek out his "temporal involvement." From the moment the Messiah entered time—in other words, from the first moment of his conception and birth as a human being—*his temporal involvement was an established fact.* As a human being he took on the customs and mores of his environment. And they were the customs and mores of the lowly people of that time and that place. De facto, and antecedent to any declaration to this effect on his part, Jesus was "temporally involved" with the poor (those poor *in* humanity as well as "poor humanity")—not with the rich.

Temporal involvement is the ineluctable law of Jesus' human existence. Jesus assumed his temporal involvement on two planes: that of being and that of activity. Hence in the life of Jesus there is an "unbroken continuity of word and effect," which is what we call, in any human life, veracity. Jesus—truthful as God himself—"lived up to his word." . . .

Thus we clearly see that it was *not with power*, strength, or human authority that Jesus entered into the social, political, or even religious life of his time. Rather he entered into that society with a personal sense of decision and resolve—and to be sure, with the supernatural authority of God himself (cf. Matt. 7:29, John 7:46), but this authority was manifested in *service.* . . .

In this conflict between the social, political, and religious (dis)order, and a "truthfully involved" human being, it is the human being to all appearances who seems to be the loser. Jesus was "destined . . . to be put to death" (Matt. 16:21). But in his very death—that triumph of weakness, that folly of the cross—he initiates the implementation-in-principle of the new order which his disciples, in all generations to come, will constantly be "fleshing out," until the day of his appearance in definitive and visible revelation.[8]

Here we have an attempt to relate the new tasks of the Latin American church—collaboration in the liberation process, commitment to the poor—to the earthly deeds of Jesus in a framework of traditional Christology. Jesus' death, of course, runs the risk of being a "show" death here, and the claim of a transformation of the old order seems pale and not very concrete.

Jesus' death as a genuine failure is clearer in Virgilio Zea's approach. For Zea, too, Jesus' truthfulness plays a role. Zea sees Jesus' death as the result of his life. Jesus loved everyone, hence could not cower in the wings in the moment of danger. He would have made his life a lie if he had. And yet the forces of the opposition punished his life and his ideas precisely as if they had been a lie; and the God of love, to whom Jesus had abandoned himself, abandoned him.

Thus Jesus is the model of human failure. Or rather: the cross is the standard of rebels everywhere who know that the only obstacle to the implementation of the works of love is the intrigue of might. The truth, which history *never tires of repeating*, is: peace is only impaled on bayonets and cannon barrel. If we take time really to listen to Jesus, if we refuse to betray him, we shall find meaning in his death. He died, it is true. *But he kept hoping*: he kept hoping for God's answer. "I know on whom I have believed!" cries Paul. Will the God and Father of our lord Jesus Christ not manage to be able to let meaning and life emerge from the failure of death itself?[9]

Zea takes the historical circumstances of Jesus' death seriously indeed, while at the same time seeking to invest it with a spiritual meaning. Its relation to praxis, however, which Zea has proclaimed in his exordium, when all is said and done, does not appear. Jesus' death becomes but a thrust and impulse for faith.

With Ruben R. Dri, as well, Jesus' death is a thrust and encouragement for hope. Dri, however, has more concern for the practical consequences. Jesus' death was the consequence of his subversive activity, which endangered the power of the mighty. Today, Dri goes on, it is Christ's mystical body which suffers in Latin America. But any resignation, or "death mystique," is out of place in Christian thinking on that continent, and Dri cites the "death loaves" of Mexico and the "holy death" cult of Argentina. Rather, the goal should be precisely the vanquishing of suffering and death.

Christ's passion and death are not the product of his express will. . . . [They occur] because his proclamation of liberation threatens the privileges of the oppressors. Christ's greatness consists precisely in his fidelity to his message to the very end, even when confronted with suffering. . . . He transforms suffering and death, those signs of momentary defeat, into signs of victory—for now they are seedlings destined to wax great, and become a tree wide enough for all the birds of the sky. . . . From suffering, life arises, yes—but not from suffering that a person seeks for its own sake. Only death can come out of that. Life arises from suffering that one takes on for love of life, for love of liberation.[10]

There can be little doubt that what Dri has in mind is a renewal of Christian praxis in Latin America. Yet his considerations remain confined to a spiritual thesis. The question of the political context of Jesus' death is broached indeed, but the key notion of "transformation" is not developed in the sense of the political.

Based on the sharp opposition he sees between Jesus and the "institution," it is clear to Enrique Maza that Jesus is headed for a violent death.

Jesus and the institution have a mutual aversion. They exclude each other. The dominating classes—religious, economic, and political—

defend the social system that Jesus turns away from, condemns, and revolutionizes. Jesus is very far from attempting to limit himself and his activity to what that system allows. He makes no attempt to reform the system. The institution understands that it cannot assimilate him, that there will be no compromise, that Jesus demands a total transformation that will strike at the basic goals of the system itself. So it is either kill or be killed.[11]

To be a Christian, to be a disciple of Jesus, then, means to fulfill in one's own life the same commitment and gift of self to the oppressed that brought Jesus to his death. A like practice will call to the field of combat the same forces that did away with Jesus himself. The following of Jesus and the loss of one's life for the sake of the gospel go together. Therefore, Maza concludes, "Jesus' death is the prime analogue of service to the poor,"[12] and he links Jesus' historical death with the meaning of that death for Christians in Latin America. After all, that continent has its own analogue in religious and social relationships surrounding Jesus' death in Palestine. This contradiction, if one is to be true to the God of love, leads straight to death. Death is the consequence of a commitment to the poor.

Raúl Vidales, as well, speaks in the same breath of the death of Jesus and the death of others who have made a like active commitment to better human relationships.

> Jesus is sentenced to death simply because he, like so many other just human beings before and after him, was not afraid to take a position outside the status quo, in words and deeds alike.[13]

This is the meaning of Jesus' death as the death of a *prophet* or a "just" one. But Vidales notes that there are two further meanings to be taken into account. Jesus is not simply a prophet, or a person who is just; he is also the messiah, and the Son of God. The death of Jesus as *messiah* is a deed of revolutionary hope, for Jesus stood in opposition to the conservative concept of a messiah who would solve all problems by power and might alone. Instead, Jesus encourages human beings to take control of their own destiny and history.

> And so his witness, along with that of other human beings, will ever raise up men and women in history who are glad to undertake, for justice and its implementation, a battle worth more than their own lives, and see it through to the end.[14]

Of course, the death of this messiah also manifests the power of the evil one in the world.

The death of Jesus as *Son of God* finally reveals the dialectical force of Christian love and its revolutionary potential. Jesus forgives those who kill him, thus showing his hope for God's forgiveness of the world and the reversal of humanity's debasement. Jesus does not fall into an act of hatred. His love is transformed into hope, and that hope will be confirmed in the resurrection.[15]

This last idea is very similar to what Ignacio Ellacuría has to say about Jesus' death and resurrection. The struggle against the social configuration of sin is an important consideration in his reflection on the task of the church in Latin America.

This confrontation operates in the dialectic of death and resurrection. Only those who die will live; only those who deny themselves can follow Christ. There is no way to Christian resurrection except through the redemption that finds expression in death on the cross. If people reject the label of sin, the reason is that they are trying to evade the necessary consequences of a recognition of the reality of sin. They are trying to evade the necessity of dying to the present situation in order to fashion a new, more authentically Christian situation. . . .

Liberation takes the historical signification of Jesus of Nazareth with full and radical seriousness. It accepts the archetypal idea of death and resurrection with all its implications. It accepts the presupposition that salvation must necessarily take the form of incarnation, granting the presence of sin in history. But it does not rest content with this archetypal idea, which might just as well be inferred from a philosophical analysis of historical reality. It also turns its attention to the concrete image of Christ in the concrete circumstances of his earthly life in history. Its aim, of course, is not mere imitation but rather an authentic following of Christ. . . .

In this Christian vision of liberation we must have both features: death and resurrection. The latter presupposes the former. But if the former is truly Christian, it is sustained and guided by the hope of a resurrection that has already begun here and now. There is no resurrection without death. Without the sorrow-laden disappearance of the existing structure of sin, we cannot enter a new earth as human beings. And since this whole treatment here is aimed at praxis, I should like to highlight some possible ways of dying to sin and of rising to new life. For both the negative and the positive aspect must be operative in a spiraling process that leads us further and further on.[16]

As examples of the sins to be overcome, Ellacuría cites the deification of luxury and private property, objective injustice and institutionalized violence, dishonesty in the mass media in the interests of "those who hold power in a consumer society," and "excesses . . . in the holding and use of political power."[17] Accordingly, the task of the church is understood to reside in a positive struggle for liberation and liberty.[18]

For these authors, then, Jesus' death is both a building block in the larger edifice of the struggle for more freedom among human beings, and a unique event, issuing in a resurrection that conquers death. Both features of Jesus' death are brought to bear on Christian conduct in Latin America today.

The key to this thesis is a hermeneutics of politics—a hermeneutics which also explains, especially in Vidales, how Jesus' death leaps its own frontiers, as it were, to find a place among the deaths of all those who have dedicated their lives to the same purpose as he. At the same time this political hermeneutics does not neglect the specifically Christian element. Faith in Jesus' resurrection deprives death of its hopelessness. It refuses to understand Jesus' deed of commitment to the death as having been in vain. Further, it protects Jesus' death and resurrection from a verticalistic "spiritualization" that would relegate the hope of resurrection to fulfillment in the next world alone.

An interpretation putting stronger emphasis on the historical context of Jesus' death is presented by Miguel Angel Campos.[19] Basing his reflections on the research of Belo, Clévenot, and Guignebert, Angel analyzes the Lucan Gospel, and analyzes the opposition between Jesus and the various groups of his adversaries from both textual and historical considerations. He comes to the following conclusions:

1. Jesus initiated a discourse of a symbolic nature, with profound and direct political implications. That is, he initiated a religious discourse that was profoundly political *as religious discourse* (not as political discourse). The political implications acquire their religious, symbolic character in an endeavor to confront power with power (Jesus and the people vs. the priests and the dominant class).

2. Jesus' symbolic discourse is pitted against the symbolic discourse of a social group consisting of the elite members of the religious (the symbolic) and the political authority and power. Hence the political implications of Jesus' discourse.

3. The opposition of confrontation from Jesus' side consists in the symbolical relativization of religious power. The Law as the dominant classes understand it is no longer of any value. It is not the temple that is the center of Jewish life, but conduct "in spirit and in truth." Israel is no longer the midpoint of the world, for Jesus' message transcends its geo-social boundaries. Consequently the dominant local political power is relativized, and its institutions—the material support of the Law—now fall into disrepute. The temple loses its very raison d'être as a locale for the gathering of Jews for religious (ideological) and economic practice, inasmuch as the economic area is now closed. Social machinery in its prevailing form has been too immobile to permit a message of blessing and liberation for human beings.

Concrete short-term conditions offered no possibilities for a radical change of the whole social machinery—the "structures"—but conditions were present for a process of radicalization of the people. What was at stake was power. Hence what could be more urgent than to kill (destroy, pull up by the roots) the person whose growing influence and power threatened the dominant power?[20]

Jesus' death is presented here as the consequence of his life and work in toto, considered as an attack on the foundations of the religious and political order of the Jewish state. A key observation, of course, is that the religious and political order did not constitute two discrete spheres, but were intimately bound up with each other, so that Jesus' religious thesis must also make its way in the political area, without Jesus himself wishing to assume political power.

There is an evolution in Leonardo Boff's characterization of the meaning of Jesus' death. One might describe it as an increasing emphasis on its political implications. In his first and most important Christological piece, *Jesus Christ Liberator*,[21] Boff does cite the historical factors leading to Jesus' death: Jesus' popularity, his interpretation of the Law (which leaves the authorities out of account), the provocation of his claim to act in God's name (which throws the established order into utter confusion), and his representation by the authorities as a blasphemer and a guerrilla—so that it was as blasphemer and guerrilla that he was executed. But the real meaning of this death lies elsewhere, says Boff in this earlier work, in a realm of timeless validity:

> The whole life of Christ was a giving, a being-for-others, an attempt to overcome all conflicts in his own existence, and a realization of this goal. Jesus lived the human archetype just as God wanted, when he made him to his own image and likeness; Jesus always judged and spoke with God as his reference and starting point. Jesus thereby revealed a life of extraordinary authenticity and originality. By his preaching of the kingdom of God he lived his being for others to the end, experiencing the depths of despair of the death (absence) of God on the cross. In spite of the total disaster and debacle he did not despair. He was confident and believed up to the end that God would accept him as he was. The meaningless still had for him a secret and ultimate meaning.
>
> The universal meaning of the life and death of Christ, therefore, is that he sustained the fundamental conflict of human existence to the end: he wanted to realize the absolute meaning of this world before God, in spite of hate, incomprehension, betrayal, and condemnation to death.[22]

But this European-style theological interpretation undergoes further development and concretization in a later work, where our author explicates the inner relationship between Jesus' liberating praxis and his death in the following step by step fashion:

1. Jesus' death stands in intimate relationship with his life, his proclamation, and his praxis. His call to conversion, the new image of God he proclaims, his freedom with respect to sanctified traditions, and his prophetic criticism of the incumbents of political, economic, and religious power provoked a conflict that led to his death.

2. Jesus did not seek death. It was imposed on him from without. But he did not passively submit to it; he took it upon himself as the expression of his freedom and of his loyalty to the cause of God and human beings. Abandoned, rejected, threatened, he nevertheless refused to make common cause with the privileged, the mighty ones, just in order to survive. He remained true to his mission to proclaim the good news to whoever would be converted. Freely he assumes the death that his constellation of historical circumstances imposes upon him.

3. The cross is the symbol of the kingdom of might and of that kingdom's power over its own duty of service, even its religious duty. It was the pious who martyred Jesus. Whenever a situation turns back inward upon itself in such a way as to obscure the future and to absolutize itself, it snips off the process of liberation and bolsters the mechanisms of repression.

4. This freely accepted death manifests [Jesus'] absolute freedom both with respect to his own person and with respect to his goals. He undergoes this death out of love, in solidarity with the vanquished of history, forgiving those who have brought it about and abandoning himself into the hands of God. Henceforward death, despite its historical character as failure, is a concretization and realization of the kingdom of God.

5. There are two motives for Jesus' murder, and both extend to the structural level. First, he is condemned as a *blasphemer* for having conceived of God in a different fashion from that of the status quo. [Here Boff quotes a passage from Sobrino's *Christology at the Crossroads*.]

As we see, his activity was liberating in the highest degree. Hence his rejection. In the eyes of the political authority he dies as a *guerrilla*. His preaching and his activity bring him close to the purposes of the Zealots: his hope for the kingdom, his radicalism, some of his statements ("The kingdom of heaven has been subjected to violence and the violent are taking it by storm"—Matthew 11:12), his freedom vis-à-vis the imperial power, his influence over the people who want to make him their leader. Yet at the same time Jesus is far removed from the spirit of the Zealots. He rejects a political-religious messianism based on power, for such a messianism would be incapable of actualizing a kingdom that presupposes a radical, total liberation, overcomes all breach in the human relationship of brothers and sisters, and calls for a new human being.

6. The cross manifests the conflictual nature of any liberation process that has to be carried on in conditions where injustice has the upper hand. Under such conditions, liberation is possible only in the form of

martyrdom and sacrifice for others in the service of God's cause in the world. This is the path Jesus consciously chose and assumed.[23]

Jesus founders on the rocks of the religious and political status quo. His death makes it clear that he sought to be true to his own liberation project, and that since this project would have meant the overthrow of all prevailing institutions, he was eliminated by the underwriters of those institutions. Wherever injustice is the stronger, the praxis of liberation leads to death, and this is something to be taken into account. Thus, in the Boffian view as well, Jesus' death is the result and sign of a perverted legality prevalent in many places in the world today.

Jesus' Death as Catastrophe

Jon Sobrino emphasizes a rather different aspect of Jesus' death. Jesus' martyrdom is unlike that of other religious and political martyrs. For, as Jesus, his project itself collapses, and he has to watch it happen. The one who steadfastly proclaimed the nearness of God now dies abandoned by that God.[24]

To appreciate what is unique about this death, one need only hear Jesus' proclamation of the imminence of the kingdom, and then hear his cry on the cross as his Father abandons him.[25]

Here, Sobrino holds, the problem of God is posed in a new form:

The cross poses the problem of God, not in terms of theology (discourse about God), but in terms of theodicy (the justification of God). On the cross theodicy is historicized. The Son is not crucified by some natural evil that embodies the creaturely limitations of nature or humanity. He is crucified by a historicized evil, i.e., the free will of human beings. What justification is there for a God who allows the sinfulness of the world to kill his Son (and hence other human beings as well)?
On the positive side the cross presents a basic affirmation about God. It says that on the cross God himself is crucified. The Father suffers the death of his Son, and takes upon himself all the sorrow and pain of history. This ultimate solidarity with humanity reveals God as a God of love in a real and credible way, not in any idealistic way. From the ultimate depths of history's negative side, this God of love thereby opens up the possibility of hope and a future.[26]

The "crucified God" is a concept borrowed from Jürgen Moltmann[27] and applied by Sobrino in his Christology for the purpose of developing its thrust for liberation.[28] Here Sobrino takes his point of departure in the observation that the cross of Jesus plays a key role in Latin American popular piety,[29] where it is generally part of a passive mystique of suffering. Only recently is there a change under way:

> The present-day situation in Latin America has brought out a somewhat different focus, particularly among groups more deeply involved in the effort for social change. This new Christian focus on the cross of Jesus is much more activist in character. While the resurrection remains the paradigm of liberation, the cross is no longer seen simply as a symbol of suffering or as the negative dialectical moment which immediately and directly gives rise to the positive moment of liberation. . . . From their concrete experience in the effort to achieve liberation, people are now beginning to realize that they cannot prescind from the cross of Jesus if their experience is to be truly Christian.[30]

This new realization is based on an important prerequisite, Sobrino holds. The "Greek" notion of God's impassibility must be overcome. In contemporary theology, Jesus' death *as such* can be considered an actual "mediation of God." This conception would have been impossible in the old church. But if the death of Jesus, and indeed death in general, is not taken seriously—as reality—then discourse on God becomes idealistic and alienating. But if the cross, and death in general, is taken seriously, then the death of God is experienced as the "death of the other." And in Latin America, this means the death of the Indian and the peasant.

> When we say that the oppressed human being is the mediation of God, we must get to the heart of that statement and analyze the exact nature of that mediation. It is a complicated task, needless to say, and here I simply want to bring out one point. Why does the "oppressed" person serve as the mediation of God? It is not because in that person we find expressed what Hegel called "the monstrous power of the negative"? It is quite correct to view God as the *power over* the negative, as its *contradiction*. But such a view remains too abstract if we do not go on to ask how and in what sense God is the power over injustice, oppression, and death. Is it from outside history or from within history?
>
> In this respect liberation theology must get beyond Greek thought. It must ask itself in what sense suffering and death can be a mode of being for God.[31]

A step in this direction, according to Sobrino, is the broadening of our epistemology.

> Greek epistemology, which was based on analogy and wonder, makes it impossible for us to recognize God in the cross of Jesus. Liberation theology must add further principles here. To the principle of analogy it must add the principle of dialectic; to the principle of wonder it must add

the notion of suffering as a font of knowledge leading us to the concrete practice of transforming love.[32]

And a little later he adds:

> The cognitive attitude that allows for some sort of authentic analogy between the believer and Jesus' cross is that of sorrow in the presence of historical crosses.[33]

Not that Sobrino has the slightest intention of subjecting the cross of Jesus to any sort of horizontal reductionism. He simply wishes to show how one can speak credibly of God in view of the cross of the human being. One can do so, he says, only if God is present in the cross of Jesus and in the cross of human beings alike—only if God shares both the lot of Jesus and the lot of all who suffer.

Sobrino also speaks of Jesus' cross as the consequence and result of his life. But he is not thinking only of the "public life"; he sees the cross as a consequence of the incarnation itself.

> If God did become incarnate in history and accepted its mechanisms, ambiguities, and contradictions, then the cross reveals God not just in himself but in conjunction with the historical path that leads Jesus to the cross.
>
> At bottom the issue at stake here is our conception of God's revelation. Is God revealed only in the highpoints in Jesus' life such as his baptism, his transfiguration, his crucifixion, and his resurrection? Or does the revelation of God take place all along in the revelation of the Son, in the process whereby Jesus *becomes the Son* through his concrete history?[34]

After all, the whole course of Jesus' life is torn by the tension of two poles of contradiction. On one side there is the hope of the kingdom. On the other, there is sin. The basic question here, then, is a proper understanding of God:

> Jesus is faced with a contradictory situation, which ultimately comes down to a choice between two deities: either a God wielding oppressive power or a God offering and effecting liberation. Framed in this context of a basic theological conflict, Jesus' trajectory to the cross is no accident. He himself provokes it by presenting the basic option between two deities. His course is also a trial of the deity, with Jesus appearing as a witness on one side and those in power as witnesses on the other side.
>
> Now before going on to a concrete analysis of Jesus' conflict, I want to make two assertions. First, the cross is not simply *the end of any biographical career*; it is the end of the career of Jesus, who seeks to be a

faithful witness to God in a world of contradiction. Second, this career is simultaneously *a trial* of God himself. For that reason Jesus' cross cannot be understood on the basis of some notion of God already held. The path to the cross is nothing else but a questioning search for the true God and for the true essence of power. Is power meant to oppress people or to liberate them?[35]

A little further on, Sobrino formulates the problem somewhat differently:

Jesus' cross is no accident. It flows directly from the self-justifying efforts of the "religious" person who tries to manipulate God rather than letting God remain a mystery. . . .
  But if we view the matter in that light, then we are faced with another unanswered question prompted by the cross itself: Who is God exactly? What God really triumphed in Jesus' cross? Either the cross is the end of "religion" or it is the end of the kingdom of God as Jesus understood it. Either it is the end of people's subjugation by human beings in the name of religion or it is the triumph of Moloch and his demand for human victims. Paradoxical as it may seem, it was "religion" that killed the Son. So we are left with the question as to why the Father allowed his death. Is it possible that he accepted Jesus' death on the cross so that he might overcome the old religious schema once and for all, so that he might show that he is a completely different sort of God who serves as the basis for a completely new kind of human existence?[36]

We find a parallel reflection in Sobrino's development of another aspect of Jesus' death he considers theologically important: the question of the authentic form and presentation of God's power:[37]

Over against the notion of God as power Jesus sets the notion of God as love. . . . By the very fact that love is situated in an unredeemed world, it can unfold and develop only by confronting the oppressive weight of power.[38]

Here again Sobrino finds a consequence of the incarnation—of incarnation into the concrete, historical situation of Palestine two thousand years ago.

The cross is not the result of some divine decision independent of history; it is the outcome of the basic option for incarnation in a given situation. That entails conflict because sin holds power in history and takes the triumphant form of religious and political oppression. Jesus had to choose between evading all that or facing up to it squarely. He chose the latter course, challenging the idolatrous use of power to oppress people and the idolatrous conception of God that justified such use. Power that subjugates human beings has nothing to do with the true God.[39]

Hence among other conclusions that may legitimately be drawn from these considerations, Christian spirituality may not be allowed to limit itself to a mystique of the cross. It must be the following of Jesus' whole path through life.[40] In other words, the "privileged mediation of God" is always the actual cross of the oppressed.[41] Theologically, it follows that what the theology of liberation must attempt to do is to "historicize theodicy."[42]

> First, the meaning of history is called into question, not so much by natural catastrophes as by the catastrophes that human freedom unleashes when it organizes society in an oppressive way. Theodicy is thus *historicized*. Second, Latin American theology turns theodicy into anthropodicy, into the question of justifying human beings rather than God, much as secularized Europe and North America did in the decade of the sixties. The question is not so much how we can find a benevolent God (Luther) as how we can find a benevolent human being (J. Robinson). Last, and most important, the possibility of justifying God is not to be found in speculating about some possible logical explanation that will reconcile God with suffering history. It is to be found in a new realization of Jesus' cross, so that we may see whether that will really give rise to a new resurrection.[43]

This last consideration leads to two further ones. First, for Sobrino the cross is the privileged locus of the revelation of God's love, and the following of Jesus means the actualization of this love of God's in history.[44] Second, this interpretation is intrinsically dependent on faith in Jesus' resurrection. But the resurrection may not be allowed to nullify the cross. "It is the cross that makes Jesus' resurrection *Christian*."[45]

In this conception, the return of a consideration of Jesus' death has a twofold function. First, it keeps us face to face with the actual reality of defeat and death. The violent death undergone by Jesus brings all unjust suffering, and every inhumane death, into the world picture. For the conflicts that led to Jesus' violent death are not unique. They are structural, and they can be experienced in Latin America today just as they could in Palestine in the time of Jesus. Second, in the death of Jesus we meet the problem of God head-on. Jesus had devoted his life entirely to proclaiming the God of love. Insofar as Jesus meets disaster, God seems to meet disaster. But it is this disaster that reveals who God really is. The God of the powerful ones who put Jesus to death is an anti-God. The God of Jesus bursts through the laws of might and reveals his love, taking suffering and death upon himself and transforming them in the hope of resurrection.

Resurrection and Liberation

It is already evident from the preceding section that many liberation theologians speak of Jesus' death and resurrection very nearly as a single concept. It seems legitimate, however, to treat the two complexes separately, for we do find a series of considerations referring exclusively to Jesus' resurrection, and developing the liberating thrust of Christian faith from this.

Let us begin by looking at some texts formulated as creedal statements, followed by others in which a reflection on Jesus' death and resurrection, condensed into brief formulae for Christian interpretation, are combined with a consideration of the peculiar Latin American situation.

Short Creedal Formulae

We believe in a new human being, liberated by the blood and resurrection of Jesus.[46]

Christ stands at the beginning, in the center, and at the end of history. In accomplishing his Pasch he destroyed evil in his death and worked all good in his resurrection. All liberations, and all other benefits of whatsoever nature they be, have their meaing through the Christ of Easter.[47]

Consequently, the dynamics of the life of Jesus Christ, through his embodiment of God, his crucifixion, and his resurrection, constitute an extraordinary prototype for an understanding of how it is possible and necessary in our times to participate in the struggle for liberation.[48]

The core of the gospel is the experience of God. But the center of this experience is freedom itself. To evangelize is to create freedom in the addressee of the word of Jesus Christ. This freedom is the new human being, the fruit of the death and resurrection of Jesus Christ and the new creation of the Spirit.[49]

Here we have the theme of the new human being and of the struggle for liberation as the way to that new human being, on the basis of a profession of faith in Jesus' death and resurrection.

The following two brief texts are similar:

Jesus delivered the human being by choosing humanity [*humanidad*— perhaps we ought to say, "incarnation"] as his point of departure and resurrection as his point of arrival. In so doing, he has overcome every system bearing the seal of sin.[50]

As the Exodus marked the deliverance of Israel, so the deed of Jesus Christ among men and women aims at the freedom of the whole human race, especially of those who writhe under the cruel yoke of oppression.[51]

The three texts which follow express an attempt to unite a traditional view of the resurrection and today's new consciousness of human reality:

[Jesus of Nazareth] claimed to be the Son of God, and he proved his claim by his resurrection. But he has had his message imprisoned in the structures of a Greco-Roman civilization over the course of twenty centuries now. This is the structure which prevails, and this is the structure which provokes, in the Christian world, the protests and reactions which so many interpret as the death of God. All these things we see happening are intimately connected with one another. We are assisting at the dawn of a new age. Promises are being kept.[52]

Jesus took upon himself the whole of humanity, in order to lead that humanity to eternal life. But the necessary preparation for eternal life is social justice—the first form of love of one's brothers and sisters. By means of his resurrection, Christ delivers humanity from death. In so doing he is conducting all human liberations to their eternal plenitude.[53]

But Christ's Paschal mystery remakes human beings completely—makes them entirely new. Now that human being is called to freedom (cf. Gal. 5:23) and delivered from every servitude that sin can cause: selfishness, ignorance, hunger, misery, injustice, even death. Christ is not satisfied with forgiving sins or preaching the good news of the Kingdom. He multiplies the loaves, he heals the sick—he raises the dead. Christ is concerned about the whole human being.[54]

Marcel van Caster seeks to integrate a human/temporal liberation with a divine/eternal one. In order to do so he distinguishes "two states of integration" and posits a relationship between the second stage and Christ's resurrection:

Our strivings for earthly liberation are a mediation of our love of God, whom, as we learn from the example of Jesus Christ, we are to love for God's own sake.[55]
    The Easter mystery, then, will be interpreted as follows: Thanks to Christ Jesus, who was faithful to the death, and who was sustained in this fidelity by his Father, the human being receives light and strength, through the mediation of the Spirit of Christ, to toil on earth for justice and peace, to conquer sin, which opposes this justice and this concord, and so to prepare a better world—that is, better living conditions and better interpersonal relationships, for a boundless future.[56]

Segundo Galilea treats the resurrection in his search for a new Christian spirituality:

We have to find this new Christianity and this "Christianity for revolutionary times" will of course have its roots in Christ's Paschal mystery: in the biblical dynamics of change, which include death and resurrection.[57]

The "worldly side" of Christ's Pasch—Christ's Pasch in its historical mystery—means basically that death and resurrection are not something purely mystical or ascetical, but that they form foci of social change. Thus the Christian discovers God in a new form. God's walking among human beings, God's presence among men and women, is divested of its purely religious dimension now. Today this presence is discovered in political and cultural occurrences and social revolutions.[58]

These two authors posit a relationship between the resurrection and social involvement.

Rafael Avila puts more emphasis on the political:

> In Jesus' case, it is the disciples who, despite the slanted reports given out by "official government sources" (cf. Matt. 28:11–15), and all manner of other pressure, proclaim the resurrection of the Word—while the political authorities would like to make sure that the Word is still in the tomb (Matt. 27:66). As if by stationing watches and bribing soldiers they could prevent that Word from rising in glory and finding a plethora of followers![59]

Avila devotes a lengthy section of his book to Jesus' resurrection. In fact, he places it at mid-point in his considerations. But he does so almost in passing. His presentation as a whole does not actually develop in the light of the resurrection: rather it is aimed at a liberating evangelization to be carried on by the church.

> The Passover and the Exodus, in their Latin American implications, are an anticipation of the eschatological deed of Christ (CELAM, introduction, nos. 5–6). For "all liberation is an anticipation of the complete redemption of Christ" (CELAM 4:9), inasmuch as Christ's liberation through his Paschal mystery is an "action of integral human liberation" (CELAM, 1:4)—a benefit to the human being in all dimensions: effectuated by the liberation of the *whole* human being, not just a part, and of *all* human beings, not just a group, and indeed of the whole cosmos and not just human beings (cf. Romans 8:21).
>
> Christ, then, is integral, universal, and cosmic liberator. The church, sprung from the mystery of the Paschal deliverance and filled with the grace of the liberating Spirit—for where the Spirit of the Lord is, there is freedom (2 Cor. 3:17)—can consequently be nothing other than a historical movement under the impulse of God for the deliverance of humankind, "a movement proclaiming the freedom of the daughters and sons

of God, and repudiating all the bondage which ultimately results from sin" (*Gaudium et Spes*, 41).

In order to be existential, and not just theoretical, this proclamation must be accompanied by the testimony and commitment of persons and institutions. Historical events, *from which God speaks to us*, indicate the direction which our commitment ought to take. Therefore when we make a commitment to the processes of personalization, socialization, and liberation as today's signs that the Paschal mystery is present and effective, we make a commitment to Christ, who is personalized, socialized, and liberated, as well—who becomes a "visible sign" for today's history—and who, in thus becoming visible, actualizes his word of admonition in our own times. Commitment to history is commitment to Christ, and vice versa. In this wise, faith appears as a salutary process of historical participation, removing all division and separation between experience of the world and experience of the living God. Any position one takes with respect to these processes is a position taken for or against Christ. And the degree of our commitment to these processes—the depth of our option—is the exact measure of our conversion.[60]

This very positive statement subsumes Easter, with its consequences for the church in Latin America, under the generic concept of liberation, and thereby posits their intimate correlation.

Interpretative Theses

Javier Alonso Hernández, whose thinking has so much in common with that of Gustavo Gutiérrez, endeavors to render the relationship between redemption and liberation more precise by a consideration of Jesus as the "animator of history."

What does it mean, in the biblical conception, to call Christ "lord of history"? Or—since the word *lord* carries connotations of power and might today—what would it mean to call Christ the "animator of history"?

It means that that lord, that animator, is present in every event that takes place in the world and in every reality obtaining anywhere at any time. Vatican Council II insisted on this point, and we shall not tarry on it here. Instead we shall proceed to a consideration of the two senses in which this lord, as present in all earthly reality, is the animator of history.

First, the goods of the earth are intended as a medium of community among human beings. When the goods of the earth do not lead human beings to convergence, when they do not unite them in view of a common goal, then Jesus fails in his animating function in history altogether. . . .

Second, the title "lord" means, for those in cognizance of cause, that these goods of the earth are not merely a bond of unity among human beings, they are also a bond of unity between human beings and God. Hence that classic acclamation of the primitive Christian community, "Jesus is Lord of history!" reveals just exactly this "real presence." My Christ—the Christ with whom I can enter into community—is not the Christ of Bethlehem, nor even the Christ of Calvary. He is the Christ of the resurrection, who, at this very moment, exercises a special manner of being present throughout all reality, wherever the bond of unity among human beings in virtue of the goods of the earth is a reality.[61]

Here Jesus' resurrection is seen as the way to universal oneness—a oneness understood not in the sense of some "spiritual" unity, but in the sense of a common participation in the goods of the earth. Hence the resurrection is not a closed event, an occurrence turned inward upon itself, but an event that finds its fulfillment in the just distribution of the world's goods.

José Comblin follows this same line of thinking, but uses a completely different example.

The risen Christ is never alone. He can never be considered as a solitary person, in isolation from others. Christ cannot exist without his body. If you prescind from a person's body, you are no longer speaking of that *person*. Christ is continuously in search of his body. He is like a person who has not yet managed to occupy his whole body, and so has gone in search of his members. Jesus, gone in search of his members, comes to us in the text that was Las Casas's "main argument": "There are other sheep I have that are not of this fold, and these I have to lead as well. They too will listen to my voice . . ." (John 10:16). These "sheep" are the Indians. They belong to Christ. Accordingly no one can say he or she loves or worships Christ while at the same time separating from Christ the sheep that belong to him. This is what is done by the large landholders and others—they divide Christ's sheep from him. For they deprive them of their freedom, and when they deprive them of their freedom they render them incapable of drawing near to Christ. Faith is freedom. The repression of the Indians makes their free approach to Christ impossible. The Indians are baptized, true. But baptism without freedom is not drawing near to Christ, and so the oppressors of the Indians destroy the body of Christ. They say they love Christ. But they cut him off from his Indians. And a Christ cut off from his Indians is a gnostic being, a bodiless phantasm, a mystification of Christ—not the true Christ, risen and alive, whose new life consists precisely in being united to his Indians.[62]

Here the traditional conception of the church as the body of Christ comes down to cases. The basic argumentation proceeds from the equivalence of the resurrection, new life, and freedom, and concludes that there can be no community with the risen Christ where there is no freedom. Hence when a group of Christians deprives the Indians of their freedom, Christ's resurrection is absent. The repression of the Indians is a perversion of faith in the resurrection of Christ.

The Chilean bishops, in their 1971 pronouncement *Gospel, Politics, and Socialisms,* likewise posit a connection between Christ's resurrection and liberation.

> Through his proclamation of the perfect liberation of the human being, the risen Christ appears as victor over the *whole* power of death—over sin rooted in human hearts as well as sin that abides in the various cultural structures that peoples have created for themselves in the course of the centuries. This is when his Paschal feast becomes the Paschal feast of the *whole* of history: when it becomes liberation. It is indispensable that Christ's liberating power not only fill the hearts of all men and women and animate the noble strivings which every age calls forth in individuals; it must also penetrate all structures that condition the life of human society on earth. Only in this wise will the liberation of each and all, together and as individuals, be assured.[63]

The accent here is on liberation from structures. Nevertheless this is another instance in which the resurrection means liberation. And once more we see that an important part, at least, of that liberation has yet to be achieved.

Hugo Assmann broaches another aspect of Christ's resurrection: the specific contribution to be made by Christians to Latin American liberation. To Assmann, it is clear that there are no theoretical premises for a genuinely comprehensive contribution. Still he seeks to formulate a thesis:

> But this does not take care of the question of Christians' "specific contribution" to liberation. The problem remains. Furthermore, it is a vital problem for us who believe that there are ways and means of actualizing in history the love that springs from the sources of our faith. Still, one must begin, and with determination. We do not see everything clearly. Nor are we the only ones who deal with love as a dimension of human community. The way to seek what is specifically Christian seems clear in principle; it is the specifically and integrally human. . . . But it is not enough theoretically to insist that we Christians possess a comprehensive view of the human being. Naturally, a genuinely historical rereading of the Bible, especially the message of Christ, has led us to a whole series of radical questions to which Marxism has not paid due attention. It may be that the core of this complex of questions lies in the Christian assurance that death is overcome—and with it this radical alienation about whose downfall Marx has nothing important or satisfactory to say. Now the problem of death does not appear in its broadest historicization at the

point where our faith assures us that there is "something beyond." This of course scarcely excludes selfish tendencies. The problem of death now appears in its broadest historical relevance where we assert that the God who raised Jesus is not a God of the dead but of the living, and that this God has willed that, since life is his own natural "ambience," it be the radical environment of humankind as well.[64]

Faith in Jesus' resurrection as the core of Christian faith is thus delivered from individualistic interpretation. Living space for everyone—meaning humane living conditions for everyone—is understood as the identifying note of faith in the resurrection. And this interpretation takes shape against a background of the social miseries of the greater part of the Latin American population.

Interpretations

Leonardo Boff's interpretation differs from those just presented. Boff sees the meaning of Jesus' resurrection more in the area of the "personal existential."[65] True, there are nuances that suggest social implications, as when he speaks of the resurrection as the realization of Jesus' liberation proclamation.[66] But this "liberation" remains rather abstract. For Boff the resurrection of Jesus is the fulfillment, in anticipation, of the kingdom of God—"this utopia realized within the world."[67] Hence "for the Christian, as of the moment of the resurrection there is no more *utopia* . . . but only *topia*."[68] In other words, "Jesus' resurrection is the anticipated irruption of the liberation of the end-time."[69]

The first consequence of the resurrection is an insight, an awareness:

> The resurrection of the crucified one demonstrates that it is not meaningless to die as Jesus died: for others and for God. The anonymous death of all throughout history who have died for justice' sake, for openness to transcendence, for an ultimate meaning in human life—finds its explanation in the resurrection.[70]

Boff even cites an anthropological meaning of Jesus' resurrection.[71] One might say he gives it a symbolic meaning, and this even in a passage in which he is emphasizing its political consequences. What he is doing is connecting these political consequences with the relationship between the kingdom of God in Jesus' preaching, and Jesus' resurrection:

> The meaning of the resurrection as total liberation only becomes clear when it is set in a context of Jesus' struggle for the establishment of the kingdom in this world. Otherwise it degenerates into pious cynicism about the injustices of this world, combined with an idealism that has no connection with history. Through his resurrection, Jesus continues his

activity among men and women and arouses them to the struggle for
liberation. All genuinely human growth, anything that can really be
called justice in social relationships, and whatever is conducive to the
multiplication of life, represent a form of the actualization of the
resurrection—the anticipation and preparation of its future plenitude.[72]

Here Willi Marxsen's famous dictum, "the Jesus affair is not over," is
specified in terms of liberation. But the liberation concept remains general-
ized, and two questions come principally to mind:
  1. Is the kerygma of Jesus' resurrection indeed as immediately bound up
with Jesus' proclamation of the kingdom as Boff sees it to be? Is there not
more discontinuity between Jesus as proclaimer and as proclaimed than
Boff is willing to admit?
  2. Is the intrinsic connection Boff posits between resurrection kerygma
and liberation struggle convincingly established?
  Boff says basically nothing in connection with Jesus' resurrection other
than what he has already said about the activity of Jesus in the world today.
Consequently it comes as little surprise that the section following the foregoing citation is entitled "Jesus' Liberation Actualized as Discipleship."[73]
  Raúl Vidales, too, places strong emphasis on the internal connection
between Jesus' proclamation and Easter. Vidales attempts to base the prophetic role Christians have in the current Latin American struggle for liberation on Jesus, and on Jesus' resurrection as part of his integral project for
establishing justice and overcoming politico-social conflict.

> Easter belongs to the life of Jesus "immanently." It is the logical out-
> come of his historical struggle, more than the inevitable accomplishment
> of a pre-established divine plan.[74]

Departing from certain traditional interpretations which he calls "reli-
giously progressive but politically conservative,"[75] Vidales searches for a
"practical reading" of Easter:[76]

> Historically Jesus' proclamation was a failure. The relatively brief his-
> tory of Jesus the messiah and just one ended with his death. The con-
> spiracy of government forces and established religion overcame and
> annihilated what his words and deeds had proclaimed: the coming of the
> kingdom, and a world based on relationships among free, reconciled
> brothers and sisters. Jesus' death, after trial and sentencing, makes it all
> too clear that this hope can only be maintained in history by constant
> struggle. His disciples make a point of setting themselves against all pes-
> simism. The Paschal event shows both them and us that his hope is not a
> naive illusion, but that the kingdom of God, the subject of the messianic
> hopes, has already begun to materialize—in the prophetic and messianic
> praxis of Jesus, culminating in the resurrection. This is the hope that

animates the faith experience of Christians who have made a revolutionary commitment to the creation of the new human being, and a new society, according to Jesus Christ.[77]

Jesus, in his life and conduct, manifested "the dialectical force of Christian love and its revolutionary strength."[78] Hence:

> Easter is God's seal on Jesus' life. God reveals himself as God in the
> resurrection only by making Jesus "Son of God in power"—only by
> revealing him as fully human, with all the grandeur and limitation this
> implies for Jesus' struggle for the justice of the promise. The inherent
> sense of the resurrection is, and can be, nothing other than the inherent
> sense of Jesus' life.[79]

As Jesus' death is the result of his uncompromising commitment to justice, so his resurrection is the result, decreed by God, of the death of the just
one. The apparent victory of inhumane established power is not actually the
last word. The last word is the dialectical "might" of love. Jesus' effort has
not been in vain. We have not seen the end of it yet.

The most detailed consideration of Jesus' resurrection is to be had in the
works of Jon Sobrino. Sobrino distinguishes in Jesus' resurrection a historical, a theological, and a hermeneutical problem. The "historical problem"
springs from the results of modern exegesis: the disciples' post-Easter faith
in the resurrection of Jesus is historically demonstrable.[80] In his exposition
of the "theological problem," Sobrino develops the notion that the resurrection is first of all a statement about God; then it is a statement about the
human being and history; finally it is a statement about Jesus himself.[81]

But Sobrino makes his key points in his exposition of the "hermeneutical
problem."

> Jesus' resurrection is not understandable simply in terms of its character
> as an eschatological event. An approach to it must be twofold. On one
> side, we must do justice to the resurrection as the New Testament under-
> stands it: otherwise we shall not be speaking of the resurrection of *Jesus*,
> but of a utopian symbol. On the other side, we must understand the res-
> urrection in its meaning for today: otherwise it is not the eschatological
> event—the event of universal significance. The correct hermeneutics will
> not be easy to find. In fact, it will depend on the human being's ultimate
> personal decisions.
>
> Here we propose, in three points, a possible hermeneutics, which, so
> we believe, will do justice alike to the New Testament texts and the mod-
> ern situation.
>
> 1. The expression "resurrection of the dead" is a utopian formula
> from Old Testament and late Judaic times. It stands in opposition to the
> Greek formula "immortality of the soul." The biblical formulation ex-

presses the total transformation of the human being and history. The first hermeneutical condition for understanding Jesus' resurrection, then, is hope for this transformation, which overcomes what is negative in the world. It is a hope *against* death and injustice, in the biblical model, and not a "beyond" death and injustice, as in the Greek model.

2. A grasp of the resurrection presupposes a grasp of history as *promise* and a grasp of a sense of mission. The disciples are aware that they are not merely spectators but witnesses—of an event that demands to be witnessed to in its very substance. The resurrection can be grasped only from within a very conscious reading of history based on trust in the promise.

3. In the New Testament, the apparitions of the resurrected one are always tied to a call to mission. The disciples are conscious that, with the resurrection of Jesus, something new is afoot in the world. Jesus' resurrection therefore sets in motion a twofold praxis: a ministry of the *kerygma* of the resurrected Jesus, and a ministry of the *content* of this resurrection—a ministry to the new creation. Jesus' resurrection cannot be grasped apart from active ministry in the transformation of an unredeemed world.

Today's understanding of the resurrection of Jesus, then, presupposes (1) a radical hope in the future, (2) a historical awareness of history as promise and as mission, and (3) a specific praxis which is nothing other than discipleship. This last condition seems to be the most necessary one, inasmuch as a praxis arising out of love concretizes Christian hope as a hope against all hope. Love is the only way to open up history. Grasping the resurrection of Jesus is like coming to a knowledge of God: it is not a once-and-for-all occurrence. One's horizon of understanding must be constantly maintained in a process of becoming. Hope and the deeds of love must be kept continuously vital and effective. Only then will the resurrection of Jesus be understood not simply as something that happened to someone named Jesus, but as the resurrection of the firstborn of all creation—a promise of the perfect fulfillment of history.[82]

At first glance one would hardly say there is anything particularly Latin American in all this. But on closer examination, the emphasis on praxis in discipleship, and on transforming the world, are accents which lend Sobrino's interpretation a genuine Latin American touch.

This is clear from his detailed discussion of the Christological theses that we have just seen. On the first point, Sobrino posits both a community and a difference between the resurrection and apocalyptical thought. The expectation of God's justice is common to both apocalyptical thought and to hope of resurrection. What is new in the Christian resurrection kerygma, by contrast with received apocalyptic, is that the one who is resurrected is the condemned, crucified Jesus, and that this is the source of the Christian expectation of God's justice. To put it another way, Jesus' resurrection is a matter of oppressor and oppressed.[83]

On the third point, Sobrino says:

In the last analysis the resurrection sets in motion a life of service designed to implement in reality the eschatological ideals of justice, peace, and human solidarity. It is the earnest attempt to make those ideals *real* that enables us to comprehend what happened in Jesus' resurrection.[84]

This statement is then concretized to the effect that the hermeneutics of the resurrection must necessarily be political. The truth of the resurrection can only be experienced in a transformation. Of course, this political hermeneutics must take the theology of the cross into account, "for the work of transforming reality goes on in the presence of the power wielded by evil and injustice."[85]

Precisely this last assertion makes it clear that Sobrino, while seeing an intrinsic relationship between Jesus' life and his resurrection, is more interested than are our other theologians in the experience of failure and in God's solidarity with the one who has failed. In Sobrino, the important correspondence is not between Jesus' praxis and that of Latin American Christians, but between the experience of post-Paschal *new beginnings* and the project of a *new world*. Jesus' death and resurrection stand in terms of a dialectical tension.

Chapter 8

The Key: The Kingdom of God

We have already entertained a number of different considerations of Jesus' proclamation of the kingdom of God in our foregoing sections. Jesus could not espouse the Zelotic concept of the kingdom. His death is connected with his proclamation. His resurrection, too, has intimate ties with the kingdom.

Still, we feel that this is a matter deserving of consideration in a section of its own. For many theologians of liberation, the key to an understanding of Jesus is precisely his proclamation of the kingdom of God, and these theologians accordingly specify the task of Latin American Christians, as well as that of the church, in terms of that proclamation.

The threads of liberation Christology all come together in our theologians' assertions on the kingdom of God. There is exhortation; there is argumentation; there is generalization; there is concretization. The very dates of these assertions have left their traces on their content: older statements are more optimistic, while recent ones tend to be more hesitant. Nowhere is the pathos of liberation so trenchant as in the discourse on the kingdom of God. Galilea writes:

> The promise holds us in suspense. We are on the lookout for a change. For we are expecting the coming of the *kingdom of God*. This kingdom, with its beginnings in history itself, and of which the present historical process in Latin America forms a part, is the enduring expression of the power of God, which comes to light in the victory of the new over the old: of resurrection over death, of the new human being over the old, of the just society over the unjust. It springs up in the Paschal dialectic, for it is the step from death to life.[1]

Thus Galilea leaves the question of the relationship between expectation and behavior open. Vidales, on the other hand, places heavier stress on the actualization of the kingdom of God. In an article taking the Latin American pentecostal movement to task for some of its political implications, Vidales says:

> The presence of the Lord . . . directs the church to fulfill its central commitment—to work for the coming of justice. In this way the task for believers is to be found in the specific challenge of making the coming of the Kingdom a reality, and the Kingdom is nothing other than God's justice expressed as brotherhood between men.[2]

With the tension between expectation, which is passive, and actualization, which is active, we broach a problem to which Gustavo Gutiérrez devotes a number of pages in his *A Theology of Liberation*.[3] His central thesis runs as follows:

> We can say that the historical, political liberating event *is* the growth of the Kingdom and *is* a salvific event; but it is not *the* coming of the Kingdom, not *all* of salvation.[4]

But this statement does not actually contribute very much to a precise determination of the relationship in question. And yet this relationship is a problem underlying practically all the cognate declarations, whether these place more stress on the prophetic role of Jesus or the church, or on cooperation in the political sphere.

Kingdom of God as Motive for Prophetic Criticism

Pironio, who is by and large closer to traditional theology,[5] speaks as follows:

> The proclamation of the kingdom, and the imminence of the kingdom, are always joined to liberation and benefit to human beings.[6]

Hence when this liberation and this benefit are trampled under foot anywhere—and Pironio leaves no doubt that they are, in many places in Latin America—then:

> The church feels the obligation to proclaim the gospel of salvation, to call those who are responsible for this state of affairs to be converted, to testify to the truth, to issue a call for justice, to thrust human beings toward love.[7]

To be sure, the language leaves the impression that this prophetism can still be fairly warm and friendly.

Galilea is more forthright. He asks why Jesus was taken for a political messiah when in fact he was not. He sees the answer in Jesus' proclamation of the kingdom of God.

> Jesus reveals the destiny and the demands for conversion of people and societies. The Kingdom of God as a promise that even now is present among us implants in society values that will allow for the criticism of all forms of social and structural sin, including all forms of exploitation and domination. Thus, the preaching of the Kingdom is not properly speaking a political discourse, but it can give rise to authentic liberation movements among human beings: insofar as it makes them conscious of various sinful situations and insofar as it inspires them to transform society because of a Gospel of the Kingdom in which they have believed.[8]

The same theses are developed in the book which Galilea and Vidales wrote together, *Cristología y pastoral popular*, on Christology and its relationship to pastoral praxis. The authors emphasize that a correct pastoral activity depends first of all on a correct Christology, and that it is therefore a matter of urgency to transmit an accurate image of Christ in pastoral theory. And so they begin by sketching an image of Christ that is preponderantly "religious," and by asking how such a religious person could have exerted so much influence on political movements in Latin America. Then they give their answer:

> Because Jesus is Master and Teacher. . . . He is Master of all human beings and of all things. He is the absolute witness to the truth. His quality of prophet and Master was recognized even by those who did not follow him (Luke 10:25). They, too, always accorded him this title. As Master and Lord he proclaims a truth that will always be valid: the truth about God, about human beings, and about the Kingdom which becomes present in our midst now that he is here.
>
> His truth about God, sole creator and liberator, implies a radical criticism of all idolatry—of any ideology, person, or form of power pretending to usurp the lordship of God by oppressing the human being. Thus he taught us that anything established on earth as an end in itself is established sin, and therefore human beings' enemy.
>
> His truth about human beings means that Jesus—more than just the founder of a new religion—actually restores to human beings their capacity to live all the values which make them "more than human beings." This is their destiny, and he enables them to achieve it. Jesus taught us to live as free persons. He taught us to love, he taught us to suffer, and he taught us to die. His message about human beings denounces a world and a system which do not keep human beings and their true destiny at the center of all things. Consequently, while instituting no politico-social programs, Jesus laid down once and for all the rules for any system or program which seeks to style itself human.

His truth about the Kingdom, which he was himself inaugurating, means that no human kingdom is definitive—and that, without a relationship to the values constituting the Kingdom of God, any human society, and any ideology, will be devoid of justice, of love, and of a communion of brothers and sisters. Jesus called the poor to form his Kingdom. In fact he proclaimed that one had to become poor in order to enter into it (Matt. 5:3; Luke 6:20, 16:19f., 18:19f.; etc.). His call is universal—but it is the blind, the infirm, the poor, and the lame who will occupy its first places (Luke 14:21). In any socio-cultural context, in any human scale of values, these facts are radically revolutionary. They are the parameters within which any ideological, social, or political movement will have to operate if it sincerely seeks justice.

The revolution of the Kingdom of Jesus has a revolutionary ethics, too. It is the ethics of the Beatitudes. The Beatitudes are the great prophecy of the Gospel. They propound the everlastingly valid ideal of the "new human being," who stands at the center of any group in search of a better society. The ideal of the "blessed" or "happy" one is not just a promise for the next life. It is the ethical condition for any transformation of a society in order to bring that society nearer the Kingdom.

Finally, this Jesus Liberator is, in this same regard, Master and Teacher over everything in the Church and its mission. He leads the Church to a true pastoral equilibrium of prophecy and politics. He teaches it that the God it is to proclaim will necessarily come into conflict with idols— ever new idols, which oppress human beings. He reminds it that the glory of God is the freedom of the human being, and that the ministry of the liberation of this human being is the grand objective of its mission. He teaches it that the Kingdom it is to preach is a historical one, and that it is in today's history that the Church is to be the critical conscience that springs from faith in justice, in truth, in love, and in a communion of sisters and brothers. He reminds it that pastoral theory and practice are deprived of a most important Christological dimension if the poor are not evangelized (Luke 4:18), and if the Church is no longer capable of making a poor person of every human being who receives the Good News: if it loses the capability of making the blind, the lame, the infirm, the little ones, the poor, the weak, the despised, and those whom the world counts foolish feel at home in the Church as its favorite children. Finally, he reminds it that the proclamation of the Beatitudes is never out of style—that it is essential to the evangelization of any society and any culture.[9]

Here the kingdom of God is mainly a truth and a value, or set of values. It is not a political reality, but a social one. It does, however, provide the basis for a critique of any political structure, as well as an encouraging sketch of what political structures could look like. It says that the concrete measuring stick will be how the poor are dealt with.

Despite our author's insistence that the kingdom is historical, one has the impression that the critical position from which history is evaluated lies outside history. The insistence upon the absolute nature of truth reinforces this impression. The tension between the unhistorical character of the truth of the kingdom and its historical actualization is unresolved. The kingdom of God is an ideal.

Similarly with Leonardo Boff:

> In any case, it is certain that the proclamation of the kingdom as victory over all the evils of this world, and as fulfillment of the whole of reality in God, represents the heart of Jesus' kerygma, as "a joy to be shared by the whole people" (Luke 2:10).[10]

Ruben R. Dri places stronger emphasis on the historical nature of the kingdom of God. He is engaged in a discussion of "piety," where he distinguishes two meanings this concept can have: the pagan, which is dualistic, static, and fatalistic; and the evangelical, which is incarnate, societal, and historical and which he calls "faith." He cites Jesus as an example of the second meaning:

> The kingdom of God proclaimed by Jesus is dynamic. It grows in this world. Christ likens it to the mustard seed that becomes a bush as big as a tree, or to a bit of leaven that causes a whole mass of dough to rise. The seed is sown in the hearts of human beings. It comes from God, who takes the initiative—but it is the human being who carries the process forward. "Happy the peace*makers*" (Matt. 5:9), he cries. The kingdom is not an edifice of theories, erected on a foundation of contemplation. The kingdom is built by doing the will of the Father.
>
> But this will is not a ready-made decree, fallen from heaven like Zeus's thunderbolt from Olympus. It is a sense and a meaning to be discovered in one's own life circumstances, to be discovered in history. Christ's disciple is the great reader and builder of history.[11]

One would like to see a concrete example of this reading and building. Gustavo Gutiérrez holds the choice open between an absolute and an historical understanding of the kingdom of God.

> This proclamation of the kingdom, this struggle for justice, leads Jesus to death. His life, and his death give us to know that the only possible justice is definitive justice. The only justice is the one that goes to the very root of all injustice, all breach with love, all sin. The only justice is the one that assaults all the consequences and expressions of this cleavage in friendship. The only justice is the definitive justice that builds, starting

right now, in our conflict-filled history, a kingdom in which God's love will be present and exploitation abolished.[12]

This is an example of a passage stressing not only prophetical criticism, but political behavior. The emphases are interconnected, of course, but there are a good many texts in which the second is the stronger, and we shall now examine some of these.

Kingdom of God as Motivation for Political Conduct

José María González Ruiz[13] places the accent on a society of brothers and sisters as the form in which the kingdom of God appears.

For Jesus, and the primitive Christian community, the kingdom of God means the overthrow and defeat of everything that is alienating for the human being—especially the inequalities that are at the basis of the opposing interests of members and groups who by rights should all constitute a single human community. The universal condition of sisters and brothers enjoyed by all men and women is rooted in the fact that they are all sons and daughters of the same Father: God is the father of each and every one of them. Thus "religion," far from being an "opium of the people," is transformed into an incentive to battle every obstacle to this universal condition.[14]

José Comblin offers a concrete example of this quality of the kingdom of God. He is thinking of the new praxis of the military regimes in Latin America:

The proclamation of human rights is not an ancillary function in the service of evangelization. Nor is it merely a new chapter in the book of Christian ethics. This proclamation is the very substance, in the proper sense, of the gospel of Jesus Christ as proclaimed to our contemporaries. It is the authentic proclamation of the kingdom of God.[15]

Fernando Azuela offers a more detailed analysis of the direction in which the battle for the kingdom of God is headed:

Jesus' death reveals sin's unexpected dimension: its capacity to annihilate the best that humankind can produce. Now this Jesus presses us to address every conversion, that of social structures as well as that of the human heart. Structural and personal sin are intrinsically interdependent. They exert their influence on each other in a vicious circle. To break out of this vicious circle, we must wage the battle on both fronts, the structural and the individual.

The Step from the Effects of Sin to the Kingdom. This irruption of the power of sin and death produces an effect: a counter-kingdom of God. Here, all oblivious of its divine worth, humanity embraces depravity. Here reign misery and hunger, disease, ignorance, the curtailment of human freedoms, inequality of opportunity, oppression, repression, and all manner of evil. . . . The kingdom of God, for which Jesus dies, battles for the exact opposite: complete, integral peace, the fruit of equality and justice. Here reigns the community of brothers and sisters. Here reign solidarity, mutual service, love!—all concretized in every manner possible: education, medical attention, economic assistance, and political decisions in favor of the common weal, and all this in harmony and concord with the dignity and value of a human being who is loved by God. . . .[16]

Here are ideal values and politically feasible programs woven into a single fabric. Obviously, Azuela considers political praxis necessary for the actualization of the kingdom of God.

Arnaldo Zenteno sees this kind of praxis actually prefigured in Jesus' own struggle. He combines his religious and political assertions: commitment to the kingdom of God means commitment to the liberation of the oppressed.

If we think about the subject of this article [that Jesus died for opposing the people's oppressors], we begin to see Jesus as liberator. And in this view of Jesus, we suddenly see a great light: *Jesus is fighting against the leaders of his people, who are maintaining a situation that is the very negation of the kingdom of God.* Jesus wages this battle against the leaders of his people not only to free the people from the oppression under which they suffer, but by the same token vigorously to invite the leaders themselves to conversion, openness to God and their brothers and sisters. Jesus means to wage a struggle that will deliver people *from* a religio-political system of repression and discrimination, and *to* the life of the kingdom, that they may be a people indeed—God's people.

This liberation implies integral liberation. After all, oppression itself is integral, being a product of religious and political power acting in concert.[17]

A glance at Zenteno's headings reveals what he understands by liberation:

1. Liberation from Human Self-Satisfaction and Closed Religious Models

2. Liberation from Salvation through the Law

3. Liberation from the Privatization of the Kingdom: Salvation Is for All, but It Begins with Love for Those Who Are Rejected by the Leaders of the People

4. The Kingdom of God Is a Kingdom of Service.

On this fourth point, among Zenteno's precisions we read the following:

In considering the Kingdom of God as a kingdom of service that calls for the transformation of human relationships, let us mark well that this means not only the transformation of interpersonal relationships, but also, and principally, the transformation of structures—the perduring forms by which human beings relate to one another in society. Thus the kingdom stands in clear antithesis to, for example, a kingdom of privileges, bribery and graft, and sinecures. Or again, it is the antithesis of a clericalism that oppresses the people.

Zenteno's fifth and last heading is: "Liberation from the Sacralization of the Past: The Eschatological Moment of the Kingdom Rejects the Absolutization of the Past." Now Zenteno concludes his article:

I have sought to emphasize Jesus' death as the climax of the process of his life—that life of proclamation and incarnation of the liberating kingdom—and as the climax of his constant collision with those who rejected the kingdom by repressing the people.
    Everything I have said can be reduced to one simple formula: *What Jesus proclaimed, and what brought him down to death, was the liberation of human beings in the kingdom of his Father. What the leaders of the people, taken as a group, incarnate, is the kingdom of human beings' oppression.*
    Jesus does battle. He is a sign of contradiction (cf. John 7:43). The proclamation of the kingdom is charged with conflict, for it is a proclamation that bursts asunder the repressive kingdom of the leaders of the people.[18]

Zenteno all but identifies Jesus with the kingdom. And surely discipleship in the struggle for the liberation of the oppressed is identified as a struggle for the kingdom. With his description of the "negation of the kingdom of God," Zenteno makes it altogether clear that what he has in mind is the politico-economic situation of the majority of the Latin American population.

Jesus and the Kingdom of God

All these considerations and reflections are inspired by Gustavo Gutiérrez. Gutiérrez makes the political dimension of the gospel central to Jesus' proclamation of the kingdom.

For Jesus, the liberation of the Jewish people was only one aspect of a universal, permanent revolution. . . . The deep human impact and the social transformation that the Gospel entails is permanent and essential because it transcends the narrow limits of specific historical situations and goes to the very root of human existence: the relationship with God in solidarity with other men. . . . The life and preaching of Jesus postulate the unceasing search for a new kind of man in a qualitatively different society. Although the Kingdom must not be confused with the establishment of a just society, this does not mean that it is indifferent to this society. Nor does it mean that this just society constitutes a "necessary condition" for the arrival of the Kingdom, nor that they are closely linked, nor that they converge. More profoundly, the announcement of the Kingdom reveals to society itself the aspiration for a just society and leads it to discover unsuspected dimensions and unexplored paths. The Kingdom is realized in a society of brotherhood and justice; and, in turn, this realization opens up the promise and hope of complete communion of all men with God. . . .

[Jesus'] testimony and his message acquire this political dimension precisely because of the radicalness of their salvific character.[19]

Here, apropos of the kingdom of God, Gutiérrez is developing a variation on his basic theme of the necessity of a new interpretation of the relationship between secular history and salvation history.[20] Gutiérrez holds that the kingdom stands for a world perfected in every way. But in view of the fact that steps toward that perfection are already given in history—this is the meaning of "anticipation"—the notion of the evolution of world history toward salvation now enters his thesis.

To be sure, this anticipation must face the power of sin and overcome that power in a dialectical process. Here is where Jesus fits into the picture. His role is to be, in his person and in his activity, the densest concentration of this anticipation of the kingdom—and at the same time the agent of its conceptual universalization: that is, Jesus liberates the notion of the kingdom from its confines as first and foremost the perfection and fulfillment of Israel and transposes it to the perfection and fulfillment of the entire world. Jesus sets afoot a comprehensive hope for a new world and a new human being by himself anticipating this new world and by issuing a challenge for commitment to it.[21]

A like conception has made its appearance in Boff's more recent thought. In *Jesus Christ Liberator* the kingdom of God is still described mainly as a basic utopia of the human heart and absolute meaning in history, and the role of Jesus is merely to demonstate that this kingdom "is no longer an unattainable human utopia."[22] But in a more recent little book entitled *Jesucristo y nuestro futuro de liberación*, Boff describes the kingdom of God as a utopia of absolute liberation *and its historical anticipations*:[23]

Jesus' basic intent is to proclaim the actualization of the absolute sense of history and to be the instrument of that actualization. That is, he seeks to be the instrument of liberation *from* whatever so cruelly scourges that history today—pain, division, death—and of liberation *for* life, *for* an open community of love, grace, and the fullness of God.[24]

Here again is Boff's view of the universal character of the kingdom of God as Jesus understands it. Hence:

No liberation within history determines the definitive aspect of the world. No historical liberation shows us the shape of utopia. The total liberation that yields total freedom is the essence of the kingdom and God's eschatological gift. History is a process in that direction. The human being can call for it, and demand it, but the kingdom of God contains an essential element of futurity that is not attainable through human activity. It remains the object of eschatological hope.

But the kingdom of God is not *only* future. It is not *only* utopia. It is present, as well, and occurs in historical concretions. Hence it is to be thought of as a process beginning in the world and culminating in its eschatological end. In Jesus we find this dialectical tension appropriately maintained: there is the goal, total liberation (the kingdom of God); and yet we find mediations (deeds, activity, attitudes) which translate this kingdom processually into history.[25]

Here Boff cites Luke 4:16–21. Then he proceeds:

Jesus' liberation has a twofold aspect. First, he proclaims a total liberation of all history, not just a part of it. But second, he begins to anticipate this totality in a process, concretized in partial liberations which open up to the totality. Were Jesus to proclaim a utopia consisting in a "happy ending" to the world without anticipating this happy ending in history, he would be nourishing false hopes in people: his proclamation would be devoid of credibility. On the other hand, were he to introduce partial liberations which failed to open up to totality and futurity, he would be frustrating people's reasonable hopes and falling into a phantasmagoric immanentism. Instead, Jesus' life and work manifest both dimensions, in dialectical tension.[26]

A little further on, Boff adds:

Jesus' *acta et facta*—his praxis—are to be understood as historicizations of what "kingdom of God" means in the concrete: a liberating change of situation. This is the sense in which Jesus works toward the goal aimed at by oppressed groups.[27]

Next, Boff points up the effects of Jesus' liberating conduct on the social sphere. But he draws a clear line of demarcation between Jesus' anticipatory actualizations of the kingdom of God and political activity:

Despite his liberating praxis, which concretized the reality of the eschatological kingdom in history, Jesus made no attempt to assume political
power. He always saw political power as a temptation of the devil. It
"regionalized" the universal kingdom. The most profound reason for
Jesus' rejection of political power resides in his basic understanding that
the kingdom God is the kingdom *of God*, hence is historicized through
human freedom alone. It is by conversion, not constraint.[28]

We see from this last citation that Boff has not managed as well as Gutiérrez to present the internal connection between Jesus' praxis with respect
to the kingdom of God and the liberation struggles of later history. Boff's
interpretation of the universality of liberation through Jesus, of which political liberation is a mere segment, ill accords with his characterization of
political praxis as a temptation of the devil. From this standpoint Jesus'
liberation struggle bears the stamp more of an individual's self-liberation.

Finally, for Jon Sobrino, Jesus' proclamation of the kingdom of God is
purely and simply a message of liberation.[29] Sobrino proceeds from the
thesis that Jesus proclaimed not himself, but the kingdom of God. This
kingdom, or lordship, of God is to be understood as God's gracious interference in history.

[God's reign] is not merely an extension of human potentialities; it
breaks in as grace. Neither is it merely a transformation of the inner person. It is also a restructuring of the visible, tangible relationships existing
between human beings. It is authentic liberation at every level of human
existence.[30]

In Jesus' outlook God's gracious condescension—God's "lordship"—
means a world transformation.

The deeds of Jesus are basically signs of the coming of the kingdom, as
he himself states in his reply to the emissaries of John the Baptist. . . .
This reply, lifted out of Isaiah, makes very clear what the coming of the
kingdom means to Jesus. It presupposes that the kingdom is the transformation of a bad situation, of an oppressive situation, and that God's
activity can only be envisioned as the *overcoming* of a negative situation.
God's action does not simply affirm the positive aspect of human existence. Rather, it affirms it through *negation*—which is to say, through a
liberation. Thus Jesus does not simply affirm the infinite possibilities of
God and then go on to affirm human possibilities. Instead his aim is to
act in such a way that human possibilities might be realized concretely in
oppressive situations.

That is why the Gospels place Jesus in the midst of situations embody-
ing divisiveness and oppression, where the good news and salvation can
only be understood as being in total discontinuity with them. The

freedom that Jesus preaches and effects in practice cannot help but take the form of liberations.[31]

This is how Sobrino understands both Jesus' "signs," and his praxis of the forgiveness of sins as a sign of the liberation that ushers in the kingdom of God. And this in turn determines Christian praxis, which Sobrino denotes as discipleship, or the following of Jesus:

> Because his God exists only insofar as he "reigns," thereby liberating people and creating human fellowship, access to God is only possible in a liberative praxis based on following Jesus.[32]

Less clearly than in Sobrino's treatment of Jesus' death, but nevertheless recognizably, this concept of Jesus' proclamation of the kingdom is dependent upon a correct concept of God. If God condescends graciously to interfere in history, if God is the one whose coming is proclaimed by Jesus, then ultimately God is the liberator, whose activity will be discernible in the liberating life and work of Jesus and Jesus' disciples alike. Our section on the death of Jesus has made it clear, of course, that this liberation is not to be expected in terms of a rectilinear evolution—"this would correspond to optimism"—but in terms of a dialectic, involving the cross of Jesus and the cross of men and women. This is hope.

Summary and Conclusions

Anyone who deals with the theology of liberation addresses a phenomenon that is still in the process of becoming. We have "not yet seen the end" of this affair, either politically or theologically. It is no easy matter, then, to set forth nicely rounded conclusions. It does seem feasible, however, to map out typical tracks along which the Jesuological and Christological argumentation of liberation theology tends to run.

1. Unlike the received theologizing of the academicians of the northern hemisphere, liberation theology demands no precise correspondence between the various elements of its product and specific traditional theological disciplines, like exegesis, dogmatics, or moral theology. Liberation theology does all its theology together. Thus exegetical and systematic problems, especially, go hand in hand, are intertwined. Even problems outside the purview of theology itself, especially those of the social sciences, are continually being introduced into theological discourse.

2. The distinction, so dear to European exegesis and dogmatics alike, between the historical Jesus and the Christ of the kerygma—along with its subsidiary distinction between Jesus' own words, *ipsissima vox Jesu*, and formulations of the primitive Christian community—go almost entirely by the board in the theology of liberation. Indeed not only is there no conceptual consistency in liberation theology's use of "Jesus" as distinguished from "Christ" but the concept of a "Jesus of history" can be applied in a new sense altogether.

3. The reason for all this is that the theologians of liberation have an interest in Jesus different from that of their European colleagues. Neither have they any interest in a "historical" Jesus in the European sense of the word—when the mechanics of their argumentation demands this sort of "historical" material they are only too glad to be able to borrow it from European exegesis and get on with it—nor are they even concerned to sketch a new systematic Christ (and so confessional lines blur almost to the vanishing point). No, they are entirely preoccupied with the *applicability* of theological reflection to the comprehensive societal process they see unfolding in Latin America today. In other words, their interest is practical. Jesuological and Christological argumentation is entirely at the service of a renewal of Christian, and ecclesial, praxis.

4. Quite as if it went without saying that this is what a Christian does, our theologians of liberation proceed from a point of departure in a confession

142

of faith in Jesus Christ. Indeed, in this point of departure itself, their theology is as good as traditional. Their "practical interest," however, yields a new interpretation of the old confession: Jesus Christ is liberator. José Míguez Bonino's formulation is especially striking:

> Far from dashing Old Testament hopes, the New Testament incorporates them right into its own proclamation of Jesus Christ. Thus Zechariah and Mary receive him as the promised Deliverer (Luke 1:46-55, 68-79). Jesus himself adopts the liberation program Isaiah proclaimed (Luke 4:18-19, Matt. 11:1-6). In Jesus' death and resurrection, a new world has dawned. A new age is inaugurated, and its sign is liberation— liberation from the "world," from sin, from death, from the Law. And in the Lord's Parousia it will be perfect and complete.[1]

5. Owing to the various levels of meaning of the concept of liberation, a number of our authors fail to elude the danger of confusing the political assertion, "The situation of dependency calls for liberation," with the theological one, "Subjection to sin calls for liberation." The difficulty is present in the Medellín documents themselves, where the current situation in Latin America is characterized as a "sinful" one. The proposition "Jesus Christ liberates" is open to the same objection, today as when it first began to be current.

6. Certain features of Jesus' praxis come in for special emphasis: his transcendence of the confinement of the Jewish faith to the Jewish nation, the precedence he accords the human element over the cultic or ritual one, his transcendence of religious, racial, and political prejudices. The intrinsic correlation between religious discourse and political praxis in the Judaism of Jesus' time is of the greatest significance to the theologians of liberation. Jesus is generally placed within the tradition of the prophets.

7. The postresurrection confession of faith in Jesus as the Christ seizes upon Jesus' concrete praxis, as well as upon his basic significance as God's commended witness. Jesus' death and resurrection demonstrate that his liberation is universal and total: that it means to win out over any and all constraint, individual or collective, and any and all enslavement, whether of a person or a group of persons. Applied to everyday secular experience—or, to put it another way, seen in the light of comprehensive liberation through Jesus Christ—faith in Jesus' death and resurrection acquire utopian characteristics. This faith then evidently becomes all the more of a motive for commitment to liberation.

8. Liberation theology's appeal to New Testament texts manifests a number of typical characteristics:

a. Biblical thought is considered to demonstrate the gross inadequacy of received "Greek" philosophical thought in theology.

b. The features of Jesus' praxis that are singled out for special consideration are those of struggle and conflict.

c. In the application of passages from the New Testament to situations in Latin America, a typological argumentation prevails: the "poor" of the Beatitudes are the exploited campesinos, and so on.

9. The priority of the practical in Latin American Christology discloses new features in old themes like theodicy, Chalcedon, grace, and so on. All acquire a new physiognomy, verifying the dictum that the theology of liberation is a "new way of doing theology."

10. On at least one count, liberation Christology seems to have made a contribution to Old World theology. Never again, we think, will it be possible to do Christology in the absence of a raised consciousness of the social reality in which this Christology has to be formulated—the reality of First World/Third World relationships—or in the absence of reflection on the political implications of the life and work of Jesus and the church. When two-thirds of the population of Latin America are hungry and yearning for social and political deliverance, Christology, even in Europe (where, incidentally, the causes of this situation are to be sought), must begin to ponder liberation—and to provide an impetus for a liberating Christian praxis.

Notes

Introduction

1. The term "Latin America" is generally taken to mean Mexico and Central and South America—the American countries whose principal languages, with very rare exceptions, are either Spanish or Portuguese. Often the Spanish-speaking islands of the Caribbean, such as Cuba, for example, are included. We may seem to be belaboring the obvious, but the breadth of the received definition would seem to be worth setting forth in explicit terms, as a good many European publications use "Latin America" and "South America" as if the two were simply interchangeable. This is inaccurate and misleading. Mexico, for example, is part of Latin America, but not of South America.

It will also be worthwhile to point out, although we shall not go into the matter, that there are good grounds for speaking of "theologies of liberation" in the plural, instead of simply lumping all approaches included in this denotation under the singular term (as we shall generally be doing).

2. See Gustavo Gutiérrez, *A Theology of Liberation*: *History, Politics, and Salvation*, trans. and ed. Caridad Inda and John Eagleson (Maryknoll, N.Y.: Orbis Books, 1973), p. 15

3. See José Loza Vera, "La tarea del exégeta en Latinoamérica," in *Liberación y cautiverio*, ed. E. Ruiz Maldonado (Mexico City: Organizing Committee, 1976) pp. 431–444; Samuel Ruiz García, "Teología bíblica de la liberación," *Servir* 20 (1974): 459–506. According to Hugo Assmann, the new theology of liberation is characterized by "a new freedom with respect to biblical scholarship. It does not simply throw the latest exegesis out the window, but neither does it accept the latter's narrow liberalism, or digressions on matters of scant historical importance ("Aspectos básicos de la refexión teológica en América Latina," *Pasos* 52 [May 28, 1973]: 5).

4. It would appear that we have an exception, in German theology, in the critical observations of L. Hödl, "Jesu Heilsweg in den Sohnesgehorsam des Kreuzes" (Hödl et al., *Das Heil und die Utopien* [Paderborn, 1977], p. 110). There is no space here for the full catalog of dissenting opinions, and we shall have to content ourselves with simply naming Blank, Küng and Schillebeeckx by way of example.

5. CELAM, *Liberación: Diálogos en el CELAM*, Documentos CELAM, no. 16 (Bogotá: CELAM, 1974), p. 371. As late as 1970, Hugo Assmann had to say that Latin American theology had simply developed no satisfactory Christology at all (*Teología de la liberación* [Montevideo: MIEC-JECI, 1970], p. 100; cf. his *Theology for a Nomad Church* [Maryknoll, N.Y.: Orbis Books, 1976], pp. 103–104). Since then, books by Leonardo Boff and Jon Sobrino have come to the rescue.

Part 1

1. Gustavo Gutiérrez, *A Theology of Liberation*, trans. and. ed. Caridad Inda and John Eagleson (Maryknoll, N.Y.: Orbis Books, 1973), p. 15.

2. For primary sources, see Gutiérrez, *A Theology of Liberation*; Claude Geffré and Gustavo Gutiérrez, eds., *The Mystical and Political Dimension of the Christian Faith*, Concilium 96 (New York: Herder/Seabury, 1974); José Míguez Bonino, *Theologie im Kontext der Befreiung* (Göttingen: Vandenhoeck and Ruprecht, 1977). For presentations of the theology of liberation see especially Gerd-Dieter Fischer, "Abhängigkeit und Protest: Der gesellschaftliche Kontext der neueren lateinamerikanischen Theologie," in *Gott im Aufbruch: Die Provokation der lateinamerikanischen Theologie*, ed. Peter Hünermann and Gerd-Dieter Fischer (Freiburg, 1974); Gerd-Dieter Fischer, "Befreiung: Zentralbegriff einer neuorientierten lateinamerikanischen Theologie, Amerkungen zu ihren theologisch-hermeneutischen Problemen," *Theologie und Glaube* 63 (1973): 1–23; idem, "Theologie in Lateinamerika als 'Theolgie der Befreiung,' " *Theologie und Glaube* 62 (1972): 161–178; Reinhard Frieling, "Die lateinamerikanische Theologie der Befreiung," *Materialdienst des kinfessionskundlichen Instituts Bensheim* 23 (1972): 26–35; Peter Hünermann, "Evangelium der Freiheit: Zur Physiognomie lateinamerikanischer Theologie," in *Gott im Aufbruch*, pp. 11–24; Miguel Manzanera, "Theologie der Befreiung: Ansatzpunkt-Ziel-Methode," in *Theologie und Befreiung*, ed. H. Bettschneider (St. Augustine, 1974); idem, "Die Theologie der Befreiung in Lateinamerika und ihre Hermeneutik," in *Theologische Akademie XII*, ed. J. Beutler and O. Semmelroth (Frankfurt, 1975), pp. 52–78; Hans Zwiefelhofer, *Bericht zur "Theologie der Befreiung"* (Munich, 1974). Discussion and critique are available in, for example, H. Bettschneider, ed., *Theologie und Befreiung* (St. Augustine, 1974); International Theological Commission (Karl Lehmann, with Heinz Schürmann, Olegario González de Cardenal, and Hans Urs von Balthazar), *Theologie und Befreiung* (Einsiedeln, 1977); Alfonso López Trujillo, "Theologie der Befreiung: 'Das erste Wort,' " *Orientierung* 38 (1974): 18–20; idem, 'Das zweite Wort,' *Orientierung* 38 (1974): 30–32. For a *general survey*, with abundant citations and references, see Christian Modehn, *Der Gott, der befreit: Glaubensimpulse aus Lateinamerika* (Meitingen/Freising, 1975).

Chapter 1

1. For a detailed study of the background of this concept, see Hans-Jürgen Prien, *Die Geschichte des Christentums in Lateinamerika* (Göttingen, 1978).

2. The original Spanish version has seen at least twenty-three editions. In English, Eduardo H. Galeano, *Open Veins of Latin America: Five Centuries of the Pillage of a Continent* (New York: Monthly Review Press, 1973).

3. In the version reported in R. and E. Grün, eds., *Die Eroberung von Peru—Pizarro und andere Konquistadoren 1526-1712: Die Augenzeugenberichte von Celso Gargía, Gasparde Carrajal, Samuel Fritz,* 2nd ed. (Tübingen, 1975).

4. Cf. Karl Josef Rivinius, "Unterdrückung und Befreiung am Beispiel der Kirchen-geschichte Lateinamerikas," in *Befreiende Theolgie: Der Beitrag Lateinamerikas zur Theologie der Gegenwart*, ed. Karl Rahner et al. (Stuttgart, 1977).

5. I have encountered this attitude—"The Indians are like animals"—rather often in Mexico. See Prien, *Geschichte des Christentums*, p. 165.

6 For a reevaluation of the prophetic role of the church in the history of Latin

America, see Joseph Barnadas, "Christian Faith and the Colonial Situation," in *Power and the Word of God*, ed. Frans Böckle and Jacques-Marie Pohier, Concilium 90 (New York: Herder/Seabury, 1973). Unfortunately Dussel's history was unavailable to me (Enrique Dussel, *Historia de la Iglesia en América Latina, 1492-1970*, 3rd ed. [Barcelona: Nova Tierra, 1974]; Eng., *The History of the Church in Latin America: Colonialism to Liberation*, trans., Alan Neely [Grand Rapids: Eerdmans, 1981]).

7. Prien gives the following example: "Dominican Father Antonio de Montesinos first held forth with his energetic Christian protest against the continued maltreatment and exploitation of the Indians in his Advent sermon of 1511 on Santo Domingo. Like a voice crying in the wilderness of this island he stormed against the stupefied Spaniards before him. They were in the state of mortal sin, he told them and their retainers, and could no more be saved than established Moors or Turks. Cruelly had they established a lawless slave regime over innocent men and women. Their demands on Indian labor went beyond all bounds, and they even failed to feed adequately the Indians of whom this forced labor was required—just as they totally neglected their Christian instruction. 'Are they not human beings?' he cried. 'Are they not endowed with rational souls? Are you not required to love them as yourselves?' None wished to hear a voice like this, and the scandal was total. The Dominicans stationed in Santo Domingo, however, agreed with Montesinos, and in 1512 Ferdinand the Catholic demanded of Governor Diego Columbus that he either bring the Dominicans to reason or dispatch them back to Spain, as they presented a danger with ideas of this sort. The superior of the Spanish Dominicans, Alonso de Loaysa, threatened his confreres with refusal of permission to leave Spain, unless they dissociated themselves from this manner of scandalous proclamation" (*Geschichte des Christentums*, p. 170).

8. Cf. ibid., p. 203.

9. Given by Prien on pages 221-228 of the *Geschichte des Christentums*.

10. Prien, again, reports: "The Franciscans had endeavored to recruit novices from among the Indians as early as 1527. They soon discovered, however, that the Indians did not share their particular ideal of perfection and preferred to marry, although they remained good Christians. And so in 1536 they launched, in the Santiago Tlatelolco quarter of Mexico City, an experimental institution of higher learning. Their project had the support of their bishop, Zumárraga, their provincial, García de Cisneros, the president of the Mexican *Audiencia*, the former bishop of Santo Domingo and Concepción, Sebastián Ramírez de Fuenleal, and the first viceroy, António [*sic*] de Mendoza (1535-50), 'who had a high opinion of the Indians' intelligence.' The very idea of higher education for the Indians was gunpowder. Neither the Augustinians nor the Dominicans had secondary schools in their missions at that time, and the latter were strictly opposed to teaching the Indians Latin: after all, a knowledge of Latin opened the way to the Bible and the corpus of theological literature. It soon became evident that many tolerated the school with a sense of high humor, certain that it would enjoy no success whatever. But many of its students, after a number of years, became absolutely brilliant in Latin—which presaged the formation of an Indian educated elite class, one that would outshine the Spaniards themselves (many an uneducated secular priest, for example), and so now a storm of opposition broke over the heads of the Tlatelolco pioneers. The prejudice was essentially racial (the Spanish upper class was automatically superior to the Indian) and colonial (the Indian should be content with the role of slave and beast of burden). Neither Church nor society gave the Indian a decent chance at the priest-

hood, and so even the Tlatelolco school ceased to function as a seminary. Further, the candidates were more inclined to marriage than to celibacy—which, to traditional Roman thinking, demonstrated their unfitness for the role that had originally been conceived for them" (p. 250).

11. As given by Metzler (cited in ibid., pp. 252 ff.).

12. Gutiérrez, "Contestation in Latin America," in Teodoro Jiménez Urresti, ed., *Contestation in the Church*, Concilium 68 (New York: Herder/Seabury, 1971), p. 45.

13. That this is still the case today is evident from the very last source cited in Prien's book: a Brazilian Indian, speaking at a meeting in 1975, states, "It is not we who pillage this soil. The white is like a wild boar . . . . Wherever he comes he destroys everything. And when he has everything he will still rob more, and he writes his robbery down on a piece of paper to make sure it is his" (*Geschichte des Christentums*, p. 1178).

14. A detailed treatment is to be found in D. Nolen and F. Nuscheler, eds., *Handbuch der Dritten Welt*, vol. 3 (Hamburg, 1976).

15. Pablo Richard, "Teología de la liberación en la situación actual de América Latina," *Servir* 13 (1977): 33-34. Richard draws up a schema of the history of the Latin American church in "periods":

1492-1808: Colonial Christianity
1808-1880: Crisis in colonial Christianity
1808-1968: Attempt to build a new Christianity
1880-1930: Conservative, anti-liberal
1930-1968: Liberal, developmentalist, antisocialist
1968-   : A new Christianity? [ibid., p. 34].

Galeano's synthesis is of another kind: "Bolívar prophesied shrewdly that the United States seemed fated by Providence to plague America with woes in the name of liberty. General Motors or IBM will not step graciously into our shoes and raise the old banners of unity and emancipation which fell in battle; nor can heroes betrayed yesterday be redeemed by the traitors of today. It is a big load of rottenness that has to be sent to the bottom of the sea on the march to Latin America's reconstruction. The task lies in the hands of the dispossessed, the humiliated, the accursed. The Latin American cause is above all a social cause: the rebirth of Latin America must start with the overthrow of its masters, country by country. We are entering times of rebellion and change. There are those who believe that destiny rests on the knees of the gods; but the truth is that it confronts the conscience of man with a burning challenge" (Galeano, *Open Veins of Latin America*, p. 283).

16. A concise presentation of the same may be found in Evers and Wogau's " 'Dependencia': Lateinamerikanische Beiträge zur Theorie der Unterentwicklung," *Das Argument* 79 (1973): 404-454; Peter Berger, *Pyramids of Sacrifice: Political Ethics and Social Change* (New York: Basic Books, 1974); or Hans Zwiefelhofer, "Zum Begriff der Dependenz," in *Befreiende Theologie: Der Beitrag Lateinamerikas zur Theologie der Gegenwart*, pp. 34-45.

17. For the origin of the theory of dependency in post-Leninist-Marxist theory of imperialism see Berger, *Pyramids of Sacrifice*, pp. 50-51. See also Berger's critique of the theory of imperialism, ibid., pp. 50-56. Berger's whole story is in terms of "rich countries" and "poor countries"; of course, from a Latin American viewpoint the Soviet Union and its East European satellites are themselves "rich countries."

18. No one today seriously disputes the economically harmful influence of wealthy countries, especially in their use of their capital, on Latin America. See Berger, *Pyramids of Sacrifice*, pp. 51, 217-218. The dependence is there. What is disputed is whether the *theory* of imperialism—and, in its framework, the *theory* of dependency—can explain all the observable facts. It is also disputed whether the Latin American situation can be described in terms of Marxist analysis without adopting Marxist theory in its entirety; Berger pleads in favor of such a possibility (*Pyramids of Sacrifice*, p. 54); Alfonso López Trujillo denies it ("Theologie der Befreiung in Lateinamerika," in *Kirche und Befreiung*, ed. F. Hengsbach and López Trujillo [Aschaffenburg, 1975], pp. 76-86).

19. The theology of liberation, insists Segundo Galilea, does not spring from a Marxist, or any other, *theory* of dependency, but from the stark *fact* of Latin American dependency. He concedes, to be sure, that the temptation is strong among some liberation theologians to base their theology on a particular theory of dependency, and says that this helps to render liberation theology suspect of "ideologism" ("La liberación en la conferencia de Medellín," *Servir* 10 [1974]).

20. Dutch theologian C. Jaime Snoek, who works in Brazil, has dealt with the question of whether theology has any contribution to make to the "Third World problem." In this connection he discerns a certain communality between the anthropological orientations of modern philosophy and of biblical thought, and writes: "Christianity is the religion of 'coming-to-be,' the active anticipation of the future. It is also the religion of development. . . . Here, as everywhere, it is impossible to conceive of any development whatsoever without Christianity, for all humanity stems from Christ. Thus development, as we understand it, becomes the salvific and humanizing activity of God himself, but within the history of humanity" ("Tercer mundo: Revolución y Cristianismo," *Cristianismo y Revolución* 1 [1966]: 9).

21. Gustavo Gutiérrez, "Involvement in the Liberation Process," in *The Power of the Poor in History*, trans. Robert Barr (Maryknoll, N.Y.: Orbis Books, 1978), p. 29. Gutiérrez is sketching the situation at the close of the 1960s. For the special tone and connotations of *dependence*, or *dependency*, see Arturo Blatezky, *Sprache des Glaubens in Lateinamerika* (Frankfurt, 1978).

22. As we are dealing with "antecedents of the theology of liberation," we should at least mention the meeting of the Jesuit provincial superiors of Latin America, in Rio de Janeiro, May 6-14, 1968, under the presidency of their general, Pedro Arrupe. The final document, programmatic in its nature, is entitled, "Carta de Rio: Orientaciones y compromisos" (Letter from Rio: directions and commitments), and is translated into German as "Die Befreiung des Menschen soll unser Ziel sein," *Orientierung* 32 (1969): 139-141.

Walter Repges, in *Christen in Lateinamerika* (Essen: ADVENIAT, 1975), considers Camilo Torres to be one of the forerunners of the theology of liberation. I can second this judgment of his only with strong reservations. No theological interpretation of the concepts of liberation and freedom occurs in Torres's writings. There are, to be sure, two loci in his essay, "La revolución, imperativo cristiano," in *Cristianismo y revolución* (Mexico City, 1970), pp. 316-345; in Eng., "The Christian Apostolate and Economic Programming," in *Revolutionary Writings* (New York: Herder and Herder, 1969), pp. 103-134. In that essay he does express notions which also occur in the theology of liberation. He writes:

"Benevolent works for our neighbor, from the theological point of view, constitute one of the surest signs of the existence of supernatural life. And from the pastoral standpoint, these good works constitute the most important objective for the apostle who lives in a pluralistic society with social problems" (*Revolutionary Writings*, p. 108).

"To seek authoritative economic planning in the indigent countries is generally an obligation for the Christian. This planning is essential to efficacy in the authentic service of the majorities and therefore it is a condition of charity in these countries.

"It is most probable that the Marxists will take over the leadership of this planning. In this case, the Christian must collaborate insofar as his moral principles will permit, keeping in mind the obligation of avoiding greater evils and of seeking the common good. Under such conditions, it is possible that in the underdeveloped countries there will be no recurrence of the struggles among groups seeking structural reforms favorable to the majorities. Without factionalism, and without conquerors or conquered, Christians will be able to participate in the building of a better world that will continually draw closer to its ideal of universal love" (*Revolutionary Writings*, pp. 133-134).

Both passages are from Torres's address to the second international congress of Pro Mundi Vita, in Louvain, Belgium, in September 1964.

23. Eduardo Pironio, "Latinoamérica: 'Iglesia de la Pascua,' " in *Panorama de la teología latinoamericana* (Salamanca: SELADOC, 1975), p. 178. Pironio has since been made a cardinal and assigned a post in the Roman Curia (1976).

24. "During these days we have gathered in the city of Medellín, moved by the spirit of the Lord, in order to orientate once again the labors of the Church in a spirit of eagerness for conversion and service" (CELAM, *The Church in the Present-Day Transformation of Latin America in the Light of the Council*, vol. 2, ed. Louis Michael Colonnese [Washington, D.C.: Latin American Bureau, USCC, 1968], p. 41).

25. Ibid., p. 165.

26. Ibid., p. 78.

27. Ibid., p. 58.

28. Ibid., p. 61.

29. Ibid., p. 42.

30. Ibid., p. 100.

31. Ibid., p. 42.

32. Ibid., p. 39.

33. There is broad consensus on the positive value of Medellín. See, for example, Hans Zwiefelhofer, *Christen und Sozialismus in Lateinamerika*, vol. 1 of *Theologie in Lateinamerika* (Düsseldorf, 1974). To be sure, Teodoro Ignacio Jiménez Urresti's omission of Medellín from among the "antecedents" of liberation theology is conspicuous ("La teología de liberación: Antecedentes, causas y contenidos," in Facultad Teológica, *Teología de la liberación, Conversaciones de Toledo, June 1973* [Burgos: Aldecoa, 1974]). A. García Rubio's observations ("Die lateinamerikanische Theologie der Befreiung [I]," *Internationale katholische Zeitschrifte* 2 [1973]: 407-409) are, it would seem to me, appropriate and instructive here. Meanwhile, the Third General Conference of Latin American Bishops was held in Puebla, Mexico, in 1979, and the debate on whether Puebla's conclusions extend, specify, restrict, or cancel those of Medellín is still in full swing. See H. Schöpfer and E. Stehle, eds., *Kontinent der Hoffnung* (Munich/Mainz, 1979), and *Puebla and Beyond: Documents and Commentary*, ed. John Eagleson and Philip Scharper, trans. John Drury (Maryknoll, N.Y.: Orbis Books, 1979).

Chapter 2

1. Our subheadings in this chapter correspond essentially to the three levels of reflection proposed by Hugo Assmann as characteristic of Latin American theology: (1) a socio-political *analysis* of the Latin American situation today, (2) an ethico-social *option* for change, and (3) a *strategy* on the level of praxis (Assmann, "Liberación: Implicaciones de un nuevo lenguaje teológico," *Stromata* 28 [1972]: 169f.). For all aspects of chap. 2, see especially (besides publications in German): Hugo Assmann, *Theology for a Nomad Church*, trans. Paul Burns (Maryknoll, N.Y.: Orbis Books, 1976); idem, *"Opresión-liberación: Desafío a los cristianos* (Montevideo: Tierra Nueva, 1971); CELAM, *Liberación: Dialogos en el CELAM,* Documentos CELAM, no. 16 (Bogotá: CELAM, 1974); *Fe cristiana y cambio social en América Latina: Encuentro de El Escorial, 1972* (Salamanca: Sígueme, 1973); Lucio Gera, "Teología de la liberación," *Perspectivas de Diálogo* 8 (1973): 39–50; Gustavo Gutiérrez, "Apuntes para una teología de la liberación," *Cristianismo y Sociedad* 8 (1970): 6–22; J. Jesús Herrera Aceves, "La historia: Lugar teológico dentro de la experiencia eclesial," in *Liberación y cautiverio: Debates en torno al método de teología en América Latina,* ed. E. Ruiz Maldonado (Mexico City: Organizing Committee, 1976); Santiago Martínez Sáez, "Teología y liberación," *Istmo* 74 (May-June 1971): 9–21; Alex Morelli, "Nuevos elementos para una teología de la liberación," *Contacto* 8 (1972): 56–68; Isidro Pérez, "La teología de la liberación: Una nueva forma de teología en la Iglesia," *Teológica Xaveriana* 26 (1976): 311–321; Eduardo Pironio, "Teología de la liberación," *Criterio* 43 (1970): 782–790, 822–824; *Religion—¿Instrumento de liberacion?,* with contributions by Gustavo Gutiérrez, Rubem Alves, and Hugo Assmann (Barcelona/Madrid: Búsqueda, 1973); Pablo Richard, "La teología de la liberación en la situación actual de América Latina," *Servir* 13 (1977): 33–54; E. Ruiz Maldonado, ed., *Liberación y cautiverio*; Juan Luis Segundo, *The Liberation of Theology,* trans. John Drury (Maryknoll, N.Y.: Orbis Books, 1976); SELADOC, *Panorama de la teología latinoamericana,* 2 vols. (Salamanca: Sígueme, 1975); Estanislão Yepes, "La teología de liberación en América Latina," *Horizontes* 17 (1973): 111–125.

2. It seems to me more appropriate to speak of a variety of content within *the* theology of liberation than to speak of various theologies of liberation. Míguez Bonino's solution—"theology in a liberation context"—does permit an important aspect to emerge in the very designation. But ultimately an explanation of the variety of content is more important than the dispute over designations. See Assmann, "Implicaciones de un nuevo lenguaje teológico," p. 162, where he cites the powerful integrating potential of the ecclesiastical system for the discourse on liberation.

3. Elsewhere this step is carried further. In the symposium "Theology of Liberation," held in Bogotá in 1970 (where prominent representatives of the theology of liberation did not take the podium), the first paper, by the sociologist Germa Bravo Casas, consisted of an analysis of the Latin American situation: "Underdevelopment as a Form of Dependency." The other papers, as well, often paralleled the theology of liberation—for instance, that of Javier Lozano Barragán, "The Church's Contribution to the Liberation of Latin America," or that of Leonidas Proaño, bishop of Riobamba, Ecuador, "Liberation's Hour Strikes." For these papers see *Aportes para la liberación: Simposio teología de la liberación, conferencias, Bogotá, Marzo 6 y 7 de 1970* (Bogotá, 1970).

4. Eg., Hugo Assmann, *Theology for a Nomad Church*, p. 65; Gustavo Gutiér-rez, "Liberation Praxis and Christian Faith," in *The Power of the Poor in History*, trans. Robert Barr (Maryknoll, N.Y.; Orbis Books, 1983), pp. 36–74.

5. Cf. Juan Carlos Scannone's article, "Liberación: El lenguaje teológico de la liberación," *Víspera* 7 (1973): 41. This is the point on which publications in German have most to say. To be sure, the matter of methodology is still in dispute, as is evinced in discussion like Segundo's "Théologie et sciences sociales" (in Enrique Dussel et al., *Les luttes de libération bousculent la theologie* [Paris, 1975], pp. 167–185), where the author lists the points he says are not handled in sociology and takes up a critique of Marxist inspired sociology; see also Ignacio Ellacuría's "Hacía una fundamentación del método teológico" (*Estudios Centroamericanos* 30 [1975]: 409–425), which contrasts two articles, from Spain and Brazil respectively, in order to isolate the character of the Latin American theological contribution.

In his article "Liberación: Notas sobre las implicaciones de un nuevo lenguaje teológico," Assmann addresses himself to quite another aspect of the problem. Among the reasons why, as he says, so many of the hopes raised by Medellín have gone unfulfilled, he lists, in the second place, the Latin American bishops' inexperience in socio-political analysis. This, says Assmann, has prevented the church from fulfilling the role that could have fallen to it in the liberation of Latin America.

6. Assmann, *Theology for a Nomad Church*, p. 44.

7. Segundo Galilea, "Liberación en la Conferencia de Medellín," *Servir* 10 (1974): 33.

8. Assmann, "The Actuation of Christ's Power in History: Notes on the Discernment of Christological Contradictions," in *Faces of Jesus*, ed. José Míguez Bonino, trans. Robert Barr (Maryknoll, N.Y.: Orbis Books, 1984), pp. 132–133.

9. Assmann, "Implicaciones de un nuevo lenguaje," p. 176.

10. Assmann, "El aporte cristiano al proceso de liberación en América Latina," *Pasos* 52 (May 28, 1973): 79.

11. Ibid., p. 80.

12. Enrique Dussel, "Histoire de la foi chrétienne et changement social in América Latina," in Dussel et al., *Les luttes de liberation bousculent la theologie*, p. 95. The present translation relies on the Spanish version as cited by Juan Gutiérrez González, *Teología de la liberación: Evaporación de la teología: La obra de Gustavo Gutiérrez vista desde ella misma* (Mexico City: Jus, 1975), p. xii n. 6.

13. José Comblin, "La liberación en el pensamiento cristiano latinoamericano," *Servir* 10 (1974): 12–13.

14. See Assmann, "Aspectos básicos de la reflexión teológica en América Latina," *Pasos* 52 (May 28, 1973): 1.

15. Assmann is surely referring to G. Mainberger, *Jesus starb umsonst: Sätze, die wir noch glauben konnen* (Freiburg im Breisgau, 1970). Assmann's editor in English cites Mainberger's pages 79ff in *Theology for a Nomad Church*, p. 108 n. 30.

16. Assmann, *Theology for a Nomad Church*, p. 79.

17. From a seminar presentation, "Necesidad y posibilidades de una teología socio-culturalmente latino-americana," in *Fe cristiana y cambio social*," pp. 371–372.

18. We could go on and on. However, I should only like to call attention to the effect this thesis can have on the whole train of thought of a Latin American theologian. Hugo Assmann, whom we cite so frequently, lists the following "common lines of theological exposition, . . . the themes that at present appear most fre-

quently in the theology of liberation": 1. The world as conflict. 2. Slavery in Egypt and Exodus. 3. A world in conflict: institutionalized violence; sin. 4. Liberation-salvation. 5. History of salvation or salvation of history? 6. Creation and the salvation process of liberation. 7. Liberating political presence and eschatological hope. 8. Christ the animator of history. 9. The significance of Christianity. 10. The choice for the church in the 1970s (*Theology for a Nomad Church*, pp. 64–70).

All attempts of theologians, be they Latin American or Northern, to sum up the theology of liberation in a short formula locate its point of departure in the concrete situation, the "historical reality," in which human beings find themselves. See Gutiérrez, *Theology of Liberation*, trans. and ed. Caridad Inda and John Eagleson (Maryknoll, N.Y.: Orbis Books, 1973), pp. 11–13, 45–50, and "Liberation, Theology, and Proclamation," in *The Mystical and Political Dimension of the Christian Faith*, Concilium 96 (New York: Herder/Seabury, 1974), pp. 64–77; Miguel Manzanera, "Theologische Anmerkungen zur 'revolutionären Gewalt' in Lateinamerika," in *Befreiende Theologie*, ed. Karl Rahner et al. (Stuttgart, 1977), p. 106; Christian Modehn, ed., *Der Gott, der befreit; Glaubensimpulse aus Lateinamerika* (Meitingen/Freising, 1975), p. 15.

19. Herrera, "La historia: Lugar teológico," in *Liberación y cautiverio*, p. 341.

20. Segundo expresses this thesis as follows. First he distinguishes two concepts of "secularization": a negative one—secularization as an evacuation of the sacral world, tending toward a theology of the death of God as its projected limit—and a positive one—secularization as the beneficent interference of a divine revelation in daily praxis. He holds an acceptance and recognition of the latter as the sine qua non of theology in Latin America today. Today, theology on that continent must take account of everyday reality. "It is simply a fact," he says, "that interaction between social praxis and theology is the decisive, determining methodological factor for Latin American theology, present and future. As we say: here there is no authentic theology without the contribution of sociology" ("Instrumentos de la teología latinoamericana," in *Encuentro teológico "Liberación en América Latina"* (Bogotá: Ed. América Latina, 1972), p. 37.

21. Segundo, *Liberation of Theology*, p. 241.

22. Isidro Pérez, "Teología de la liberación: Una nueva forma de teología en la Iglesia," *Teológica Xaveriana* 26 (1976): 313.

23. Gutiérrez, *Theology of Liberation*, p. 11.

24. Ibid.

25. "Theological reflection is defined as critical reflection on the praxis of the faith of the church" (Juan Carlos Scannone, "El lenguaje teológico de la liberación," *Víspera* 7 [1973]: 41).

26. Casiano Floristán, "Método teológico de la teología pastoral," in *Liberación y cautiverio*, p. 249.

27. Segundo Galilea, "Salvación de los pecadores y liberación de los pobres según el Evangelio," *Christus* (Mexico) 40, no. 473 (1974): 28.

28. Gustavo Gutiérrez, "Involvement in the Liberation Process," in *The Power of the Poor in History*, trans. Robert Barr (Maryknoll, N.Y.: Orbis Books, 1983), p. 29. A cursury glance at René Laurentin's *Liberation, Development and Salvation* (Maryknoll, N.Y.: Orbis Books, 1972), which appeared at about the same time as Gutiérrez's article (I had access to Laurentin only in English, but the French appeared in 1969), and which is the result of a collaboration between Laurentin and Mexican sociologists and theologians, shows that it develops a number of reflections

having analogues in the theology of liberation. For example, he has chapters entitled, "The Life of the Church as a Theological Locus," "Is There a Theology of Development?" and "Mission and Development." The principal differences between Laurentin and Gutiérrez are that Laurentin's considerations are more ecclesiocentric and place more emphasis on development. In his last chapter, Laurentin states his formula for the next step to be taken: "Today, development calls for a profound conversion: a conversion from good intentions to scientific realism and effective action. A conversion from chauvinism to universalism—from bilateral to multilateral aid. A conversion from economic materialism (which may be worse with capitalism than with Marxism) to cultural humanism: a humanism that is open to man's divinization" (*Liberation, Development and Salvation*, p. 210).

29. José Porfirio Miranda, *Von der Unmoral gegenwärtiger Strukturen: Dargestellt am Beispiel Mexio* (Wuppertal: Jugendienst, 1973), p. 15.

30. Enrique Dussel, "Domination–Liberation: A New Approach," in *The Mystical and Political Dimension of the Christian Faith*, Concilium 96, p. 56.

31. Scannone, "El lenguaje teológico," p. 47.

32. Pedro Negre, "Biblia y liberación," *Cristianismo y Sociedad* 2 (1970): 72–73.

33. Gera, "Teología de la liberación," p. 50.

34. On the problems in this area, see Sergio Silva, *Glaube und Politik: Herausforderung Lateinamerikas* (Frankfurt, 1973).

35. CELAM, "Elementos relevantes sobre la teología de la liberación: Documento de trabajo de la tercera Reunión de Coordinación del Equipo de Reflexión Teológica Pastoral del CELAM," *Contacto* 11 (1974): 53.

36. Scannone, "El lenguaje teológico," p. 44.

37. Luis Alberto Gomez de Souza, "Los condicionamientos socio-politicos actuales de la teología en América Latina," in *Liberación y cautiverio*, p. 74.

38. Leonardo Boff, "¿Qué es hacer teología desde América Latina?", in *Liberación y cautiverio*, p. 138.

39. Enrique Dussell, "Sobre la teología de la liberación," *IPLA* 11 (1971): 1.

40. Ibid., p. 2.

41. Segundo, *Liberation of Theology*, p. 3.

42. Cf. Roberto Oliveros Maqueo, *Liberación y teología: Génesis y crecimiento de una reflexión, 1966–77* (Lima: CEP, 1977). The abiding interest of this subject is evinced in the fact of two thematic issues of the Mexican review, *Christus*: "The God of the Poor" (vol. 44 [1979], no. 519), and "Priests and Commitment to the Poor" (ibid., no. 524).

43. See CELAM, *Present-Day Transformation*, pp. 57–58, 71–73, 81, 169, 215–217.

44. See, for example, Samuel Ruiz García's synopsis of the Old Testament's approach to liberation and dependency:

1. God pledges himself more and more to the concerns of the poor and identifies more and more strongly with their hopes.

2. God promises to be with them definitively.

3. The world and human beings will be transformed, through consecration to the justice of a God who liberates the oppressed;

4. With this justice of his, God opens the future to us ("Teología bíblica de la liberación," *Servir* 20 [1974]:502).

45. Julio de Santa Ana, "Notas para una ética de la liberación: A partir de la Biblia," *Cristianismo y Sociedad* 8 (1970):55.

46. Gustavo Gutiérrez, "Liberation Praxis and Christian Faith," in *The Power of the Poor in History*, p. 55.

47. Gutiérrez, "Apuntes para una teología de la libertión," *Christianismo y Sociedad* 8 (1970) 21ff.

48. Gutiérrez, "God's Revelation and Proclamation in History," in *The Power of the Poor in History*, p. 18.

49. Luís Fernando Rivera, "Socialismo de Santiago 2:1-13," in *Panorama de la teologíalatino americana*, vol. 1, p. 142.

50. In the English edition of the Jerusalem Bible the heading reads "Respect for the Poor."

51. Rivera, "Socialismo de Santiago," *Panorama*, vol. 1, p. 143.

52. Segundo Galilea, *¿A los pobres se les anuncia el Evangelio?* (Bogotá: CELAM-IPLA, 1975), pp. 59-64.

Chapter 3

1. The following works take a critical position, in varying degrees and with different nuances, toward the theology of liberation or toward one or more of its authors or approaches: Ph.-I. Andre-Vincent, "Les 'théologies de la liberation,' " *Nouvelle Revue Théologique* 98 (1976): 109-125; Héctor Borrat, "Entre la proclama y los programas," *Víspera* 7 (1973): 47-52; Lothar Bossle, "Praxeologischer Obskurentismus: Mangelnder Praxisbezug in der 'Theologie der Befreiung,' " *Stimmen der Zeit* 194 (1976): 473-486; Carlos Bravo, "Notas marginales a la teología de la liberación," *Ecclesiastica Xaveriana* 24 (1974): 3-60; Juan Gutiérrez Gonzalez, *Teología de la liberación: Evaporación de la teología: La obra de Gustavo Gutiérrez vista desde ella misma* (Mexico City: Jus, 1975); F. Hengsbach and Alfonso López Trujillo, *Kirche und Befreiung* (Aschaffenburg, 1975), especially López Trujillo's article, "Die Theologie der Befreiung in Lateinamerika"; International Theological Commission, *Theologie der Befreiung* (Einsiedeln, 1977); François Hubert Lepargneur, "Théologies de la liberation et théologie tout court," *Nouvelle Revue Théologique* 98 (1976): 126-169; Alfonso López Trujillo, *¿Liberación o revolución?* (Bogotá: Paulinas 1975); idem, "Panorama de la teología de la liberación," in Facultad Teológica del Norte de España, *Teología de la liberación, conversaciones de Toledo, June 1973* (Burgos: Aldecoa, 1974); idem, "Secularización, liberación y ateísmo," *Revista Javeriana* 74 (1970): 553-567; Santiago Martínez Saez, "Teología y liberación," *Istma* 74 (May-June 1971): 9-21; Alberto Methol Ferré, "Política y teología de la liberación," *Víspera* 8 (1974): 30-52; P. Melecio Picazo Galvez, "Elementos cristológicos para una teología de la liberación," in CELAM, *Liberación: Diálogos en el CELAM*, Documentos CELAM, no. 16 (Bogotá: CELAM, 1974), pp. 323-336; Eduardo Pironio, "Teología de la liberación," *Criterio* 43 (1970): 782-790, 822-824; Juan Luis Segundo, *The Liberation of Theology* (Maryknoll, N.Y.: Orbis Books, 1976); and Virgilio Zea G., "Resurrección: Revelación de Dios, liberación del hombre," *Teológica Xaveriana* 25 (1975): 17-27. Antonio Bentue offers a preliminary reflection on Puebla, shortly after the close of that general conference of Latin American bishops, in his "Teología de la liberación: ¿si o no?", *Mensaje* 28 (1979): 440-450.

2. Luís Alberto Gómez de Souza, "Los condicionamientos socio-politicos actuales de la teología en América Latina," in *Liberación y cautiverio*, ed. Enrique Ruiz Maldonado (Mexico City: Organizing Committee, 1976), p. 78.

3. Pope Paul VI, *Evangelii Nuntiandi* (Dec. 8, 1975), especially nos. 6-39. Eng., "On Evangelization in the Modern World" (Washington, D.C.: USCC Publication Office, 1976).

4. International Theological Commission, *Theologie der Befreiung* (Einsiedeln, 1977).

5. See note 1 above. Also Yves M.-J. Congar, *Peuple messianique* (Paris, 1975).

6. Héctor Borrat, "Entre la proclama y los programas."

7. See the literature on the "basic Christian communities," the "grassroots Christian communities." For an example of their self-concept see *Orientierung* 41 (1977): 177. See also Alvaro Barreiro, *Basic Ecclesial Communities: The Evangelization of the Poor*, trans. Barbara Campbell (Maryknoll, N.Y.: Orbis Books, 1982).

8. Alfonso López Trujillo, "Theologie der Befreiung in Lateinamerika," in *Kirche und Befreiung*, pp. 74-76. For a discussion of the entire problem see Peter Berger, *Pyramids of Sacrifice: Political Ethics and Social Change* (New York: Basic Books, 1974), pp. 32-65.

9. Juan Carlos Scannone concedes liberation theology's dependence on Marxist analysis, but sees the possibility of its deliverance from determinism through application of a perspective of salvation history—especially of the "eschatological reservation," the "already-but-not-yet." Thus, Scannone holds, the theology of liberation can interpret each new situation as *open* to the liberating activity of God ("El lenguaje teológico de la liberación," *Víspera* 7 [1973], p. 42).

10. López Trujillo, "Theologie der Befreiung," in *Kirche und Befreiung*, ed. Hengsbach and López Trujillo, pp. 76-86. See also his *¿Liberación o revolución?*, pp. 11-69, and his "Secularización, liberación y ateísmo."

11. *Evaporación de la teología: Obra de G. Gutiérrez.* Juan Gutiérrez Gonzalez devotes 146 pages to a discussion of 20 pages of Gustavo Gutiérrez, taking him to task point by point and labeling as false or inexact both his general lines of approach and his specific assertions. G. Gutiérrez is reproached with horizontalism, Marxism, and, as J. Gutiérrez's title suggests, "flight from theology."

There is some justification in some of this criticism. But all of it is open to the objection that it refuses a priori to admit the possibility that the new ideas and goals of theology as formulated by Gustavo Gutiérrez are legitimate. Juan Gutiérrez remains the prisoner of a dualistic conception of love of God and neighbor, natural and supernatural, faith and reason. The most generous response to a like critique can only be that it is based on a different understanding of the nature of theology.

The same will have to be said of Martínez Saez's polemics. Martínez defines the task of theology as "that of penetrating, elucidating, and defending the teaching of the church" ("Teología y liberación," p. 10).

12. Cf. his argumentation in *Evaporación de la teología*, pp. 94-99.

13. Ibid., pp. 98-99.

14. See "Liberation Praxis and Christian Faith," in *The Power of the Poor in History* (Maryknoll, N.Y.: Orbis Books, 1982). Gustavo Gutiérrez strongly insists that liberation theology represents a break with the old way of thinking, as well as the dominant social class. (Is this a reflection of the Latin American ruling class's new awareness of its failure in the social area?)

15. Picazo, "Elementos crisotológicos para una teología de liberación," p. 578.

16. See the Medellín documents (CELAM, *Present-Day Transformation*) vol. 2, pp. 48, 58 (twice), 59, 99 (twice), 100 (twice), 101, 114, 141, 165, 167, 169, 213, 215.

17. Cf. ibid., pp. 48, 58, 100, 141.

18. Eduardo Pironio, "Der neue Mensch: Theologische Besinnung auf das Wesen der Befreiung," in *Gott im Aufbruch: Die Provokation der lateinamerikanischen Theologie,*ed. Peter Hünermann and Gerd Dieter-Fischer (Freiburg, 1974), p. 41.

19. Ibid., p. 42.

20. Ibid., p. 48.

21. Pironio's theology of liberation stresses three points: (1) Religion must play a sufficiently broad role in liberation. (2) There must be no violence. (3) Political relationships must be improved.

22. Pironio, "Neue Mensch," p. 50.

23. Quite by chance I came upon an article by G. Marquínez-Argote in the Salvadoran periodical *Estudios Centroamericanos* (1977): 475-484. The article, entitled "The Way Zubiri Looks from Latin America," states: "The new generation of Latin American philosophers is sketching a concept of philosophy as commitment to the liberation of the masses, who, to our very day, are dependent and oppressed." Part of his article is entitled "Primacy of Reality over Being." Philosophy, it would seem, is taking its cue from theology.

24. Gilberto Giménez, "De la 'doctrina social de la Iglesia' a la ética de liberación," in SELADOC, *Panorama de la teología latinoamericana* (Salamanca: Sígueme, 1975), p. 46.

25. Javier Lozano, "El compromiso de la Iglesia en la liberación de América Latina," in *Aportes para la liberación: Simposio teología de la liberación, conferencias, Bogotá, marzo 6 y 7, 1970* (Bogotá, 1970), pp. 93-94.

26. This would be the appropriate place to refer to an explanation of the rise of liberation theology in cultural psychology. Horacio Bojorge holds that the theology of liberation springs from a fear on the part of white theologians that their intellectual enterprise could meet the same fate as whites have generally inflicted on the Indian masses of Latin America (Horacio Bojorge, "Goel: Dios libera la los suyos," *Revista Bíblica* 32 [1970]: 8-12).

27. Lamberto Schuurmann, "Teología de la liberación, *Respuesta* 16 (1973): 22.

28. Gustavo Gutiérrez writes: "To characterize Latin America as a dominated and repressed continent naturally leads one to speak of liberation and above all to participate in the process" (*Theology of Liberation*, [Maryknoll, N.Y.: Orbis Books, 1973], p. 88).

29. Zea, "Resurrección: Revelación de Dios, liberacion del hombre," p. 25.

30. Eduardo Pironio, "Sentido, caminos y espiritualidad de la liberación," in CELAM, *Liberación: Diálogos*, p. 19.

31. Picazo, "Elementos cristológicos," p. 576.

32. José Míguez Bonino, "Fundamentos bíblicos y teológicos de la responsibilidad cristiana," in *Encuentro y desafío* (Buenes Aires: Iglesia y Sociedad en América Latina, 1961), pp. 22ff.; citation is from p. 25.

33. Carlos Bravo, "Notas mariginales a la teología de la liberación," pp. 59. It is unfortunate that Gutiérrez's subtitle in Spanish, *Perspectivas,* is missing in the German and English translations of his main work.

34. Ibid., p. 45. For possible objections here from the side of liberation theology see Segundo, "Capitalism-Socialism: A Theological Crux," in *The Mystical and Political Dimension of the Christian Faith*, Concilium 96 (New York: Herder/ Seabury, 1974).

Chapter 4

1. *Liberación y cautiverio: Debates en torno al método de la teología en América Latina*, ed. Enrique Ruiz Maldonado (Mexico City: Organizing Committee, 1976).

2. What was given out as "liberation theology" in Chile shortly after the coup can be gathered from a statement by Father Raúl Hasbún, Television Programming Director of Santiago's Catholic University (whose evaluation differed radically, to be sure, from that of Archbishop Raúl Silva Henríquez of Santiago). Hasbún wrote in *El Mercurio*, November 18, 1973: "The only way to wipe out Marxism is to face up to it . . . with moral and spiritual forces that are stronger than it is. This is what has now happened here. The moral reserves of the Chilean woman, farmer, miner, settler, and trucker have made common cause with the spiritual forces of the army, the university, and the church" (quoted in "El reino de Dios sufre violencia [Mateo 11, 12] y en Chile,. . ." typewritten message of certain groups of Christians in Chile, November 1973, p. 38).

3. U.S. Congress, Senate Committee on Foreign Relations, Subcommittee on Western Hemisphere Affairs, *Rockefeller Report on Latin America* (Washington: Government Printing Office, 1970). One passage reads:

The Cross and the Sword

"Although it is not yet widely recognized, the military establishments and the Catholic Church are also among today's forces for social and political change in the other American republics. This is a new role for them. For since the arrival of the Conquistadores more than 400 years ago, the history of the military and the Catholic Church, working hand in hand with the landowners to provide 'stability,' has been a legend in the Americas.

"Few people realize the extent to which both these institutions are now breaking with their pasts. They are, in fact, moving rapidly to the forefront as forces for social, economic, and political change. In the case of the Church, this is a recognition of a need to be more responsive to the popular will. In the case of the military, it is a reflection of a broadening of opportunities for young men regardless of family background.

The Church

"Modern communications and increasing education have brought about a stirring among the people that has had a tremendous impact on the Church, making it a force dedicated to change—revolutionary change if necessary.

"Actually, the Church may be somewhat in the same situation as the young—with a profound idealism, but as a result, in some cases, vulnerable to subversive penetration; ready to undertake a revolution if necessary to end injustice but not clear either as to the ultimate nature of the revolution itself or as to the governmental system by which the justice it seeks can be realized" (pp. 84ff.).

4. See the testimonials recorded by Marietta Peitz, *Das Risiko, ein Christ zu sein: Zeugnisse aus Asien, Lateinamerika, Afrika* (Graz, 1973), pp. 84–159. See also Martin Lange and Reinhold Iblacker, eds., *Witnesses of Hope: The Persecution of Christians in Latin America*, trans. William E. Jerman (Maryknoll, N.Y.: Orbis Books, 1981).

5. Segundo, "Condicionamientos actuales de la reflexión teológica en Latino-américa," in *Liberación y cautiverio*.

6. Leonardo Boff, "¿Que es hacer teología desde América Latina?", in *Liberación y cautiverio*, p. 141.

7. Ibid., p. 129.

8. Pablo Richard, "Teología de la Liberación en la situatión actual de América Latina," p. 54.

9. Gustavo Gutiérrez, "Theology from the Underside of History," in *The Power of the Poor in History*, trans. Robert Barr (Maryknoll, N.Y.: Orbis Books, 1983), p. 170.

10. Ibid., p. 214. See also Boff, *Teología desde el cautiverio* (Bogotá: Indo-American Press Service, 1975).

Part II

1. See note 5 of our introduction. See also Estanislão Yépez, "La teología de la liberación en América Latina," *Horizontes* 17 (1973): 113; and cf. Raúl Vidales: "We also need an express reflection on Jesus and his political posture. True, some study has been done here and there—Galilea or Comblin, for example. But this is too important a matter to be handled helter-skelter. What we need is a comprehensive study of it, in the whole framework and context of the 'theology of liberation'! Last, in the final document of the Second Golconda Group conference in May 1968, although there is a passage entitled 'Reflection in the Light of the Gospel,' there is actually no reference to the gospel, but only to the creation accounts of Genesis, along with a great deal of reliance on the teaching of Medellín. Christ is mentioned only twice, and only in quotations from Medellín" (Raúl Vidales, "Ausencias y limitationes de la teología de la liberación," *Servir* 9 [1970]: 198; Vidales's reference is to Golconda, *El libro rojo de los "curas rebeldes"* [Bogotá: MINIPROC, 1969], pp. 117-119).

2. In addition to Leonardo Boff, *Jesus Christ Liberator* (Maryknoll, N.Y.: Orbis Books, 1978) and Jon Sobrino, *Christology at the Crossroads* (Maryknoll, N.Y.: Orbis Books, 1978), I refer the reader to: Gustavo Gutiérrez, *A Theology of Liberation* (Maryknoll, N.Y.: Orbis Books, 1973), pp. 225-232; Hugo Assmann, "The Actuation of the Power of Christ in History," in *Faces of Jesus*, ed. José Míguez Bonino, trans. Robert Barr (Maryknoll, N.Y.: Orbis Books, 1984, pp. 125-136; Leonardo Boff, "El Jesus histórico y la Iglesia," *Servir* 12 (1976): 263-284; Héctor Borrat, "Para una cristología de la vanguardia," *Equipos Docentes de América Latina* 14 (April-June 1971): 51-56; Rubén Cabello, "La misión de Jesús y el 'Año acepto al Señor,' " *Christus* (Mexico) 40, no. 472 (1975): 28-32; Marcel van Caster, "Liberación del hombre y misterio pascual," *Perspectivas de Diálogo* 7 (1972): 50-59; Ignacio Ellacuría, *Freedom Made Flesh: The Mission of Christ and His Church*, trans. John Drury (Maryknoll, N.Y.: Orbis Books, 1976), pp. 11-43; Segundo Galilea, "Jesus' Attitude toward Politics: Some Working Hypotheses," in *Faces of Jesus*, pp. 93-101; idem, "Cristología y 'ortopraxis' cristiana," *Christus* (Mexico) 39, no. 458 (1973): 16-20; Segundo Galilea and Raúl Vidales, *Cristología y pastoral popular* (Bogotá: Paulinas, 1974); Francisco Interdonata, "Jesús y la política," *Revista Teológica Limense* 10 (1976): 179-202; Javier Jiménez Limón, "Jesús y el poder," *Christus* (Mexico) 41, no. 492 (1976): 46-55; Enrique Maza, "Jesús y la institución," *Christus* (Mexico) 40, no. 480 (1975): 34-38; Melecio Picazo Gálvez, "Elementos cristológicas para una teología de la

liberación, in CELAM, *Liberación: Diálogos*, Documentos CELAM, no. 16 (Bogotá: CELAM, 1974), pp. 323-336; Raúl Vidales, "La práctica histórica de Jesús: Notas provisorias," *Christus* (Mexico) 40, no. 481 (1974): 162-171; Virgilio Zea G., "Jesús, el hombre," *Revista Javeriana* 82 (1974): 36-48; idem, "Jesús o el riesgo de la existencia," *Revista Javeriana* 82 (1974): 162-171. Cf. Manfred Hofmann, *Identifikation mit dem Anderen: Theologische Themen und ihr hermeneutischer Ort bei lateinamerikanischen Theologen der Befreiung* (Stockholm/Göttingen, 1978), pp. 69-85.

3. Horst Goldstein speaks of the Exodus theme as having been "promoted to a program" in liberation theology. See his "Skizze einer biblischen Begründung der Theologie der Befreiung," in Karl Rahner et al., eds., *Befreiung Theologie: Der Beitrag Lateinamerikas zur Theologie Gegenwart* (Stuttgart, 1977), p. 66.

4. Arnaldo Zenteno, "Liberación y esclavitud en la sacrada escritura," *Servir* 7 (1971): 276.

5. Ibid., p. 287.

6. Juan Hernández Pico, "Método teológico latinoamericano y normatividad de Jesús histórico para la praxis política mediada por el análisis de la realidad," in *Liberación y cautiverio*, p. 598.

Chapter 5

1. When I am referring to the Jew of Nazareth, I call him simply "Jesus." Even in the theology of liberation he is often referred to as "Jesus of Nazareth," the "historical Jesus," or the "human Jesus." But since these designations tend to reflect a particular position or approach, I prefer to use simply his name.

2. José Porfirio Miranda, *Being and the Messiah: The Message of St. John,* trans. John Eagleson (Maryknoll, N.Y.: Orbis Books, 1977), p. ix.

3. Ibid.

4. See Reinhard Frieling, "Jesus Christus, der Befreier: Eine Skizze lateinamerikanischer Christologien," *Materialdienst des konfessionskundlichen Instituts Bensheim* 29 (1978): 53.

5. Hugo Assmann, *Opresión-Liberación: Desafío a los cristianos* (Montevideo: Tierra Nueva, 1971), pp. 103-105; citation is from p. 104.

6. Hugo Assmann, "Evangelización y liberación: Elementos para un cuadro teológico de referencias," *Teología desde la praxis de la liberación: Ensayo teológico desde la América dependiente* (Salamanca: Sígueme, 1973), pp. 149f.

7. Gustavo Gutiérrez, *A Theology of Liberation: History, Politics and Salvation*, trans. and ed. Sister Caridad Inda and John Eagleson (Maryknoll, N.Y.: Orbis Books, 1973), pp. 225-232.

8. Gustavo Gutiérrez, "Jesús y el mundo político," *Perspectivas del Diálogo* 7 (1972): 76-81.

9. Gutiérrez, *Theology of Liberation*, "Christ and Complete Liberation," pp. 168-187; "Christ the Liberator," pp. 175-78.

10. Ibid., p. 226.

11. Ibid., pp. 177-78.

12. The same concern is discernible in a talk by Gutiérrez in July 1968 (see *Hacía una teología de la liberación: Apuntes de una conferencia del P. Gustavo Gutiérrez*, July 21-25, 1968, Servicio de Documentación, series 1., doc. 16 [Montevideo: MIEC-JECI, 1969] p. 11). In the framework of a redefinition of the relationship

between salvation and freedom, he cites Luke 4:18 (Jesus' inaugural sermon in the synagogue at Nazareth), and reproaches traditional hermeneutics with "spiritualizing" the passage. He calls for its reinterpretation in function of Leviticus 25:10 (the Year of Jubilee, in which all may reclaim the land they once possessed), and claims that this will demonstrate the intrinsic connection between the coming of the messiah (to fulfill the "Year of the Lord," as in Jesus' inaugural sermon) and the defeat of injustice (by which, for example, peasants are robbed of *their* land).

13. Frieling, "Jesus Christus, der Befreier," p. 57.

14. The title of one of Galilea's essays ("Kontemplation und Engagement: Das prophetisch-mystische Element in der politisch-gesellschaftlichen Aktion," in *Gott im Aufbruch: Die Provokation der lateinamerikanischen Theologie*, ed. Peter Hünermann and Gerd-Dieter Fischer [Freiburg, 1974]; cf. *Following Jesus*, chap. 6, "Contemplation and Commitment" [Maryknoll, N.Y.: Orbis Books, 1981]).

15. Ibid., "Kontemplation und Engagement," pp. 178–179; cf. *Following Jesus*, p. 65.

16. Segundo Galilea, *¿A los pobres se les anuncia el Evanglio?* (Bogotá: CELAM-IPLA, 1975), pp. 59–64.

17. Juan Luis Segundo, "Capitalism–Socialism: A Theological Crux," in *The Mystical and Political Dimension of the Christian Faith*, Concilium 96, pp. 104–123.

18. Ibid., p. 117.

19. Ibid., p. 120.

20. Ibid., pp. 120–121.

21. Juan Hernández Pico, "Método teológico latinoamericano y normatividad de Jesús histórico para la praxis política mediada por el análisis de la realidad," in *Liberación y cautiverio*, pp. 597–598.

22. Cristianos por el Socialismo, *El pueblo camina . . . ¿y los Cristianos?* (Santiago de Chile: Christians for Socialism, 1972).

23. Ibid., p. 43.

24. "He eschuchado los clamores de mi pueblo: Documento de obispos del Nordeste [de Brasil]," in *Signos de liberación: Testimonios de la Iglesia en América Latina, 1969–1973* (Lima: CEP, 1973).

25. Ibid., pp. 133–134.

26. Leonardo Boff, *Jesus Christ Liberator: A Critical Christology for Our Time*, trans. Patrick Hughes (Maryknoll, N.Y.: Orbis Books, 1978). Chapter titles: 1. The History of the History of Jesus. 2. How Can We Know Christ? The Hermeneutic Problem. 3. What Did Jesus Really Want? 4. Jesus Christ, Liberator of the Human Condition. 5. Jesus, a Person of Extraordinary Good Sense, Creative Imagination, and Originality. 6. The Meaning of the Death of Jesus. 7. Resurrection: The Realization of a Human Utopia. 8. Who Really Was Jesus of Nazareth? 9. The Christological Process Continues: The Accounts of Jesus' Infancy—Theology or History? 10. Only a God Could Be So Human! Jesus, the Man Who Is God. 11. Where Can We Find the Resurrected Christ Today? 12. What Name Can We Call Jesus Christ Today? 13. Jesus Christ and Christianity: Reflections on the Essence of Christianity. The English edition has an Epilogue, "A Christological View from the Periphery."

27. The same observation is made by theologian and jurist Héctor Borrat in his preface to the Spanish edition of this same book, *Jesus Christ Liberator* (*Jesucristo el liberador: Ensayo de Cristología crítica para nuestro tiempo*, 2nd ed. [Buenos Aires: Vozes, 1975], p. 14).

28. *Jesus Christ Liberator*, p. 46.

29. Leonardo Boff, "Salvation in Jesus Christ and the Process of Liberation," in *The Mystical and Political Dimension of the Christian Faith*, Concilium 96, p. 79. See also his *Jesucristo y nuestro futuro de liberación* (Bogotá: Indo-American Press Service, 1978), p. 9, where he posits an intrinsic connection between social context and Christology.

30. Jon Sobrino, *Christology at the Crossroads: A Latin American Approach*, trans. John Drury (Maryknoll, N.Y.: Orbis Books, 1978), p. 274. Reinhard Frieling, in his "Jesus Christus, der Befreier," p. 55, cites a passage from the "Prólogo" of the second Spanish edition in which, Frieling says, Sobrino asserts that the only appropriate way to approach the historical Jesus will be actual discipleship—the actual following of Christ. Doubtless this is Sobrino's thinking indeed as we see in Sobrino's own text (*Crossroads*, p. 275). The passage Frieling cites, however, is signed by the publisher, Centro de Reflexión Teológica (*Crossroads*, Preface to the Spanish edition, p. xiii).

31. Here see Sobrino's "El concimiento teológico en la teología europea y latinoamericana," *Estudios Centroamericanos* 30 (1973): 426–445, cited here in its German translation in Karl Rahner et al., eds., *Befreiende Theologie: Der Beitrag Lateinamerikas zur Theologie der Gegenwart* (Stuttgart, 1977), pp. 123–143.

32. Rahner, *Befreiende Theologie*, p. 128.

33. Ibid., p. 133.

34. *Christology at the Crossroads*, p. 275.

35. Javier Jiménez Limón, "Jesús y el poder," *Christus* (Mexico) 41, no. 492 (1976): 46–55.

36. Ibid., p. 47.

37. Ignacio Ellacuría, *Freedom Made Flesh: The Mission of Christ and His Church*, trans. John Drury (Maryknoll, N.Y.: Orbis Books, 1976).

38. Ibid., p. 47.

39. Some of Ellacuría's headings: "Part One: The Political Character of Jesus' Mission." "2. The Prophetic Mission of Jesus." "Part Two: The Historicity of the Church's Mission [originally, "The Proclamation of the Gospel and the Mission of the Church"] "5. Liberation: Mission and Charism of the Latin American Church." "Part Three: Violence and the Cross."

40. Ellacuría, *Freedom Made Flesh*, pp. 23–24.

41. Ibid., p. 29.

42. Eduardo Pironio, "Sentido, caminos y espiritualidad de la liberación," in CELAM, *Liberación: Diálogos*, Documentos CELAM, no. 16 (Bogotá: CELAM, 1974), p. 17.

43. Ibid., p. 20.

44. Eduardo Pironio, "Der neue Mensch: Theologische Besinnung auf der Wesen der Befreiung," in *Gott im Aufbruch*, p. 41.

45. Eduardo Pironio, "Teología de la liberación," *Teología* 7 (1970): 8.

46. Cf. Gerd-Dieter Fischer, "Theologie in Lateinamerika als 'Theologie der Befreiung,' " *Theologie und Glaube* 63 (1972): 173.

47. The same question of political involvement by Christians (or by the church) in the struggle for liberation in Latin America occupies the critics, as well: they protest Jesus' "preemption" by the theology of liberation. Jorge Mejía, for example, commenting on Acts 4:34, where the community of believers is said to have sold what they had and donated the proceeds, avers: "But again, this is not a direct transfor-

mation of the prevailing social order, but an anticipation of the kingdom" ("La liberación, aspectos bíblicos: Evaluación crítica," in CELAM, *Liberación: Diálogos*, p. 300). Or Interdonato, after a consideration of the points of contact between Jesus and the Zealots: "If this were to be the only source of political and revolutionary motivation, we should, it would seem to us, have to admit that we were being motivated by something sinful in these simple Jewish and Gentile societies: their sacralization of secular might, and their desacralization of religious authority by the attribution to it of earthly dimensions. Jesus fought this sin, as he fought all sin, but he did not eradicate it—hence the continual recurrence of this same misjudgment throughout the course of Christian history, on the part of people who are incapable of grasping the eschatological nature of Jesus' position and attitude. But what is surprising, and truly dangerous, is that a full-fledged Catholic theological movement—the theology of liberation—has contributed to its resurrection in our own day" (Francisco Interdonato, "Jesús y la política," *Revista Teológica Limense* 10 [1976]: 181).

Chapter 6

1. "Biblia y liberación de los pueblos" (editorial), *SIC* 37 (1974): 345-346. José Comblin could be cited here as well. Every fruitful movement in the church, he says, has had its "ideology of the Bible"—its own time-bound, and timely, hermeneutics. He reproaches European theology with refusing to answer the call of the times, by eschewing an ideology of its own. Then he goes on: "One can even say that the Bible only has meaning in those manifold provisional meanings with which the Holy Spirit himself endows it in the course of the ages" ("La liberación en el pensamiento cristiano latinoamericano," *Servir* 10 [1974]: 22). But Carlos Bravo objects: "The return to the Bible has generally fallen into the same errors as we ascribe to decadent scholasticism: that of using biblical texts to prove its *own* theses—whereas in actuality it is the precious quality of the Bible to be able to bear witness to an original experience, unique and unrepeatable" ("Notas marginales a la teología de la liberación," *Ecclesiastica Xaveriana* 24 [1974]:59).

2. For example, Gustavo Gutiérrez's work in *A Theology of Liberation*, (trans. and ed. Caridad Inda and John Eagleson [Maryknoll, N.Y.: Orbis Books, 1973], pp. 225–232) has had a great deal of influence, especially on liberation theology's approach to Jesus' trial before the Sanhedrin and Pilate.

3. Cf. Arturo Blatezky, *Sprache de Glaubens in Lateinamerika* (Frankfurt, 1978), pp. 250–256.

4. Gustavo Gutiérrez, "Jesús y el mundo político," *Perspectivas de Diálogo* 7 (1972):76.

5. Segundo Galilea, "Jesús y la liberación de su pueblo," *Christus* (Mexico) 38, no. 449 (1973): 60. See the same locus for Galilea's thinking in the paragraph just above.

6. Samuel Ruiz García, "Teología bíblica de la liberación," *Servir* 20 (1974): 478.

7. Juan Luis Segundo, *The Liberation of Theology*, trans. John Drury (Maryknoll, N.Y.: Orbis Books, 1976), pp. 111–112.

8. Movimiento Sacerdotes para el Tercer Mundo, *Nuestra reflexión: Carta a los obispos argentinos* (Buenos Aires: Publicaciones MSTM, 1970), p. 44.

9. Segundo Galilea, "Liberation as an Encounter with Politics and Contempla-

tion," in *The Mystical and Political Dimension of the Christian Faith*, Concilium 96 (New York: Herder/Seabury, 1974), pp. 23-33, esp. pp. 31-33. See also his *Following Jesus* (Maryknoll, N.Y.: Orbis Books, 1981), pp. 56-61.

10. Segundo Galilea, "Jesus' Attitude toward Politics: Some Hypotheses," in *Faces of Jesus*, ed. José Míguez Bonino, trans. Robert Barr (Maryknoll, N.Y.: Orbis Books, 1984), p. 95. In similar terms, but with altogether different purport, Jorge Mejía expresses his own view: "Thus the light shed by the Evangelists on the 'liberating' mission of the lord is wholly unpolitical" ("La liberación, aspectos bíblicos: Evaluación crítica," in CELAM, *Liberación: Diálogos*, p. 299). Mejía, of course, is concerned to demonstrate that the theology of liberation cannot justifiably appeal to Jesus' life in support of its argumentation inviting Christians to political activity. To Mejía's credit it must be pointed out that his concept of the "political" is a negative one, rather in the sense of the temptation narrative in Matthew and Luke.

11. Galilea, "Jesus' Attitude toward Politics," p. 96.

12. This attitude, often encountered in the theology of liberation, renders Christians, in spite of all they may have in common with many exclusively political non-Christian groups of a Marxist bent, "bad risks" in the eyes of the latter as comrades in a struggle for liberation.

13. Galilea, "Jesus' Attitude toward Politics," p. 96.

14. Ibid., pp. 96-97.

15. Ibid., p. 98.

16. Ibid.

17. Ibid., p. 100.

18. Gutiérrez, *Theology of Liberation*, p. 231 (or, identically, "Jesús y el mundo político," *Perspectivas de Diálogo* 7 [1972]: 80).

19. Hugo Assmann, *Teología desde la praxis de la liberación: Ensayo teológico desde la América dependiente* (Salamanca: Sígueme, 1973), p. 146.

20. Gutiérrez "Liberation Praxis and Christian Faith," in *The Power of the Poor in History*, trans. Robert Barr (Maryknoll, N.Y.: Orbis Books, 1983), p. 47.

21. Gutiérrez, *Theology of Liberation*, p. 231.

22. Another writer who appeals to Jesus' praxis (though not to its political aspects) is Julio de Santa Ana: "Freedom is infectious. It can be slowed, but not stopped. It keeps moving forward. It cannot be dammed up. However, it does not possess this communicability by nature. There is a 'pedagogy of freedom.' Freedom must be learned and applied. Here again the example of Jesus is instructive in the highest degree. In dealing with other human beings Jesus never forced anything on them in any way. He questioned them, he sought opportunities to speak with them, and thereby he created the necessary conditions for them to make their own decisions, on their own responsibility. And thus it came about that oppressed consciences began to be free ("Notas para una ética de la liberación: A partir de la Biblia," *Cristianismo y Sociedad* 8 [1970]: 58- 59).

Hugo Assmann calls our attention to another facet of the problem. To him it is clear that a particular Christology will issue in a particular manner of activity, and he cites the "Christ in Agony" of Latin American popular piety as a case in point: here is indeed a "Christ of the Oppressed." Assmann also holds that attempts to suppress the theses of the Christology of liberation (by Bekemans and López Trujillo, for example, as he asserts) are motivated not so much from consideration of theology as from a fear of the political consequences these theses may have (see "The Actualization of the Power of Christ in History: Notes on the

Discernment of Christological Contradictions," in *Faces of Jesus*, p. 125-36).

23. Segundo, *Liberation of Theology*, p. 78. See also his "Capitalism-Socialism: A Theological Crux," in *The Mystical and Political Dimension of the Christian Faith*, Concilium 96 (New York: Herder/Seabury, 1974), pp. 119-123.

24. Segundo, *Liberation of Theology*, p. 79.

25. Ibid., p. 80.

26. Ibid.

27. Ibid., p. 81.

28. We find all this in the last chapter of José Comblin's *Teología de la revolución* (Bilbao, 1973). I cite the Spanish version, as this was the version I used in Mexico City. The original is in French, *Théologie de la révolution* (Paris: Editions Universitaires, 1970).

29. Ibid., p. 292.

30. Ibid., p. 306.

31. Ibid., pp. 307ff.

32. In the chapter entitled, "From Proclamation to Action," pp. 308-336.

33. Ibid., pp. 312ff.

34. Ibid., p. 313.

35. Ibid., pp. 314ff.

36. This is the usual term for the National Socialist movement of the 1940s and 1950s, for example in Peron's Argentina.

37. Comblin, *Teología de la revolución*, pp. 315-321.

38. "Socialización y socialismo: Documento de los Sacerdotes para el Tercer Mundo," *Signos de liberación: Testimonios de la Iglesia en América Latina, 1969-1973* (Lima: CEP, 1973), pp. 226-232; citation is from p. 228. Other arguments cited are: There is nothing in the gospel to the effect that one is bound to abide by the status quo. The basic thrust of the gospel is communitarian (*"Our* Father . . . give *us* this day *our* daily bread."). Material things have no importance (Matt. 6:24-34). Service to one's neighbor is of central importance.

39. Eduardo Pironio, "Der neue Mensch: Theologische Besinnung auf das Wesen der Befreiung," in *Gott im Aufbruch*, ed. Peter Hünermann and Gerd-Dieter Fischer (Freiburg, 1974), p. 41.

40. Ibid., p. 66.

41. Ignacio Ellacuría, *Freedom Made Flesh:The Mission of Christ and His Church*, trans. John Drury (Maryknoll, N.Y.: Orbis Books, 1976), p. 40; cf. p. 101.

42. Leonardo Boff, *Jesus Christ Liberator: A Critical Christology for Our Times*, trans. Patrick Hughes (Maryknoll, N.Y.: Orbis Books, 1978), pp. 52-54. Boff makes this connection under the heading "Jesus Preaches an Absolute Meaning for Our World." Cf. his "Salvation in Jesus Christ and the Process of Liberation," in *The Mystical and Political Dimension of the Christian Faith*, Concilium 96 (New York: Herder/Seabury, 1974), p. 81.

43. Jon Sobrino, *Christology at the Crossroads: A Latin American Approach*, trans. John Drury (Maryknoll, N.Y.: Orbis Books, 1978), pp. 84, 166.

44. Hugo Assmann, *Opresión-Liberación: Desafío a los cristianos"'* (Montevideo: Tierra Nueva, 1971), p. 154.

45. Gustavo Gutiérrez, "God's Revelation and Proclamation in History," in *The Power of the Poor in History*, trans. Robert Barr (Maryknoll, N.Y.: Orbis Books, 1983), p. 14.

46. *El Congreso Eucarístico de Colombia y la lucha de clases* (Córdoba: Instituto de Reflexión y Orientación Ideológica, 1968), p. 14.

47. Alfonso López Trujilo, *¿Liberacióno revolución?* (Bogotá: Paulinas, 1975), p. 20.

48. Alfonso López Trujilo, "Secularización, liberación y ateismo," *Revista Javeriana* 74 (1970): 599-600.

49. A less socially oriented analysis of our text is presented by Rubén Cabello, "La misión de Jesús el Áño acepto al Señor," *Christus* (Mexico) 40, no. 472 (1975): 28-32, where he relates the Lord's "year of favor," or Jubilee Year, with the Holy Year, 1975.

50. The archbishop of Goiânia, the bishops of Anápolis, Goiás, São Félix, and Marabá, and the bishop-elect of Porto Nacional.

51. *Randexistenzweise eines Volkes: Aufschrei der Kirchen*, pastoral message of the bishops of West-Central Brazil, Goiânia, 1973 (Mettingen, n.d.), pp. 42-44.

52. Ibid., pp. 45-48.

53. Ibid., p. 48.

54. Juan Luis Segundo, "Conversión y reconciliación en la perspectiva de la moderna teología de la liberación," *Cristianismo y Sociedad* 13 (1975).

55. Héctor Borrat, "Las bienaventuranzas y el cambio social," in *Fe cristiana y el cambio social en América Latina: Encuentro de El Escorial, 1972* (Salamanca: Sígueme, 1973).

56. Ibid., p. 215.

57. Ibid.

58. It is striking that he bases his argumentation on Luke alone and speaks of the "poor" in the social sense of the word—whereas he has just made it clear that Matthew's "poor in spirit" means the same as Luke's "poor."

59. Borrat, "Bienaventuranzas," p. 200.

60. Ibid., p. 223.

61. Ibid., p. 225.

62. Ibid.

63. Note that the Beatitudes play almost no role in Boff's Christology—as indeed we might expect, in view of his disinclination for paradox. See the detailed discussion of his book in Hermann Brandt's "*Jesus Cristo Libertador:* Zum Verständnis der 'kritischen Theologie' bei Leonardo Boff," *Neue Zeitschrift für systematische Theologie* 15 (1973): 229-253.

64. Jon Sobrino, *Christology at the Crossroads: A Latin American Approach,* trans. John Drury (Maryknoll, N.Y.: Orbis Books, 1978), p. 166.

65. Segundo Galilea, "La espiritualidad de la liberación como espiritualidad política," *Christus* (Mexico) 42, no. 499 (1977): 30.

66. Ibid.

67. Ibid. Two authors whom we shall examine only very briefly—one because of his jejune approach, the other because of his remarkably unsuccessful attempt to combine the theses of liberation theology with a traditional spirituality—are Arnaldo Zenteno and Alfonso Rincón González.

Zenteno understands the demands of the Sermon on the Mount to be the consequence of liberation through Christ: "As we have already said when discussing slavery, we must take notice of the social extensions of the liberation Christ has brought us. I am thinking of the Sermon on the Mount, and especially the transcendence of the *Jus Talionis* and love of enemies. For we are to be children of our heavenly Father (Matt. 5:38-48)" ("Liberación y esclavitud en la sagrada escritura," *Servir* 7 [1971]: 296).

Rincón begins with an interpretation of the first Beatitude, the one concerning the poor. First, he assures us, there is a distinction between being "happy" and being "blessed." Happiness is "having in order to be." Blessedness is "fullness of being." Next, he observes that, in Jesus' teaching, the kingdom of God is a reality in which it is possible to overcome poverty through a proper sharing of goods—even today, by anticipation. Where this sharing does not yet prevail, the Christian may forthwith commit himself or herself as a revolutionary, in order to establish just relationships. But this is not all. For, Rincón avers, in the third place, a person must be guided by the "not yet" of the kingdom, as well: "In this perspective, the 'poor people,' for Christ, are those who 'cannot change,' those who are dissatisfied with the status quo, those who hope—people who hope for the promises of the kingdom" ("¿Alienación o liberación? . . . A propósito de una frase de Jésus," *Equipos Docentes de América Latina* 14 [1971]: 31). This interpretation enables Rincón to identify the rich as "slaves," and the poor as "free": "Jesus is called the 'Poor One.' Now, he was 'poor' not only in the sense that he identified himself with a particular social class, and became involved in the battle for justice, but also, and more basically, in the sense that he was completely open to God and human beings. His poverty—which he demands of his disciples as well—leads not to 'nothingness,' or alienation, but to *being*, to *service*, to *liberation*. He was poor in order to enrich us by his poverty. He was poor in order to enjoy *full freedom*—in order to proclaim the kingdom of God, whose power is destined to transform human relationships and the world, and lead human beings to the love of God himself" (ibid., p. 32).

68. MOAC, "Informe del IV Encuentro Latinoamericano," in *Signos de liberación*, pp. 161-70; citation is from p. 167.

69. "Carta pastoral del Episcopado [de Cuba]," in *Signos de Liberación*, p. 173.

70. This was before Salvador Allende's election as president in 1970.

71. A.U. Gerling and E. Scholl, eds., *Kirche der Armen? Neue Tendenzen in Lateinamerika: Ein Dokumentation* (Munich, 1972), p. 174.

72. For example, Iglesia Joven, and Cristianos por el Socialismo ("Church Youth," and "Christians for Socialism").

73. Chilean Bishops, *Evangelio, política y socialismos* (Santiago, 1971), pp. 20-22.

74. Ibid. The entire pastoral letter is reproduced in the Dokumente/Projekte Series of ADVENIAT, no. 12 (Essen: Geschäftsstelle der Bischöflichen Aktion, 1972), pp. 45-142.

75. "El reino de Dios sufre violencia (Mateo 11,12) y en Chile, . . ." unpublished document (1973), pp. 40-41.

76. That is, one might add, socialism. But I shall do without the word because of the negative connotations of the concept in Northern theological circles. In a context of liberation theology, on the contrary, it awakens positive associations. For Latin American Christians, "socialism" is a utopian notion, while in the Northern world it recalls the social system of the Soviet Union and its dependent states.

77. *Congreso Eucharístico y la lucha*; see above note 46.

78. Ibid., pp. 12-14.

79. Helder Camara, *Race against Time* (Denville, N.J.: Dimension, 1971), p. 63.

80. See above p. 23.

81. Julio de Santa Ana, "Notas para una ética de la liberación: A partir de la Biblia," *Cristianismo y Sociedad* 8 (1970): 55.

82. Raúl Vidales, "Evangelización y liberación popular," in *Liberación y cautive-*

rio: Debates en torno al método de la teología en América Latina (Mexico City: Organizing Committee, 1976), pp. 225-226.

83. Ibid., pp. 232-233.

84. Segundo Galilea, *¿A los pobres se les anuncia el Evangelio?* (Bogotá: CELAM-IPLA, 1975), p. 59.

85. Ibid., p. 60. All the material in ibid., pp. 59-64, deals with this subject.

86. Ibid., p. 60.

87. Ibid., p. 61.

88. Segundo Galilea, "Salvación de los pecadores y liberación de los pobres según el Evangelio," *Christus* (Mexico) 40, no. 473 (1975): 27-31.

89. Gustavo Gutiérrez, "Liberation Praxis and Christian Faith," in *The Power of the Poor in History*, p. 44.

90. Gutiérrez, "Liberation, Theology and Proclamation," in Concilium 96, p. 64.

91. Gutiérrez, "God's Revelation and Proclamation in History," in *The Power of the Poor in History*, p. 13.

92. Gutiérrez, *Theology of Liberation*, pp. 196-203.

93. Ibid., p. 198.

94. Segundo Galilea, "Liberation as an Encounter with Politics and Contemplation," in Concilium 96; *Following Jesus*, trans. Helen Phillips (Maryknoll, N.Y.: Orbis Books, 1981), pp. 54-67. In the Parable of the Last Judgment (Matt. 25:31-46), Galilea finds the "prototypical presentation" of *contemplatio in actione,* ("Liberation as an Encounter," p. 35; *Following Jesus,* p. 59; the Spanish originals are identical at this point).

95. *Following Jesus,* pp. 59-60.

96. Pedro Negre Rigol, "Los cristianos, la liberación y sus opciones pastorales," *Cristianismo y Sociedad* 12 (1974): 34-35.

97. Raúl Vidales, "Evangelización y liberación popular," in *Liberación y cautiverio,* pp. 227-228.

98. Helder Camara, too, writes: "Christ healed on the Sabbath and reminded the Pharisees that nobody lets a donkey drown in a well on the Sabbath. We may very well be put in mind of the majority of humanity, languishing in misery and hunger. Most do not know Christ, it is true. But Christ is there anyway, groveling in misery and hunger, living in ramshackle huts, without medical attention, without work, and without a future" ("El Evangelio y la liberación humana," *Perspectivas de Diálogo* 9 (1974): 196.

99. José María Casabó Suque, "Violencia y revolución (II)," *CIAS* 18 (1969): 34-35.

100. Héctor Borrat, "Para una cristología de la vanguardia," *Equipos Docentes de América Latina* 14 (1971). For example: "But the identification of Christ with the neediest very often succumbs to the most egregious errors. Christ tends to be seen as just another needy person. Just some poor person or other. Or as a name, to symbolize the matchless worth of the poor. And so Jesus' actual, particular identity—and his unique power over history—falls out of consideration. His traits here may be rather more positive than the traditional ones, but the latter are still recognizable: crushed under the weight of his sufferings, this sweet, poor Jesus makes no demand of his own but to be served through philanthropy toward the lower classes. Or perhaps indeed he demands that these proletarian lands known as Latin America be

liberated, but in no case has he done anything about it himself. His proclamation is stifled: obviously it is too 'ideological.' Not a word of his own does he have to say. For revolutionary humanism, he is the Great Naught. No champion of humankind, this Jesus—humankind will deliver itself, in the measure of its 'love,' its 'devotion,' its 'openness,' its 'commitment,' and its 'revolutionary activity.' Precisely here is where the neo-Pharisaism that has so many Catholic leftists in its clutches has its deepest roots" ("Cristología de la vanguardia," p. 55).

101. Ellacuría, *Freedom Made Flesh,* p. 39.

102. See Martin Hengel, *Was Jesus a Revolutionist?* (Philadelphia: Fortress Press, 1971), and his bibliography.

103. Gutiérrez, *Theology of Liberation,* pp. 225-232.

104. Ibid., p. 227.

105. Ibid.

106. Ibid., p. 228.

107. Ellacuría, *Freedom Made Flesh,* pp. 21-79, esp. pp. 60-79.

108. Ibid., p. 49.

109. Ibid., p. 60.

110. Ibid., p. 63.

111. Ibid., pp. 63-64.

112. Ellacuría remarks parenthetically that there are people in Latin America today, as well, who are unable or unwilling to distinguish between the political activity of the church and subversive activity of a communist type (ibid., p. 68).

113. Ibid., pp. 68-69.

114. Sobrino, *Christology at the Crossroads,* pp. 210-213.

115. Ibid., p. 213.

116. Boff, *Jesus Christ Liberator,* p. 59.

117. Ibid.

118. Ibid., p. 60.

119. Raúl Vidales, "La práctica histórica de Jesús: Notas provisorias," *Christus* (Mexico) 40, no. 481 (1975): 51.

120. Ibid., p. 50.

121. Ibid. (citing Baumbach).

122. Ibid., p. 51.

123. Ibid.

124. Galilea, "Jesús y la liberación de su pueblo," p. 62. Cf. *Following Jesus,* p. 108.

125. Enrique Maza, "Jesús y la institución," *Christus* (Mexico) 40, no. 480 (1975): 34-38.

126. Ibid., pp. 34-35.

127. Ibid., p. 35.

128. Ibid., p. 37.

129. Sobrino, *Christology at the Crossroads,* pp. 92-94; idem, "Tésis sobre una cristología histórica," *Estudios Centroamericanos* 30 (1975): 444-469.

130. Sobrino, "Cristología histórica," p. 465; cf. *Christology at the Crossroads,* p. 359.

131. "Cristología histórica," p. 465.

132. Ibid., p. 467.

133. Ibid., p. 468. Cf. *Christology at the Crossroads,* p. 204.

134. For such an investigation see Franz Mussner, "Gab es eine galiläische Krise?" in *Orientierung an Jesus: Festschrift für J. Schmid* (Freiburg, 1973), pp. 238-252.

135. Boff, *Jesus Christ Liberator,* pp. 105-110. Boff does not let the opportunity go by to make the connection with contemporary Latin America: "He is made an object of derision, struck, spat upon in the face, and tortured, scenes described by the Synoptics (and today quite frequent in police circles throughout the world)" (ibid., p. 107).

136. Sobrino, *Christology at the Crossroads,* pp. 204-209.

137. Ibid., p. 206.

138. Ibid., pp. 206-207.

139. Ibid., p. 208.

140. Ellacuría, *Freedom Made Flesh,* pp. 72-77.

141. Ibid., p. 74.

142. Ibid., p. 77.

Excursus: The Use of Violence

1. Segundo Galilea, *¿A los pobres se les anuncia el Evangelio?* (Bogotá: CELAM-IPLA, 1975), p. 60.

2. Samuel Ruiz García, "Teología bíblica de la liberación," *Servir* 20 (1974): 476.

3. Ibid., p. 482.

4. Eduardo Pironio, "Teología de la liberación," *Teología* 8 (1970): 9.

5. José María Casabó Suque, "Violencia y revolución (II)," *CIAS* 18 (1969): 26.

6. José Míguez Bonino, *Theologie im Kontext der Befreiung* (Göttingen, 1977), pp. 95-115.

7. Ibid., p. 107.

8. Ibid., p. 108.

9. Ibid., p. 109.

10. Ibid., p. 110.

11. Ibid., p. 112. Here Míguez cites Dom Helder Camara to the same effect: "Armed rebellion is legitimate, but impossible. It is legitimate because it is provoked, and impossible because it would be put down. . . . My position here is based not on religion but on tactics. It rests not on some idealism or other, but on purely political calculations. . . . I feel an antipathy for anyone who fails to be disturbed, or who keeps silence. I love only those who fight, who dare to do something."

12. Ibid., pp. 113-14. Hugo Assmann, as well, emphasizes that the basic Christian attitude is not *non*violence, but the *defeat* of violence ("Crítica al concepto corriente de violencia," *Cristianismo y Sociedad* 9 (1971): 12-20.

13. Juan Luis Segundo, *The Liberation of Theology,* trans. John Drury (Maryknoll, N.Y.: Orbis Books, 1976), pp. 162-165.

14. Ibid., p. 165.

15. Míguez Bonino traces this contradiction to two basically different theological frameworks. One conceives the world in terms of ordered structures—and so violence, as a disturbance of order, will be negative. The other conceives it as a movement toward liberation—and so violence, as a possible contribution to liberation, will be ambivalent (*Theologie im Kontext der Befreiung,* pp. 102-104). Cf.

Miguel Manzanera, "Theologische Anmerkungen zur 'revolutionären Gewalt' in Lateinamerika," in Rahner et al., *Befreiende Theologie: Der Beitrag Lateinamerikas zur Theologie der Gegenwart* (Stuttgart, 1977), p. 109.

Chapter 7

1. Leonardo Boff, *Jesucristo y nuestro futuro de liberación* (Bogotá: Inter-American Press Service, 1978), p. 23.

2. Ignacio Ellacuría, "Hacía una fundamentación de método teológico latinoamericano," *Estudios Centroamericanos* (San Salvador) 30 (1975): 616. The article by Boff to which he is alluding is "Christ's Liberation via Oppression: An Attempt at Theological Construction from the Standpoint of Latin America," in *Frontiers of Theology in Latin America*, ed. Rosino Gibellini (Maryknoll, N.Y.: Orbis Books, 1983), pp. 100–132. The quotations are from p. 103.

3. Boff, *Jesucristo y nuestro futuro,* p. 32.

4. *El Congreso Eucarístico de Cólombia y la lucha de clases* (Córdoba: Instituto de Reflexión y Orientación Ideológica, 1968), p. 25.

5. "Carta pastoral de Arzobispo de Montevideo y su Presbiterio," in *Signos de liberación: Testimonios de la Iglesia en América Latina, 1967–1973* (Lima: CEP, 1974), p. 264.

6. As cited by Hans Zwiefelhofer, *Christen und Sozialismus in Lateinamerika,* vol. 1 of *Theologie in Lateinamerika* (Düsseldorf, 1974), p. 81.

7. Alejandro Cussiánovich, *Para ser libres nos ha liberado CRISTO, Gálatas, 5, 1,* vol. 4 (Lima: CEP, 1972), p. 62. Part of the passage is identical with the Spanish original on p. 229 of Gustavo Gutiérrez's *Theology of Liberation.* Since both appeared in 1972 I was unable to determine the original source.

8. Bruno Renaud, "Iglesia y compromiso temporal," *SIC* 35 (1972): 157–160.

9. Virgilio Zea, "Jesús o el riesgo de la existencia," *Revista Javeriana* 82 (1974): 171.

10. Ruben R. Dri, "El dolor de los hombres latinoamericanos y muerte de Jesús," *Christus* (Mexico) 40, no. 496 (1977): 25.

11. Enrique Maza, "Jesus y la institución," *Christus* (Mexico) 40, no. 480 (1975): 37.

12. Ibid., p. 38.

13. Raúl Vidales, "La práctica histórica de Jesús: Notas provisorias," *Christus* (Mexico) 40, no. 481 (1975): 52.

14. Ibid., p. 48.

15. Ibid.

16. Ignacio Ellacuría, *Freedom Made Flesh* (Maryknoll, N.Y.: Orbis Books, 1976), pp. 151–152.

17. Ibid., pp. 153–155.

18. Ibid., p. 158.

19. Miguel Angel Campos, "¿Por qué murió Jesús?" *Christus* (Mexico) 42, no. 496 (1977): 17–21.

20. Ibid., p. 21.

21. Leonardo Boff, *Jesus Christ Liberator* (Maryknoll, N.Y.: Orbis Books, 1978), pp. 100–120. The Portuguese original was published in 1972.

22. Ibid., pp. 118–119.

23. Boff, *Jesucristo y nuestro futuro,* pp. 30–32. The theses themselves had already appeared, three years earlier, in Boff's *Teología desde el cautiverio* (Bogotá: Indo-American Press Service, 1975).

24. Jon Sobrino, "Tésis sobre una cristología histórica," *Estudios Centroamericanos* 30 (1975): 469; *Christology at the Crossroads,* p. 370.

25. Sobrino, "Tesís sobre una cristología histórica," p. 469.

26. Ibid., p. 470; *Christology at the Crossroads,* p. 371.

27. Jürgen Moltmann, *The Crucified God: The Cross of Christ as the Foundation of Christian Theology* (New York: Harper & Row, 1974).

28. Sobrino, *Christology at the Crossroads,* pp. 179–235.

29. Ibid., p. 180. M. Velasquez M. offers some examples in his "Breve introducción en torno al arte popular como expresión del ser del Mexicano" (manuscript of an address delivered in Oberhausen, Germany, on September 19, 1978).

30. Sobrino, *Christology at the Crossroads,* p. 180.

31. Ibid., p. 196.

32. Ibid., p. 198.

33. Ibid., p. 199.

34. Ibid., p. 202.

35. Ibid., pp. 203–204.

36. Ibid., p. 209.

37. Cf. chap. 5 above.

38. Sobrino, *Christology at the Crossroads,* p. 214.

39. Ibid., pp. 214–215.

40. Ibid., p. 215.

41. Ibid., pp. 222–223.

42. Ibid., p. 224.

43. Ibid.

44. Ibid., pp. 226, 227.

45. Ibid., pp. 233–234.

46. Francisco (Néstor Paz Zamora), "Al pueblo de Bolivia," in *Signos de liberación,* p. 44.

47. CELAM, "Elementos revelantes sobre la teología de la liberación," *Contacto* 11 (1974): 55.

48. Julio de Santa Ana, "Notas para una ética de la liberación: A partir de la Biblia," *Cristianismo y Sociedad* 8 (1970): 52.

49. José Comblin, "La nueva práctica de la Iglesia en el sistema de la securidad nacional: Exposición de sus principios teóricos," in *Liberación y cautiverio* (Mexico City: Organizing Committee, 1976), p. 163.

50. Samuel Ruiz García, "Teología bíblica de la liberación," *Servir* 20 (1974): 503.

51. De Santa Ana, "Notas para una ética," p. 51. The "deed of Jesus Christ among men and women" is the resurrection.

52. Gerardo Valencia, "Estructuras para las tierras de misión," in *Signos de liberación,* p. 199.

53. "Mensaje de obispos del Tercer Mundo," in *Signos de renovación: Documentos post-conciliares de la Iglesia en América Latina,* 2nd ed. (Lima: Comisión Episcopal de Acción Social, 1969), p. 28.

54. Eduardo Pironio, "Latinoamérica: 'Iglesia de la Pascua,' " in SELADOC,

Panorama de la teología latinoamericana, vol. 1 (Salamanca: Sígueme, 1975), p. 180.

55. Marcel van Caster, "Liberación del hombre y misterio pascual," *Perspectivas de Diálogo* 7 (1972): 54.

56. Ibid., p. 56.

57. Segundo Galilea, "Un cristianismo para tiempo de revolución," *Mensaje* 20 (1971): 334.

58. Ibid., p. 335.

59. Rafael Avila, *Elementos para una evangelización liberadora* (Salamanca: Sígueme, 1971), p. 36.

60. Ibid., pp. 68f. Avila's references to "CELAM" are to Medellín's Conclusions (CELAM, *The Church in the Present-Day Transformation of Latin America in the Light of the Council*, vol. 2, ed. Louis Michael Colonnese [Washington, D.C.: Latin American Bureau, USCC, 1970], pp. 48, 100, and 59, respectively).

61. Javier Alonso Hernández, "Esbozo para una teología de liberación," in *Aportes para la liberación: Simposio teología de la liberación, conferencias, Bogotá, marzo 6 y 7 de 1970* (Bogotá, 1970).

62. Comblin, "La nueva práctica de la Iglesia," p. 167.

63. Chilean Bishops, *Evangelio, política y socialismos* (Santiago, 1971), p. 15, as given in ADVENIAT, *Evangelium, Politik und Sozialismus,* Dokumente/Projekte, no. 12 (Essen: Geschäftsstelle der Bischöflichen Aktion, 1972), p. 59.

64. Hugo Assmann, "El aporte cristiana al proceso de liberación en América Latina: Movilización popular y fe cristiana" (Montevideo: ISAL, 1971), pp. 93ff. The limits of the Marxist view are also cited by Alfonso López Trujillo, *¿Liberación o revolución?* (Bogotá, 1975), p. 31.

65. Successively in *Jesus Christ Liberator,* "Salvation in Jesus Christ and the Process of Liberation," in Concilium 96, and *Jesucristo y nuestro futuro.*

66. Boff, *Jesus Christ Liberator,* p. 122.

67. Ibid., p. 135.

68. Ibid.

69. *Jesucristo y nuestro futuro,* p. 32.

70. Ibid.

71. *Jesus Christ Liberator,* pp. 134–136.

72. *Jesucristo y nuestro futuro,* p. 33.

73. Ibid.

74. Raúl Vidales, "La práctica de Jesús: Notas provisorias," *Christus* (Mexico) 40, no. 481 (1975): 44.

75. Ibid.

76. Ibid., p. 46.

77. Ibid., p. 44.

78. Ibid., p. 53.

79. Ibid.

80. Sobrino, "Tésis sobre un cristología histórica," pp. 472 f.

81. Ibid., p. 473. For the resurrection in its first "statement," cf. *Christology at the Crossroads,* p. 240: "Let us assume that the resurrection of Jesus is not simply the resuscitation of a cadaver or some great 'miracle' performed by God. Let us assume that it is the *event that reveals God.* In that case our talk about the resurrection and our hermeneutics of the resurrection bring us to the same set of problems

we face with regard to knowledge of God in general. In other words, we cannot assume at the start that we already know who God is and move from there to an understanding of the resurrection. As was the case with the cross of Jesus, we can only learn who God is from the cross and resurrection of Jesus."

82. "Tésis sobre un cristología histórica," pp. 474 ff.

83. *Christology at the Crossroads,* pp. 242–244.

84. Ibid., p. 255.

85. Ibid.

Chapter 8

1. Segundo Galilea, "Un Cristianismo para tiempo de revolución," *Mensaje* 20 (1971): 335.

2. Raúl Vidales, "Charisms and Political Action," in *Charisms in the Church,* ed. Christian Duquoc and Casiano Floristan, Concilium 109 (New York: Seabury, 1978), pp. 74–75.

3. Gustavo Gutiérrez, *A Theology of Liberation,* trans. and ed. Caridad Inda and John Eagleson (Maryknoll, N.Y.: Orbis Books, 1973), pp. 160–178.

4. Ibid., p. 177.

5. As evinced by his concept that Christ is at work in history "in order to achieve all humanity's transformation into the people of God, and the redeemed world into church" (Eduardo Pironio, "Der neue Mensch: Theologische Besinnung auf das Wesen der Befreiung," in *Gott im Aufbruch,* ed. Peter Hünermann and Gerd-Dieter Fischer [Freiburg, 1974], p. 56).

6. Ibid., p. 68.

7. Ibid.

8. Segundo Galilea, *Following Jesus* (Maryknoll, N.Y.: Orbis Books, 1981), p. 103.

9. Segundo Galilea and Raúl Vidales, *Cristología y pastoral popular* (Bogotá: Paulinas, 1974), pp. 41–43.

10. Leonardo Boff, "El Jesús histórico y la Iglesia," *Servir* 13 (1976): 276.

11. Ruben R. Dri, "Alienación y liberación," *Cristianismo y Revolución* 4 (1970): 62.

12. Gustavo Gutiérrez, "God's Revelation and Proclamation in History," in *The Power of the Poor in History,* trans. Robert Barr (Maryknoll, N.Y.: Orbis Books, 1983), p. 14.

13. This Spanish theologian, a professor in Barcelona, may be included here, inasmuch as he has had a great deal of influence on the theology of liberation, especially in the biblical area, and is very close to that theology in his own thinking.

14. José María González Ruiz, "La fraternidad nacida del Evangelio de Jesús," *Misión Abierta* 70 (1977): 36.

15. José Comblin, "La nueva práctica de la Iglesia en el sistema de la securidad nacional: Exposición de sus principios teóricos," in *Liberación y cautiverio: Debates en torno al método de la teología en América Latina* (Mexico City: Organizing Committee, 1976), p. 162.

16. Fernando Azuela, "¿Como predicar la muerte de Jesús en un continente crucificado?" *Christus* (Mexico) 42, no. 496 (1977): 33.

17. Arnaldo Zenteno, "Muerto por oponerse a los opresores del pueblo," *Christus* (Mexico) 42, no. 496 (1977): 13–14.

18. Ibid., pp. 14–16.

19. Gutiérrez, *Theology of Liberation,* pp. 231–232.

20. Ibid., pp. 145–187.

21. This thesis is developed and concretized in José Míguez Bonino, *Theologie im Kontext der Befreiung* (Göttingen, 1973), pp. 116–133.

22. Leonardo Boff, *Jesus Christ Liberator: A Critical Christology for Our Time,* trans. Patrick Hughes (Maryknoll, N.Y.: Orbis Books, 1978), pp. 49–62; citation is from p. 61. The original Portuguese edition was published in 1972.

23. Leonardo Boff, *Jesucristo y nuestro futuro de liberación* (Bogotá: Indo-American Press Service, 1978), p. 24.

24. Ibid.

25. Ibid., pp. 24–25.

26. Ibid., p. 25.

27. Ibid., p. 26.

28. Ibid., p. 28.

29. Jon Sobrino, *Christology at the Crossroads* (Maryknoll, N.Y.: Orbis Books, 1978), pp. 41–78.

30. Ibid., p. 44.

31. Ibid., p. 47.

32. Ibid., p. 59.

SUMMARY AND CONCLUSIONS

1. José Míguez Bonino, "Teología y liberacíon," *ISAL* 3 (1970): 2.

Bibliography

Note: For complete bibliographic information for sources of articles see listings below under "Anthologies of Essays."

Alves, Rubem. *A Theology of Human Hope.* Washington, D.C.: Corpus, 1971.
Assmann, Hugo. "The Actuation of the Power of Christ in History: Notes on the Discernment of Christological Contradictions." In *Faces of Jesus.*
———. "The Power of Christ in History: Conflicting Christologies and Discernment." In *Frontiers of Theology in Latin America.*
———. *Theology for a Nomad Church.* Maryknoll, N.Y.: Orbis Books, 1976.
Avila, Rafael. *Worship and Politics.* Maryknoll, N.Y.: Orbis Books, 1981.
Berger, Peter. *Pyramids of Sacrifice: Political Ethics and Social Change.* New York: Basic Books, 1974.
Boff, Leonardo. "Christ's Liberation via Oppression: An Attempt at Theological Construction from the Standpoint of Latin America." In *Frontiers of Theology in Latin America.*
———. "Images of Jesus in Brazilian 'Liberal Christianity.' " In *Faces of Jesus.*
———. *Jesus Christ Liberator: A Critical Christology for Our Time.* Maryknoll, N.Y.: Orbis Books, 1978.
———. "Salvation in Jesus Christ and the Process of Liberation." In *The Mystical and Political Dimension of the Christian Faith.*
Comblin, José. "Freedom and Liberation as Theological Concepts." In *The Mystical and Political Dimension of the Christian Faith.*
———. *Jesus of Nazareth: Meditations on His Humanity.* Maryknoll, N.Y.: Orbis Books, 1975.
———. *Sent from the Father: Meditations on the Fourth Gospel.* Maryknoll, N.Y.: Orbis Books, 1979.
Conference of Latin American Bishops (CELAM). *The Church in the Present-Day Transformation of Latin America in the Light of the Council.* 2 vols. Ed. Louis M. Colonnese. Washington, D.C.: USCC, 1970.
———. *Official Conclusions of the Third General Conference of Latin American Bishops, Convened at Puebla, Mexico, January 1979.* Washington, D.C.: NCCB, 1979.
Croatto, J. Severino. "The Political Dimension of Christ the Liberator." In *Faces of Jesus.*
Dussel, Enrique. "Domination–Liberation: A New Approach." In *The Mystical and Political Dimension of the Christian Faith.*
Eagleson, John, and Philip Scharper, eds. *Puebla and Beyond.* Maryknoll, N.Y.: Orbis Books, 1980.
Echegaray, Hugo. *The Practice of Jesus.* Maryknoll, N.Y.: Orbis Books, 1984.

Ellacuría, Ignacio. *Freedom Made Flesh: The Mission of Christ and His Church.* Maryknoll, N.Y.: Orbis Books, 1976.

———. "The Political Nature of Jesus' Mission." In *Faces of Jesus.*

Galeano, Eduardo H. *Open Veins of Latin America: Five Centuries of the Pillage of a Continent.* New York: Monthly Review Press, 1973.

Galilea, Segundo. *Following Jesus.* Maryknoll, N.Y.: Orbis Books, 1981.

———. "Jesus' Attitude toward Politics: Some Working Hypotheses." In *Faces of Jesus.*

———. "Liberation as an Encounter with Politics and Contemplation." In *The Mystical and Political Dimension of the Christian Faith.*

Gutiérrez, Gustavo. "Liberation Praxis and Christian Faith." In *Frontiers of Theology in Latin America.*

———. "Liberation, Theology and Proclamation." In *The Mystical and Political Dimension of the Christian Faith.*

———. *The Power of the Poor in History.* Maryknoll, N.Y.: Orbis Books, 1983.

———. *A Theology of Liberation: History, Politics and Salvation.* Maryknoll, N.Y.: Orbis Books, 1973.

———. *We Drink from Our Own Wells: The Spiritual Journey of a People.* Maryknoll, N.Y.: Orbis Books, 1984.

Hengel, Martin. *Was Jesus a Revolutionist?* Philadelphia: Fortress Press, 1971.

Jiménez Limón, Javier. "Meditation on the God of the Poor." In *The Idols of Death and the God of Life.*

Lange, Martin, and Reinhold Iblacker, eds. *Witnesses of Hope: The Persecution of Christians in Latin America.* Maryknoll, N.Y.: Orbis Books, 1981.

Míguez Bonino, José. "Who Is Jesus Christ in Latin America Today?" In *Faces of Jesus.*

Miranda, José Porfirio. *Being and the Messiah: The Message of St. John.* Maryknoll, N.Y.: Orbis Books, 1977.

Moltmann, Jürgen. *The Crucified God: The Cross of Christ as the Foundation and Criticism of Christian Theology.* New York: Harper and Row, 1974.

Negre Rigol, Pedro. "Popular Christology—Alienation or Irony?" In *Faces of Jesus.*

Schuurman, Lamberto. "Christology in Latin America." In *Faces of Jesus.*

Segundo, Juan Luis. "Capitalism–Socialism: A Theological Crux." In the *Mystical and Political Dimension of the Christian Faith.*

———. *Faith and Ideologies.* Vol. 1 of *Jesus of Nazareth Yesterday and Today.* Maryknoll, N.Y.: Orbis Books, 1984.

———. *The Liberation of Theology.* Maryknoll, N.Y.: Orbis Books, 1976.

Sobrino, Jon. *Christology at the Crossroads: A Latin American Approach.* Maryknoll, N.Y.: Orbis Books, 1978.

———. "The Epiphany of the God of Life in Jesus of Nazareth." In *The Idols of Death and the God of Life.*

Torres, Camilo. *Revolutionary Writings.* New York: Herder and Herder, 1969.

Vidales, Raúl. "How Should We Speak of Christ Today?" In *Faces of Jesus.*

Anthologies of Essays

Faces of Jesus: Latin American Christologies. Ed. José Míguez Bonino. Maryknoll, N.Y.: Orbis Books, 1984.

Frontiers of Theology in Latin America. Ed. Rosino Gibellini. Maryknoll, N.Y.: Orbis Books, 1979.

The Idols of Death and the God of Life: A Theology. Pablo Richard et al. Maryknoll, N.Y.: Orbis Books, 1983.

The Mystical and Political Dimension of the Christian Faith. Concilium 96, ed. Claude Geffré and Gustavo Gutiérrez. New York: Herder and Herder, 1974.

Index

Compiled by James Sullivan

on dependence, 12; interpreters of, 28, 106; liberation theme of, 27, 35, 106, 143, 152, 156-57; on methodology of liberation theology, 18; Pironio and, 12, 26, 47, 150, 162; and poor, 23, 71-72, 106; on praxis, 14, 19-29; Puebla and, 150; and Vatican II, 13; on violence, 103. *See also* CELAM
media, 110, 158
Mejía, Jorge, 162, 164
Mendoza, António de, 147
messianism: hope of, 62-63, 86-93, 109, 126; praxis and, 126; rejection of political-religious, 113, 131-32
Mestizos, 8. *See also* Indians
methodology, 15, 17, 18, 32, 42, 56, 104-05, 152, 153
Methol Ferré, Alberto, 155
Metz, Johannes B., 2, 25
Metzler, 148
Mexico, 145, 146, 147, 153; "death loaves" of, 108; native clergy in, 9
Míguez Bonino, José, 146, 151, 152, 164, 175, 177; on Christology, 159; on class struggle, 101, 170; criticism of, 26; on liberation, 143; Protestant tradition of, 146, 151, 152, 164, 175, 177; on violence, 101-03, 170
military, 33, 158; in Argentina, 32; in Bolivia, 32; in Chile, 32, 72, 158; in Peru, 32; praxis of, 135; refusal of kingdom to rely on, 97; in Uruguay, 32
Miranda, José Porfirio, 20, 37, 154, 160, 177
mission: of church, 46, 52, 66; history as, 128; of Jesus, 162
missions (missionaries): colonialism and, 8-10. *See also* colonialism; evangelization
MOAC, 167
Modehn, Christian, 146, 153
Moltmann, Jürgen, 114, 172, 177
Montesinos, Antonio de, 147
Morelli, Alex, 151
Moses, 52; Jesus as new, 35, 36; Law of, 98; mission of, 54; tradition of, 76
Mussner, Franz, 170
national security, 33, 34. *See also* military
National Socialist movement, 165
Neely, Alan, 147
Negre Rigol, Pedro, 83, 154, 168, 177
Nolen, D., 148
nonviolence: Assmann on, 170; Jesus and, 99-103; love and, 102; Pironio on, 157; revolution and, 102; Segundo on, 102-103. *See also* violence
Nuevas Leyes de Indias, 8
Nuschler, F. 148
Oliveros Maqueo, Roberto, 154
option for the poor. *See* poor
orthodoxy, 82. *See also* praxis
orthopraxis. *See* praxis

parables, 82-85, 91
Passover, 121
pastoral ministry: class structure and, 70-82; of Jesus, 53; kingdom of God and, 52, 133; practice of, 12, 52, 81, 83, 128, 133; theology of, 19, 21, 34, 76; theory of, 12, 133
Paul, 45, 64
Paul VI, 156
Paz Zamora, Néstor, 172
Peitz, Marietta, 158
Pentecostalism, 61, 130-31
Pérez, Isidro, 151, 153
Perón, 32, 165
Peru: conquest of, 7; episcopacy in, 12; military in, 32
Peter, 86
Pharisees: contemporary, 169; culture of, 62; Jesus and conflict with, 43, 57, 59-65, 90, 96, 101, 102, 106, 168; priestly aristocracy of, 77, 97, 98; repression of conscience by, 106; theology of, 55-57
Phillips, Helen, 168
philosophy, 28, 143, 149
Picazo Gálvez, Melecio, 30, 155, 156, 157, 159
Pilate, 95, 97, 98, 163
Pironio, Eduardo, 151; on Beatitudes, 100, 170; and CELAM, 47, 162; and Christology, 47, 162, 172; criticism of liberation theologians by, 26, 28, 66, 155, 157, 165; on kingdom of God, 100, 131, 170, 174; and Medellín, 12, 26, 47, 150, 162; on politics, 30, 157; on violence, 100, 157, 170
Pizarro, Francisco, 7
Platonism, 82
Pohier, Jacques-Marie, 147
politics: analysis of, applied to poor, 70; and faith, 26, 29-31, 34, 55, 98, 157; hermeneutics of, 111; Jesus and, of his time, 39, 50-103; Jewish, 61; kingdom of God and, 135-37; praxis of, 52, 136, 143; and resurrection, 129, 130; and violence, 75
Poma de Ayela, Guamán, 8
poor, 70-82; of Beatitudes, 144, 167; and Bible, 71-85, 167; Borrat on, 168-69; and conversion, 62; death as consequence of commitment to, 109; evangelization of, 133; Galilea on, 78-83, 155, 168; Gutiérrez on, 23-24, 34, 66, 80-82, 155, 156, 159, 165, 168; and kingdom of God, 66, 67-82, 99; and Medellín, 23, 71-72, 106; option for the, 23, 59, 65, 73, 80, 81, 101, 167; as result of sin, 24, 54, 71-72, 75-76; of Roman Empire, 62; and slavery, 62, 75, 167; sociological and political analysis of, 70; triumph of, 57; Vidales on, 76, 78, 167-68
Portugal, 7-8